The British Film Industry in the 1970s

Also by Sian Barber

CENSORING THE 1970s: The BBFC and the Decade That Taste Forgot

The British Film Industry in the 1970s

Capital, Culture and Creativity

Sian Barber

Royal Holloway, University of London, UK

palgrave
macmillan

First published 2013 by
PALGRAVE MACMILLAN

Palgrave Macmillan in the UK is an imprint of Macmillan Publishers Limited, registered in England, company number 785998, of Houndmills, Basingstoke, Hampshire RG21 6XS.

Palgrave Macmillan in the US is a division of St Martin's Press LLC, 175 Fifth Avenue, New York, NY 10010.

Palgrave Macmillan is the global academic imprint of the above companies and has companies and representatives throughout the world.

Palgrave® and Macmillan® are registered trademarks in the United States, the United Kingdom, Europe and other countries.

ISBN 978–0–230–36095–2

This book is printed on paper suitable for recycling and made from fully managed and sustained forest sources. Logging, pulping and manufacturing processes are expected to conform to the environmental regulations of the country of origin.

A catalogue record for this book is available from the British Library.

A catalog record for this book is available from the Library of Congress.

10   9   8   7   6   5   4   3   2   1
22 21 20 19 18 17 16 15 14 13

Printed and bound in Great Britain by
CPI Antony Rowe, Chippenham and Eastbourne

For Paul, for always being there

Contents

Illustrations

Figure

Tables

Foreword

The 1970s are British cinema's most overlooked and least understood decade. In contrast to the vibrant and exciting film culture of the 1960s – the decade that put British cinema back on the international map in a way that it had not enjoyed since the golden age of Rank, Cineguild, Lean, and Powell and Pressburger – the 1970s seemed to mark the moment when British filmmaking ran out of residual cultural and economic energy. The 1970s have either been seen as a period of stagnation and decline, witnessing the fragmentation of British film culture, or been characterised as 'the decade that taste forgot' due to the prevalence of lowbrow populism exemplified by the *Confessions* films and the seemingly ubiquitous television sitcom adaptations. In recent years, however, this picture has been challenged by the rise of a revisionist scholarship that has looked afresh at the decade and the distinctive cultural forms and practices to which it gave rise.

Sian Barber's new study of the British film industry in the 1970s is a welcome addition to this growing body of work. It is also the first major single-authored monograph on the subject, following several edited collections and multiple-author volumes that, however valuable their insights, do not offer the same degree of intellectual rigour or analytical consistency. It will be useful to outline, briefly, the particular merits of Barber's work. First, she provides a comprehensive historical map of the economic and industrial structures of the film industry during this decade: no mean feat considering the chronic instability that beset the industry and the legislative uncertainty of the successive Conservative and Labour governments. This is the kind of nitty-gritty nuts-and-bolts film history that I like, but which is unfashionable for those who worship at the high temple of film theory. Yet, as Barber demonstrates throughout, an understanding of the economic framework is essential to make sense of the kind of films produced in the 1970s. For, as so often in the film and cultural industries, the instability of the production sector created the conditions in which both creativity and commerce could flourish. Barber argues persuasively that innovation in British cinema during this period was not merely a matter of creative *auteur* directors as varied as Joseph Losey and Ken Russell, but was also apparent in the strategies through which filmmakers found new entertainment forms and genre variations that would respond to the diverse and changing tastes of British audiences. The nexus of capital, culture and creativity, identified in the book's subtitle, is expertly analysed and documented.

But there is much more to this book than a study of the industry. Barber really comes into her own in her close and nuanced readings of a range of British films of the 1970s. These range from traditional genres, such as the costume film (*The Go-Between*), to the zany world of the British pop musical (*Stardust*) and from high art (*The Tempest*) to the lowest of the lowbrow (*Confessions of a Window Cleaner*). What is refreshing here, however, is that the analysis is free from either the aesthetic snobbery of the traditional realist school of film criticism or the intellectual and ideological prejudices of high theory (and Barber reminds us that the 1970s was the heyday of *Screen*). The films are analysed as cultural artefacts in their own right, which, regardless of their quality – good, bad or indifferent, offer insights into social values and cultural tastes. The recurring preoccupations – class, gender, youth – are expressed in different ways, often finding expression in the motifs of mobility and the crossing of boundaries that characterise this period in particular. This was not a film culture in decline but rather one in transition. And what emerges is a picture of a more diverse and varied film culture than has hitherto been acknowledged.

The British Film Industry in the 1970s exemplifies the best kind of film studies today: solidly based in empirical research yet informed by cultural theory, nuanced rather than dogmatic in its textual analysis, alert to the nature of films as complex cultural and visual artefacts, and understanding the relationships between industrial processes and individual agency that brought them to the screen in the first place. It deserves to be afforded significant intellectual currency in the ongoing debate over the nature of British cinema both as an industrial practice and as an art form.

James Chapman

James Chapman is Professor of Film at the University of Leicester. His books include *Past and Present: National Identity and the British Historical Film* (2005) and *Licence to Thrill: A Cultural History of the James Bond Films* (2nd edn 2007).

Acknowledgements

This work would never have evolved without the help and support of a large number of people. I would like to thank Sue Harper for her guidance and help throughout my PhD. Her knowledge of and enthusiasm for British cinema were matched only by her dedicated support. I would also like to thank Justin Smith for his creative ideas and meticulous attention to detail as well as the rest of the 1970s project team at the University of Portsmouth, particularly Sally Shaw and Patti Gaal-Holmes. Many thanks go to James Chapman for his contribution to this work and for providing the foreword.

None of the archival research would have been possible without the help of the staff from the BFI Special Collections and Fiona Liddell and Ed Lamberti at the British Board of Film Classification. Thanks also go to Phil Wickham and the staff of the Bill Douglas Centre at the University of Exeter, and to Andrew Spicer for his kindness in letting me use the Michael Klinger material.

I would like to thank Michael Winner, David Puttnam, Don Boyd, Ray Connolly and Glenda Jackson, who were all kind enough to share their memories of the 1970s with me. I am particularly grateful to Don Boyd for allowing me to use an image from his own collection for the cover image of this work.

Abbreviations

ABC	Associated British Picture Corporation, later EMI
ACTT	Association of Cinema and Television Technicians
AIP	Association of Independent Producers
BBFC	British Board of Film Classification
BFI	British Film Institute
CFC	Cinematograph Films Council
FPA	Film Production Association, later Film Producers Association
NFFC	National Film Finance Corporation

Abbreviation of Archival Papers

DB	Don Boyd papers pertaining to *Scum* and *The Tempest*
DJ	Derek Jarman papers pertaining to *The Tempest*
JF	James Ferman papers pertaining to film censorship
JRS	John Schlesinger papers pertaining to *Sunday Bloody Sunday*
LPGB	Joseph Losey papers pertaining to *The Go-Between*
LPRE	Joseph Losey papers pertaining to *The Romantic Englishwoman*
MKP	Michael Klinger papers pertaining to the *Confessions* series
PR	Peter Rogers papers pertaining to the *Carry On* series
TNA	The National Archives

Note:

1. When I used the Michael Klinger papers they had yet to be catalogued. They have now been catalogued and a comprehensive catalogue is available at http://michaelklingerpapers.uwe.ac.uk/catalogue.htm.
2. The BBFC changed its name 1984 from the British Board of Film Censors to the British Board of Film Classification.

Introduction

From scholarly and historic accounts to cultural and cinematic studies, the same clichés about the 1970s as a decade of decline and as a time of crisis abound. It has been too easy to limit explorations of British culture to selective considerations of obvious examples. Some of these accounts actively celebrate the low-culture appeal of the 1970s, while others lean towards the autobiographical. There is, of course, an important place for personal historical accounts and anecdotal history, but that place is not here. The limitations of the existing material open up a space for a rigorous cultural investigation of the 1970s. This account has emerged from the archival sources and combines the methodology of the cultural historian with the approach of the film scholar. Its aim is to definitively map the legislative and economic constraints on the British film industry in the 1970s.

The precarious nature of the British film industry in the 1970s, combined with a steady decline in investment, had a heavy impact on the cinematic product created. Not all these impacts were negative: the uncertain culture of production offered British filmmakers unique opportunities for innovation. But how precisely did this new economic and creative freedom affect the films that were made, and how can the texts which emerged from this polarised industry be linked to the wider social and political climate? The technical basis and financial logic of the industry were also changing. For example, the rising costs of hiring studio space led to an increase in filming on location, which was made possible by cheaper, lighter cameras, which in turn had a massive impact upon the films produced.

This analysis of 1970s British films begins with an attempt to move beyond the predictable clichés of an industry in crisis and a decade dominated by the lowbrow. But neither of these interpretations can be

1

applied to the period as a whole. The film culture of the decade is simply too diverse. Due to the instability of the economic base and the wide range of films produced, it is too straightforward to simply see the films of the 1970s as a direct result of economic factors. Although the financial retrenchment of the American studios and lack of government support did bring about a crisis in film production in the early years of the decade, the films created must be related to deeper social and political contexts, as well as to more specific issues of niche audiences, production trends and popular taste. Perhaps it is more fruitful to consider why the economic base failed to produce a coherent and easily identifiable cultural product?

The films of the 1970s cannot be easily characterised, despite some textual and thematic similarities. The massive social changes of the 1960s became manifest in the 1970s and particularly within the visual culture of this decade. Not only does cultural change lag behind social change, but the effects of such change also take time before becoming evident in methods of working. The temporal distance observed between social change and changes in culture firmly refutes the notion that film 'mirrors' society. What films do choose to suggest, invoke or manifest in reference to social change is highly selective. Much that occurs in the society of the 1970s simply does not feature in the films of the decade. There are rare examples of films which deal with contemporary issues. For example, *Carry On at Your Convenience* (1971) dealt with strikes and trade unionism, but was a box office flop, demonstrating that even a popular series had to choose its topics carefully in this decade. Many films of the 1970s are characterised by the omission of specific contemporary issues. This not only suggests the unrepresentative social function of films in the period but also draws attention to the manner in which they deal with their own omissions. Evasion and obliqueness permeate the decade's film culture, and this can be seen in much of the visual style and manner of performance, as well as within the narrative and setting of the films.

While films of the 1970s rarely dealt with contemporaneous issues, the decade did shake loose definitions of class, gender and national identity, which had all been actively challenged in the 1960s. As well as evaluating and critiquing the challenges of the 1960s, films from a range of genres and from differing production contexts began to assess the implications of cultural change from earlier periods. The instability of gender identity, class distinctions and shifts in national identity *are* evident in films of the period, but they should be linked to the changes which had taken place in post-war British society rather than in the

1970s. The massive changes effected in this post-war period can be helpfully used to consider some of the inconsistencies and incoherence of many of the films of the 1970s.

In films of the 1970s the class system and all that pertains to it are shown to have shaky foundations. Unlike earlier cinematic periods, such as the 1940s, which rely upon class conventions and restrictions, the films of the 1970s demonstrate the fracture of class and social structures. Films such as *Virgin Witch* (1971), *Dracula AD 1972* (1972) and *Alfie Darling* (1975) are peopled with rootless, youthful, classless characters who move easily within society and demonstrate the breakdown of previously fixed class boundaries. The link between the class system and the past is shown to be irrevocably broken in the 1970s. The meanings of the past are shown to be no longer fixed and settled. In revealing how the past is free from the bonds which kept it firmly moored, films allow the past to be plundered for a variety of purposes. Within the cinema of the 1970s, history and the past is utilised for many different purposes in a postmodern, eclectic way.

The lack of cohesion which has been seen to characterise 1970s British cinema and the uncertainty of hitherto fixed constructs, such as genre and the mass audience, are evidenced by the lack of a unified critical discourse surrounding film in the 1970s. This period manifests a proliferation of academic discourses that seek to define or explain the film culture using theoretical models, such as postmodernism, psychoanalysis or feminism. It is no coincidence that seminal film journal *Screen* became extravagantly theoreticist in the 1970s. The decade demands a thorough reappraisal and an examination of its films and its culture based solely on its own merits.

1
Film and Cultural History

Cinema and film form an integral part of the culture of any period of the 20th century. The thematic preoccupations of film, music, fashion, art and literature can all offer important contributions to our understanding of any given historical period. Just as the film historian must strive for a rigorous methodology which acknowledges issues of historical research, the political and social historian should not ignore important cultural indicators. However, despite their importance as social and cultural texts, all film must be interpreted cautiously. Anyone can interpret a film and see within it relevant themes, political motivations, ideological messages and easily identifiable characters and narrative. It is also easy to ally particular films with particular social moments. Yet the relationship between film and culture is rarely as straightforward as it first appears. Any study of film must consider carefully the experiences of audiences and the implications of popular taste. Box office figures, letters to popular magazines and critical reviews all allow an insight into popular taste, but recovering the experiences of audiences is difficult and many of the surviving sources of material which can be used to document popular taste are frequently sparse and uneven.

The film historian needs to move beyond straightforward observations and consider the wider context in which the film was produced. As with any field of historical enquiry, the film historian must pose a number of questions when approaching a film: Who made it? Who funded it? Who saw it? Where, when and why was it produced?

Mainstream films are produced for commercial purposes; their intention is to make money. As Harper and Porter note in their study of the 1950s, 'too often the analysis of film texts has proceeded as though they can be simply plucked out of the cultural ether, rather than products which have to be financed and marketed.'[1] Abstracting film texts from the wider context of production negates the importance of both critical agency and social and economic determinants.

All films offer important insights into the period in which they were made, yet they must be considered as crafted and sculpted artefacts rather than as uncritical mirrors of contemporary culture. It is too straightforward to see films as mirrors, yet they do offer an insight into culture, which is then carefully and deliberately reconfigured for audience consumption through negotiated creativity. Films select, amplify, refract, distort, convey, idealise or reposition a partial impression of a society and its culture.

The notion of films as mirrors is closely allied to the idea of audience, specifically the mass audience, the 'anonymous multitude' who, Kracauer believed, watched and absorbed films which embodied and therefore satisfied their mass desires.[2] Raymond Durgnat in *A Mirror for England* also suggested that cinema reflects the desires of the mass audience as cinema is *the* mass entertainment medium.[3] Films are therefore made to reiterate and reinforce the desires, needs and ideological position of the audience. This may have been the case in earlier periods, when the cinema dominated leisure time but, as Jeffrey Richards points out, by the 1970s, the audience was fragmented and television had replaced cinema as the mass entertainment medium.[4] In this era, cinema and films could not and did not reflect the desires and needs of the mass audience as this audience no longer existed. While it is true that cinema could no longer be considered the dominant mass medium during the 1970s, it was still highly significant. While audience numbers were certainly declining, people were still going to the cinema. However, the fact that people did not go to the cinema as frequently as they had done in previous periods makes it hard to utilise the reflectionist model or draw upon the theory of the mass audience.

A more useful model for understanding the 1970s is perhaps the base/superstructure model proposed by Raymond Williams, which utilises Marxist cultural theory to suggest that the economic base creates the cultural products which form the superstructure of any given society.[5] While it is true that in the 1970s the financial instability of the industry and wider economic recession gave rise to many films which had been funded – through necessity – in an unorthodox way, this does not adequately recognise the role played by creative agency. For example, *The Go-Between* (1971) arose from the economic base of the early 1970s, but the artistic endeavour of Joseph Losey, Harold Pinter and Carmen Dillon, along with the post-production involvement of Bryan Forbes and Bernard Delfont at EMI Films, greatly influenced the final product. Furthermore, cinema in the 1970s was not a stable or predictable cultural form, and the economic base itself was highly unstable and fluctuated wildly throughout the decade.

This relationship between culture and society is pivotal to any study of film for, as Allen and Gomery state emphatically, 'films do not just appear; they are produced and consumed within specific historical contexts.'[6] In order to adequately understand and acknowledge this historical context, a careful analysis of film production and reception must be undertaken. This is not to underplay the importance of visual and textual analysis, but rather to show that any such analysis should be firmly grounded in order to avoid speculation and modern interpretation.

As with the study of any historical period, it is crucial to understand and acknowledge the historical specificity of the period. In his analysis of historical films, James Chapman suggests that 'interpretative analysis of films becomes justified only when the historical circumstances of production and reception have first been established.'[7] To ignore these issues of historical location is to remove films from their social, political and economic space. As Allen and Gomery remind us, 'film histories are works of historical explanation and as such cannot escape basic questions of historiography.'[8] In order to fully comprehend these issues of historiography, it is necessary to consider how historical evidence can be used to study film and how such approaches can be carefully combined with textual and visual analysis.

Film history verses film studies?

As Jeffery Richards outlines in 'Rethinking British Cinema,' any approach which is grounded in firm archival practice must take note of what close textual analysis can offer.[9] Richards argues that despite the differences in approach – film studies' concern is with the text itself as opposed to film history's overriding preoccupation with the contexts of production and reception – scholars of film need not privilege one approach over the other. Chapman, Glancy and Harper also suggest in *The New Film History* that film scholars must now acknowledge the importance of a balanced approach which utilises contextual evidence within a theoretical framework.[10] As Andrew Spicer has also noted, 'each side has learned from the strengths of the other's approaches' and it is this balancing of the twin approaches of film history and film studies which adds strength and depth to this work.[11] I will endeavour to tread a careful path between over-reliance upon the archival sources and over-dependence on textual analysis. In this way it is possible to pay equal attention to the archive and to the text.

Adopting the archival approaches favoured by Richards in his work on the 1930s and Harper and Porter's study of the 1950s will allow for an investigation of a range of historical sources pertaining to the study of film, as well as foregrounding the importance of production and reception.[12] Historical and archive work will be complemented by investigating the attention given to the cultural, social and political importance of film, as demonstrated by Robert Murphy and John Hill in their studies of the 1960s and 1980s.[13] Hill's work on the 1980s charts the development of different thematic trends and issues within film texts of the period, and considers the social and political implications of Thatcherism for film culture. By contrast, the 1970s saw no such cohesive and unified political movement. In fact, it was the political instability of the 1970s which created such an uneasy and often incoherent relationship between successive governments and the film industry, thereby preventing any attempt to contextualise the films of the period in terms of overriding political trends and motivations.

Just as it is not sufficient to base an analysis of film solely on the film texts itself, it is equally inappropriate to limit the study of film to the confines of the archive. Such an approach would allow for adequate contextualisation, but would demonstrate little understanding of the visual culture of the period; without a consideration of visual style, a study risks being nothing more than a map of contexts. It is crucial to consider the way films *look* as this can help map trends in technology, innovation and industry. Such analysis allows for an examination of the work of cinematographers, visual artists and production and set designers and, as Harper and Porter suggest, 'to establish categories or criteria by which to assess the competence of visual discourses.'[14] These visual discourses are a vital part of film analysis. As well as illuminating the cultural and visual codes contained within the film text, the 'look' of the film can immediately suggest a great deal. For example, the colour, style and texture of the costumes and sets in *Tommy* (1975) suggest character, class and status as well as detail pertaining to narrative and setting. The visual style and 'look' of this film locates it as a 1970s cultural text but also reinforces the psychedelic influence of the music and the contemporary characters and locations.

The visual impact of film texts needs to be considered in order to examine the pleasures offered to an audience. Notions of visual pleasure in the text should not be limited to discussions of costumes, colour and set design, but rather should be developed to include style, performance and manner. Any discussion of film reception may shed light upon the pleasures found in the text, but how can we speculate about the nature of visual pleasure for an audience and where can we find evidence of agency and stylistic decisions? The answers can perhaps be found in the archive. As Sarah Street recently noted, when considering visual style, the work of set designers and art directors must be analysed through archival material such as pre-production sketches, storyboards and notes.[15] Street persuasively argues that such material must be examined alongside other production data and, of course, the film itself. It is only through a consideration of all this evidence that an understanding of visual style and its specific objectives can be reached. Engaging with issues of visual style and expanding the textual analysis to include details on costumes, set design and performance allows for an expansion of the role of the film historian. The film historian must be conscious of issues of visual style, just as the film scholar who focuses upon the text and its visual pleasures must be aware of the archive.

The archive offers untold riches to the film historian and there are not the sorts of problems of calligraphy, discourse and paper quality which assail, for example, the medieval historian. Yet the film archive does pose problems of its own. Many of the papers which form the basis of film archives are personal material relating to the work of successful producers and directors. Much of this may have been carefully filleted to avoid issues of contention or embarrassment. In order to avoid reliance on such personal and subjective material, the film historian must often seek sources from elsewhere. As Sarah Street reminds us, 'in order to tease out the diverse relations and meanings, the film historian has to draw on a plethora of source material, often not directly concerned with the films in question.'[16] Drawing upon a breadth of archival material allows a wider picture of the filmmaking process to emerge. As Andrew Spicer has recently shown in his work on the personal papers of producer Michael Klinger, extensive material exists for Klinger's successful film projects, but further material also exists for projects which were never made.[17] This effectively illustrates the possible problems of beginning an exploration of film culture with the text itself, as the text, in certain cases, does not exist. An investigation which begins in the archive allows for the entire production process of a film to be unearthed, in such cases where sources remain. Sources which relate to film are diverse and eclectic, and range from personal accounts, production ledgers, unpublished letters, interviews and correspondence to scripts, bills and receipts. As with any archival work, the reliability and worth of these sources must be rigorously questioned.

However, as Ludmilla Jordanova points out, it is not the role of any historian to 'fetishise' the primary sources, but rather to scrutinise all the types of source and actively and consciously seek out what is useful.[18] In this way, the film historian is able to call upon a range of source and archival material in order to further his or her discussions of film and culture, unfettered by uneasy and often unhelpful distinctions between primary and secondary material.

It is also not the case that once this archival material has been used, it holds no other use for future film historians. As John Tosh has noted, 'the modern discipline of history rests not only on what has been handed down by earlier historians, but on a constant reassessment of the original resources.'[19] This is a key idea and it is this process of reassessment and active questioning of archival material which forms a vital part of my work here. I will not only be considering archival accounts which have been overlooked or inadequately considered, but also be actively re-evaluating material which has previously been utilised. It is the role of all historians, be they concerned with culture, politics, economics or society, to reconsider, challenge, oppose, question and re-examine the interpretations of existing sources.

As Raphael Samuel reminds us, history is 'a social form of knowledge: the work in any given instance of a thousand different historical hands.'[20] As historians, we need to remember that the work we undertake on particular subjects and on particular decades contributes to and builds upon the work already undertaken by other scholars. All such scholarship should never be seen as the last word on a given topic or period, but rather should exist simply as part of a broader body of knowledge.

An integrated approach: Archive and text

The paucity of archival work in much of the scholarship of the 1970s period allows me to adopt a fresh approach which foregrounds the source material. I will use archival evidence to excavate beneath long-held assumptions of 1970s film culture and actively challenge perceptions about the decade. Although the 1970s has frequently been characterised as a period without adequate evidence for the study of film, diverse, eclectic and useful sources do exist. Along with the more traditional repositories of information for the film historian, such as the trade press and the library at the British Film Institute (BFI), I will draw on material from the National Archives, the British Library, the BFI Special Collections and the British Board of Film Classification. As well as the BFI Special Collections, which holds the papers of Joseph Losey, John Schlesinger, David Puttnam, Peter Rogers and Derek Jarman, I will also reference the papers of Michael Klinger held at the University of the West of England archive in Bristol and the Don Boyd papers held within the Bill Douglas Centre at the University of Exeter.

Although offering wonderful insights, the archival material does pose certain methodological, ethical and historical problems. For example, the papers of John Schlesinger are very detailed, yet there are definite omissions which suggest certain documents have been removed. These absences within the archive have to be recognised; these omissions, just as much as the inclusions, are highly significant. Secondly, inflammatory and possibly libellous material can often be found in these collections of private papers – for example, personal correspondence often yields unflattering and scandalous remarks, such as Dirk Bogarde's opinions on Glenda Jackson's acting abilities, which he conveys in a private letter to Joseph Losey.[21] In the case of such sensitive material, the researcher must ask not only how such material could be used, but also whether it should be used at all. Such letters are usually private and not intended to be read by anyone other than the recipient, but what happens when they are placed, as both the Schlesinger and Losey papers have been, in a collection which can be accessed by members of the public? Finally, the preoccupations of the researcher must be considered. I have chosen certain extracts from a range of archival material, yet there are certain documents which I have utilised more heavily than others. All archival work is highly subjective; individual researchers take what they want and leave what they do not.

While these particular concerns of selectivity, nuance and omission relate most pertinently to personal papers, there are other concerns relating to wider archival material which must also be acknowledged. In addition to the filleting of personal papers which has taken place, some areas of the film industry suffer from a complete lack of sources altogether. For example, few records exist for the pornography industry. The shadowy world of sex-film production offers little in the way of paper archives or even records of investment capital. Even the extensive papers of producer Michael Klinger, who worked with Tony Tenser on a number of sex films, yield little for this early part of his career. Certain aspects of the industry were very poorly documented, but for the film industry as a whole, much that would be valuable to the historian has not been preserved. This is not necessarily on the grounds of the quality of the films themselves, but rather that much of the material has not been considered worth preserving. The material which has been chosen for preservation must yet again be considered alongside what has not been preserved. As with any archival study, a great deal depends upon the quality of the available evidence, which may be poorly curated or patchy, yet every detail helps contribute to the most rigorous, objective and critically balanced work possible.

The sources

Contrary to established narratives about the period, important sources exist which allow for an investigation of 1970s film culture. Personal and industrial papers are becoming available all the time, and new deposits of archival material are coming to light. While many conventional sources which have been utilised in the historical study of film and cinema, such as audience figures, Mass Observation data and fan magazines, do not exist for the 1970s, other material does offer information on aspects of film production and reception if considered imaginatively. For example, the figures from the Eady Levy issued by the Film Fund Agency have not been adequately considered as a source to indicate the successes of specific companies, yet they offer vital clues as to the success of production companies and the financial stability of the industry.

The film industry comprises companies, individuals, unions, pressure groups and government-funded organisations, all of which contribute to the films produced. During any period, the various positions of these stakeholders shift, and with them shifts the balance of power. In order to discuss and evaluate the structure of the film industry, I have used production details and end-of-year accounts from Associated British Picture Corp (ABC), EMI Films, Rank and British Lion, as well as material pertaining to the activities of groups such as the Film Producers Association, the Association of Independent Producers and the Association of Cinema and Television Technicians. This material will be supplemented by additional material from trade press publications *Kinematograph Weekly* (later *CinemaTV Today*) and *Screen International*. Material from the National Archives pertaining to the National Film Finance Corporation, Film Fund Agency and Cinematograph Films Council also offer important details about the involvement of successive governments in the industry. Missing from this study is the work of the British Board of Film Censors (BBFC) in the period and the reason for its exclusion here is simply that it has been published elsewhere and so will not be duplicated here. A full-length study of the archive material from the BBFC in the 1970s has been published as *Censoring the 1970s: The BBFC and the Decade That Taste Forgot* but will be referred to where relevant here, particularly when highlighting issues of popular taste and drawing attention to cultural taboos.[22]

Articles, letters and reviews from *ABC Film Review, Cosmopolitan, Films and Filming, Monthly Film Bulletin* and *Film Review* will be used to acknowledge the important role played by audiences and critics and how such publications documented and shaped popular taste. I will, of course, be considering the differing readerships of these publications and what this suggests about the tone, content and focus of the material. Further evidence will be gathered from newspapers to balance the critical perspectives of industry publications with more mainstream observations. While it is often difficult to establish who saw a film, what they thought about it and how they responded to it, such information is a vital part of film history. Audience response is notoriously difficult to obtain, yet the relationship between film and spectator is a crucial one which can shed light on popular taste and audience preferences.

Recent work undertaken on film audiences by Robert James, Mark Glancy and Sue Harper draws upon data which offer unique insights into the world of the audience.[23] However, such finds are rare and the information they offer is usually restricted to a particular geographical area, making it difficult to establish wider trends. For example, Harper's work on Portsmouth is based upon the accounts of a single cinema in the city for the 1930s and 1940s. The admission figures, which form the basis of this work, are useful indicators of popularity and of audience taste, but can only tentatively be applied to the wider city and wider cinema-going practices of the period. Other sources which have been frequently used to analyse the responses of audiences to films include the Mass Observation material held at the University of Sussex. While this material is extensive for the 1930s and 1940s, Mass Observation data ceased to be collected in the early 1950s, so these important documentations of personal response do not exist for the 1970s period.

In the absence of such data on the 1970s, other sources must be found. One crucial find has been the personal ledgers of James Tilmouth, who managed the Odeon cinemas in Gloucester and Southampton during the 1970s. These records reveal which films were shown in these particular cinemas, how many people saw them, and how much money each film made. It is possible from this data to speculate about the popularity and success of individual films as well as map regional trends. However, it is unwise to generalise using such sparse data. As well as the possible inaccuracies and omissions within the records, these accounts only offer an insight into films shown in a single cinema, and they cannot be used to create a full picture of cinema-going in either Southampton or

Gloucester. What the data do permit is for trends to be mapped and tentative conclusions to be reached. When juxtaposed with institutional evidence, such material can also be used to suggest stronger trends. An exploration and analysis of this work has already been published in the journal *Postscript: Essays in the Arts and Humanities*, and so to avoid repetition this work is not included in full here but rather the evidence from the ledgers is cited only when relevant.[24] The importance of these ledgers and the fact that they were recently discovered attest to the vast amount of source material which is emerging. New material emerges all the time and can be used to challenge established narratives, as well as develop and enhance existing work.

Interviews conducted with important members of the film industry are also used to draw out key issues pertaining to the film industry and the films themselves. The views and information offered by Don Boyd, Michael Winner, Glenda Jackson, Ray Connolly, David Puttnam and Sandy Lieberson all provide insights into the decade. Yet, while remembered stories, events and anecdotes can provide riches for the researcher, it is wise to be cautious. In asking people to recall events which took place 30 years ago, it is inevitable that memories will become cloudy and accounts will change over time. It is also important to consider that in retelling or recalling past events, the interviewee also comments on what has occurred for the benefit of the interviewer. As Perks and Thomson observe, 'the narrator not only recalls the past, but also asserts his or her interpretation of the past.'[25] Interviews are not about facts, but are rather about how the interviewee interprets and relays information through the filter of memory. Like any other historical source, interviews offer valuable evidence, yet must be used carefully and their fallibility fully acknowledged. As Spicer has commented on Annette Kuhn's substantial work on audiences and film culture, 'the great strength of this study is that this oral history is not taken as unproblematic evidence [. . .] but understood as a complex discourse that is produced in the activity of remembering itself.'[26] This is a crucial point for any work which draws upon interview material and oral history.

Structure of this work

This work will be structured around three key themes; firstly, the importance of works about the film industry and cinema and their relevance to broader cultural histories, particularly for undervalued periods like the 1970s; secondly, a detailed exploration of cultures of production, specifically the people, pressure groups, production companies and financiers of the British film industry, to construct a picture of an industry torn between commerce and culture; thirdly, a series of case studies based on archival evidence to further elucidate the themes, visual style, technological developments and economic determinants identified in earlier parts of this work.

The case studies selected are not representative of 'typical' 1970s films, but have been selected for inclusion because they offer rich and detailed accompanying archival evidence. Of course, in selecting these films I am making choices, but have hopefully provided a range of films which represent the rich cultural spread of the decade. As I will demonstrate, due to the eclectic and uneven nature of the film culture, there are no 'typical' 1970s films, but rather a series of interesting examples, which can be used to explore broader issues.

Such an approach makes it perfectly appropriate to consider a film such as *Eskimo Nell* (1975) alongside *Ryan's Daughter* (1970). The purpose is not to differentiate or strive to find similarities, but rather to investigate how such different films can be a product of the same period and what this suggests about that period. I will also be considering the popularity of the texts, in order to speculate about the different cultural tasks they performed and what this in turn suggests about audience preferences and popular taste.

Although ambitious in scope, this study does not aim to be exhaustive or all-encompassing; the study of any historical period can never include everything. I want to offer a re-evaluation of this period to allow space for new ideas to be explored and for the decade to be considered on its own merits without resorting to tired clichés. Such an investigation is intended to free the decade from the frequently inaccurate and limited representations that have hitherto prevailed. The study of film as a cultural object is important in any period but never more so than for Britain in the 1970s.

2
Understanding the 1970s

Although frequently overlooked, the 1970s was a pivotal decade in post-war British history. As with histories of its visual culture, most historical accounts fail to consider the cultural, social and political diversity of the decade, focusing instead on significant events or broader trends. Conventional histories focus on issues such as the economic instability partially caused by the oil crisis of 1973, and the massive rise in inflation which peaked at 24.2% in 1975.[1]

Along with economic instability, political histories have frequently recounted the battles between the government and the trade unions which occurred in 1973–1974 and later in 'the winter of discontent' of 1978–1979. These events played a major part in bringing down the respective Heath and Callaghan governments and call attention to the parlous state of British politics. Party politics within the decade has also received a great deal of attention, with much focus being given to the polarisation and decline of the Left and a swing towards the Right, culminating in the election of Margaret Thatcher in 1979. However, even in the well-told narratives of economic and political instability, there are important omissions. Despite its characterisation as a repressive and gloomy decade, in which the political Left was in disarray, the 1970s saw a mass of liberalising legislation, including the Equal Pay Act (1970), the Matrimonial Causes Act (1973), which offered no-fault divorce for the first time, and the Race Relations Act (1976). Although much of this legislation had its roots in the previous decade, the enacting of such important and life-changing legislation stands testament to some of the successes of various administrations. These successes have been consistently overlooked in favour of accounts which emphasise the notable failures of government in the decade.

15

The 1970s was a decade which ran the gamut of political and social upheavals, yet conventional narratives do not reflect this diversity. Even the recent publication by Dominic Sandbrook, which extends his series of accessible social histories into the 1970s, tells a tale of decline, unease and conflict.[2] While Sandbrook does account for the uncertainty of the decade and notes that 'the point is not that Britain was a stagnant unchanging society but that the overall picture was so messy, diverse and variegated that any generalisation is bound to be risky,' he resorts to focusing on the most easily accessible cultural forms using *Confessions of a Window Cleaner* (1974) to discuss changes in permissiveness and *Love Thy Neighbour* to address issues of race.[3] In doing so, he falls into the trap of identifying a straightforward and reflexive relationship between society and culture. He tells the well-established tale of a film industry in decline in the decade, whilst paradoxically acknowledging the 'enormous richness and diversity' of the cultural landscape.[4]

The Sandbrook narrative has moved on from Norman Shrapnel's description of the decade as a 'splitting headache of unemployment, class and racial friction and economic slump,' but still fails to provide more than a brief glimpse into popular culture. Christopher Booker and Alexander Walker have both perceived the decade as the 'morning after' which followed the excesses and euphoria of the 1960s.[5] However, the political minefield of Northern Ireland, the intricacies of European politics and Organisation of the Petroleum Exporting Countries (OPEC), the political activism of second-wave feminism and gay rights and the music industry's defiant Rock against Racism all refute the notion of the 1970s as a decade of stagnation and crisis. Rather, this was a decade of confusion and change. It is no longer enough to fall back upon the tired narratives and old cliché of a 'decade in crisis.'

This labelling of the decade as a period of crisis has also been freely applied to the culture of the 1970s; some individual trends have been mapped and numerous accounts document the nostalgic appeal of glam rock, children's television and the *Carry On* series, yet few studies have considered the political, social and cultural implications of the decade as a whole. The period, like any other historical period, needs to be considered on its own merits to allow academic scholarship to sift through the well-told narratives to recognise, as Marc Bloch has identified, that 'the knowledge of the past is something progressive which is constantly transforming and perfecting itself.'[6] As new sources come to light and older sources are critically re-evaluated, our understanding of the past grows and allows for new interpretations. Our knowledge and understanding of the past is not finite and the 1970s, like any other historical period, cannot and should not be seen as a decade which has yielded everything possible of value.

Some recent attempts have imagined the 1970s more thoughtfully. Both Richard Weight's *Patriots: National Identity in Britain 1940–2000* and Andrew Marr's *A History of Modern Britain* firmly locate the 1970s within the wider context of post-war British politics and address the crucial issue of periodisation.[7] Neither historical, political nor cultural change can be mapped in tidy decades; there is overlap and continuity as well as rifts and fragmentations. The parameters of the 1970s period do not sit firmly between 1970 and 1979; so much that blossomed in the 1970s began with the political activism of 1968 and culminated with the election victory of Margaret Thatcher in 1979. This would seem to position the notion of 'the long 1970s' in a similar way to the figuring of 'the long 1960s' which began with the rise of rock and roll in the late 1950s. Arguably, films such as *Performance* (1970), *Sunday Bloody Sunday* (1971) and *10 Rillington Place* (1971) owe much of their script, narrative and character development to work undertaken in the 1960s rather than the 1970s. So, for the purposes of this work, I will contend that the film culture of the 1970s period extends far beyond 1970 and 1979. As Arthur Marwick identifies in his study of the 1960s, 'decades as defined by the calendar do not usually coincide with the analytical periods of the historian.'[8]

The 1970s decade has also consistently been likened to other historical periods, most commonly the 1930s, with both Shrapnel and Alwyn Turner noting similarities in inflation, unemployment and militant trade unionism.[9] This was refuted by Hobsbawm who rejected such economic comparisons as 'seriously flawed' and instead located the period from 1973 to 1991 amidst worldwide patterns of political and economic change.[10] While it is important to acknowledge the increasing globalisation of this period, this approach yet again minimises the importance of the 1970s as a discrete period in British social and cultural history.

In *From Apathy to Anger: The Story of Politics, Society and Popular Culture in Britain Since 1975* Mark Garnett refrains from the usual diatribes about the 1970s as a forgotten decade, and instead sees it as an important era in the development of post-war Britain.[11] In tracing thematic developments in politics and culture Garnett establishes the long cultural roots of social periods, and links changes in politics and social attitudes to significant cultural shifts. Andy Beckett draws attention to the way in which the decade has been studied, suggesting 'the Seventies as an era has been simplified more than most.'[12] This indicates how interpretations of this decade are based upon existing narratives and personal memories.

Although many of these historical studies do not offer a great deal of space to the centrality of culture, certain key ideas identified can also be applied to the study of culture and film. Film culture, like historical events, often has its roots in earlier periods. Arthur Marwick considered that the 1970s saw a widespread decline of Britain's popular culture which had failed to live up to the promises of the previous decade, while journalist Andrew Marr perceives the decade as, 'a nightmare inversion of the 60s dream.'[13] Yet these traditional narratives are contested by Richard Weight, who argues persuasively for a history which combines the popular with the political. He notes:

> It is impossible to write this or any other history without looking at what the great majority of people were consuming and then trying to assess how they thought about it... history without popular culture is not history with a stiff upper lip. It is something much worse. It is... incoherent and quite unable to communicate the full breadth of human experience.[14]

Personal experience must be considered within political narratives, just as the cultural must consider wider political and economic contexts. However, personal experiences should not be used to construct a historical or scholarly account of the decade. In the same way, it is not sufficient to seek to 'explain' a decade through its dominant occurrences and simply trace the course of events unquestioningly, without challenging long-held assumptions and previous findings.

Howard Sounes' *Seventies: The Sights, Sounds and Ideas of a Brilliant Decade* adopts a case-study approach which focuses, as Beckett's political history does, on episodes of personal interest, and neither challenge many of the established myths about the decade.[15] Alwyn Turner attempts to consider high politics alongside low culture, but fails to account for the diversity of culture, both high and low, which characterised the 1970s.[16] By considering the decade's cultural high points to be football, the TV sitcom and pop music, Turner presents a cultural hegemony which leaves little room for anything else.

Cultural accounts

Bart Moore-Gilbert's *The Arts in the 1970s: Cultural Closure?* contains a chapter by Andrew Higson on film in the decade, but in separating the arts into standalone entities, this approach does not allow for an examination of the ways in which the arts overlapped and informed each other.[17] Robert Hewison's *Too Much: Art and Society in the Sixties 1960–75* does consider the relationship between arts and culture, spanning the conventional breaks between the decades and ensuring his work is untroubled by issues of periodisation.[18] Hewison sees these overlapping decades as periods of continuity and development, yet does not consider mainstream film culture alongside a wider discussion of the arts. John A Walker's *Left Shift: Radical Art in 1970s Britain*, utilises a chronological approach, highlighting important cultural events from each year and incorporates avant-garde film practices, painting, design and sculpture alongside mainstream film, television and music references.[19] While identifying some of the important changes which took place in art during the 1970s, including its ideological and political struggles, Walker also highlights the increasing pluralism of artistic practice which permeated society and demonstrates the high level of cultural exchange which was taking place between the artistic fringe and the mainstream. In accounting for much of the neglected artistic culture of the period, Walker dispenses with notions of the 'dominant' and 'popular' and offers a careful reading of the decade in terms of cultural influences and ideas.

A period cannot be defined solely by its dominant culture, and its cultural diversity must be adequately explored. As Raymond Williams suggested, the dominant culture of a period comprises a system of 'practices, meanings and values...which are not merely abstract but which are organised and lived.'[20] This culture is constantly shifting to incorporate and reject different cultural components while simultaneously drawing upon residual cultural motifs from previous social formations which frequently resurface in different periods as part of or at some distance from the dominant culture.[21] Williams also identifies the importance of emergent cultural forms, which offer 'new meanings and values, new practices, new significances and experiences' and which exist in relation to dominant cultural discourses.[22] Conventional cultural accounts of the 1970s have focused upon dominant and easily identifiable cultural forms, for example, Hammer horror, *Carry On* and James Bond, or seek to examine newly emergent cultural practices which are specific to the period such as sexploitation films, glam rock and punk.

One of the few book-length studies of the period is Alexander Walker's *National Heroes*, which draws upon the author's experience as a journalist and film critic.[23] John Walker's *The Once and Future Film: British Films of the 1970s and 1980s,* offers a helpful overview of the two decades, but fails to recognise the 1970s as a discrete historical or cinematic period.[24] Ernest Betts' *The Film Business,* Sarah Street and Margaret Dickinson's *Cinema and State: The Film Industry and the British Government* and Bill Baillieu and John Goodchild's *The British Film Business* all address the legislative and economic problems faced by the industry in the 1970s.[25] By positioning the 1970s as a period characterised by circuit domination and a lack of governmental aid, these studies run the risk of adopting the more general historical approach of 'Britain in crisis.' Other work on British cinema has contained some detail on the 1970s, but the individual accounts of Street, Leach and Sargeant survey the period, rather than analyse the decade in depth.[26]

One full-length account which does attempt to address the cinematic culture of the 1970s is Leon Hunt's *British Low Culture: From Safari Suits to Sexploitation.*[27] However, Hunt is concerned predominantly with lowbrow material and does not compare this material with other dominant trends at the box office. While Hunt argues persuasively for the need for the critical reappraisal of such material, he does not actively consider the relationship of such material to the wider contexts of production. Hunt approaches this material from a postmodern perspective by actively celebrating the mass popular appeal of lowbrow texts. Yet, as Andrew Higson has identified, cinema in this period was wide-ranging in scope and included 'minority cinemas,' for example, the avant-garde film movement and art cinema.[28]

Other approaches to the 1970s have focused on specific genres of filmmaking, including Steve Chibnall and Julian Petley's work on horror, Andy Medhurst's writings on the *Carry On* series and Peter Hutchings' focus on Hammer.[29] Such work evaluates specific texts and genres, shedding light on many neglected aspects of production, including the roles played by Amicus, Tigon and director Pete Walker within the British horror genre.[30] Studies of the sexploitation film and saucy comedy are also plentiful, although these tend towards a celebration of low cultural production, rather than a critical dissection of the place of these films within the wider canon of British film.[31] There are also publications which analyse iconic films including *Performance* (1970), *Get Carter* (1971) and *Don't Look Now* (1973).[32] These publications celebrate the most obvious successes and points of reference for the period, but do not look to other examples which are just as worthy. James Chapman has also shed new light on different aspects of 1970s film culture which have been critically neglected, including the 'lost world' fantasy adventure films and historical films.[33]

Such investigations add to the body of work on British film and affirm that the period is finally being recognised as worthy of study. Studies of industry figures comprise biographies of directors Ken Russell, Nicolas Roeg, Derek Jarman and Joseph Losey and producers David Puttnam and Michael Deeley and there is a great deal of celebration of these 'auteurs' of 1970s cinema.[34] For most periods of film history, the model of sole authorship has been shown to be flawed, but for the 1970s specifically, it does not work. The changing culture of production actively prevented the concentration of power within the hands of any individual within the filmmaking process. More useful for the 1970s are the studies of production companies including Handmade, Goldcrest and Goodtimes, which and again focus attention upon neglected areas of 1970s film culture.[35]

Recent years have seen an explosion in 1970s film scholarship and a renewed interest in the 1970s as a period. The majority of this work is structured as edited collections, which draw together a range of case studies and examples to shed light on a complex and diverse period of cinema, but which offer no cohesive and detailed exploration of the industrial, financial and governmental frameworks of the period. *Seventies British Cinema*, edited by Robert Shail contains a number of useful essays which highlight under-researched aspects of 1970s film culture, including James Leggott's work on realist cinema, Justin Smith's valuable consideration of funding and production and Dan North's focus on producer Don Boyd.[36] The Paul Newland edited collection *Don't Look Now* emerged from a conference on 1970s cinema and offers a range of material, notably contributions on popular genres, stardom and production.[37] Both of these collections offer useful and varied insights into a decade which has been consistently under-researched, but such an approach does not allow for a consideration of the period as a whole. Forster and Harper's collection of essays on the 1970s eschews a focus on film in favour of an exploration of material as diverse as art, architecture, television, newspapers, magazines, children's programmes and social and political movements.[38]

Although important contributions to the scholarship of the period, these edited collections do not address the wider questions of cultural, social and historical context and there is little attempt to account for the diversity of film texts produced in the period. The most substantial work to emerge about the period is *British Film Culture in the 1970s: The Boundaries of Pleasure* by Harper and Smith.[39] This work explores key aspects of visual culture such as black British film, censorship, avant-garde film practice, cinematography and the impact of television, and draws them

skilfully together using a wide range of archival research, detailed textual analysis and broader thematic concerns. Detailed though this work
is, its focus is the diversity and eclecticism of film culture in the 1970s,
and the structure of the work is based around the contributions made
by a range of project members, myself included. My work does not seek
to duplicate any of the work undertaken by Harper and Smith in this
volume, and the chapters which I contributed are either absent from
this current work (in the case of censorship) or have been restructured
(in the case of the chapter on government).

My own book fits into the space left by Newland, Shail, Harper and
Smith and offers a careful exploration of the film industry in the period.
Within this work, an examination of important archival material –
much of it newly discovered or previously underused – offers an insight
into the industry and the ways in which British filmmaking operated
in the 1970s. Case studies will examine a selection of films to present
a detailed picture of the eclectic, diverse and often challenging film
culture of the period. These case studies are used to draw out issues of
authorship, casting, finance, control and conflict during the production
process, marketing, censorship, exhibition and audience response.

Setting up my study in this way allows me to draw attention to
the way in which the industry and its culture of production created
and informed the film texts of the period. This book considers issues
and themes such as visual style, technological developments, government and the impact of television, but these are all carefully situated in
relation to the film industry itself.

3
Film and Government

The following chapters will explore the cultures of production which shaped, influenced and impacted upon filmmaking in the 1970s. They focus on methods of funding, key personnel, important production companies and crucial industry organisations and institutions. They also consider the influence of the unions, the increasing popularity of television and Britain's decision to join the European Economic Community (EEC) in 1973 and how all of these factors impacted upon film production. The purpose of these chapters is to suggest the link between, for example, the streams of funding and the texts which emerged, and the attitude of successive governments and the impact this had on the films which were funded and produced. Each chapter will shed light on a different aspect of production and suggest how an exploration of these contextual factors can develop our knowledge of the visual texts which emerge in this specific decade.

One of the most important influences on the film industry in this decade, and indeed in any period, was the government. Government attitudes towards the film industry fundamentally determined what methods of support were available to filmmakers. This chapter examines the attitudes towards the industry expressed by the different political administrations through the 1970s, comparing Conservative and Labour film policy and the way in which they imagined the British film industry.

By 1970, there were three established pillars of government support for the film industry: the quota, the National Film Finance Corporation (NFFC) and the Eady Levy. All of these measures were intended to protect the film industry from Hollywood dominance, to provide film projects with adequate funding and to ensure that profits from successful films were ploughed back into the industry. The film quota was established in 1927 and stipulated that British cinemas must show a defined percentage of British films. It was believed that this would help to protect the domestic industry from domination by foreign film products, and ensure that British-made films found exhibition spaces. The quota did stimulate film production and the number of British-made films rose from 34 in 1926 to 131 in 1928, injecting much-needed capital into the film industry.[1] As recent work by Laurence Napper and Steve Chibnall has shown, while the 'quota quickies' were often derided as being of poor quality, they were an important facet of British film production and cannot be overlooked.[2] However, while the quota did improve levels of production, it only served to stimulate the production of small-budget British films, and American productions continued to dominate at the British box office. Addressing this domination and encouraging a competitive domestic industry was one of the objectives of the NFFC.[3]

Initially conceived by the then President of the Board of Trade (and later Prime Minister) Harold Wilson, the NFFC was formed in 1949. Wilson recognised that although close collaboration with Hollywood was inevitable, the British industry should not be entirely dependent on this relationship. He considered the best way to ensure independence was through a strong domestic industry. Following its creation, the NFFC was endowed with £6 million from the government, which Vincent Porter maintains was to be used to finance films on 'a commercial basis.'[4] While the NFFC was expected to become independent of government support and operate as a bank, it was hampered by an early decision to loan over £2 million of its funds to the struggling production company British Lion. Between 1949 and 1972, the NFFC played an active part in film production, financing 731 long films and 173 shorts at a cost of £28 million, while continuing to make further payments to British Lion.[5]

While the NFFC did fund a number of important British productions, many of its investments were small-budget feature films. These had little chance of generating enough profit to pay back the initial loans, let alone to guarantee a return on the investment. The money which the NFFC supplied for film production was neither the riskier 'end' money nor the 'front' money. The suppliers of the 'front' money, who got their investment back first, only came to the project when the 'end' money, usually committed by the producer and underwritten by a loan, was already in place. The NFFC's investment sat between the front money and the end money. In operating between these two types of funding, the NFFC was again unable to commit itself to risky projects as this could mean the loss of its investment, yet, paradoxically, it would only make a substantial return on its investment if the film project was a major financial success.[6] By the start of the 1970s, following the American incursion into the British industry throughout the 1960s, the NFFC was not in a position to make an important contribution due to its chaotic finances.

The final pillar of support for the film industry was a tax levied on exhibitors set up in 1954. Exhibitors were required to repay a percentage of cinema admissions, which were then passed back to the producers of successful films. Named after the Treasury official who implemented it, the Eady Levy offered a conduit through which successful companies could channel money back into production. Unfortunately, it also meant that successful films were the ones who benefited most from the system. For example, major beneficiaries included the already successful *Carry On* films and the James Bond franchise. As well as supporting successful franchises, figures from the Film Fund Agency reveal that the major American companies were also major beneficiaries of Eady money.[7] By filming in Britain or using shell companies based in the UK, American companies were able to register their films as British and become eligible for the Levy. In 1970, United Artists and Columbia took over 40% of the available Levy, a combined amount of £1.3 million.[8] In the same year, Anglo-EMI took only 7%, while British Lion received 1.5%. The Rank Corporation did better, with a 16% percentage share during this year but this dropped to a mere 2% of the total fund available by 1975.[9] These figures indicate that, despite its specified objectives, large amounts of the Levy fund ended up in Hollywood rather than in Britain.

In addition to these three pillars of government support, there was also the BFI Production Board. In 1966, the Production Board replaced the Experimental Film Fund which had been created in 1952 to subsidise young filmmakers. By the 1970s, the Board was receiving substantial sums of money from the British Film Institute as well as from the Eady fund, with its total operating annual figure estimated in 1976 to be £120,000.[10] However, the Board was plagued with similar issues to the NFFC. Alan Lovell, writing in 1976, noted the need for the Board to 'decide what kind of role it should play' and how the parameters of experimental and independent filmmaking should be defined.[11] Like the NFFC, the Production Board was uncertain as to what kind of films it should fund.

The measures set in place by previous governments had not created and sustained a stable British film industry. Yet, distributors, producers and exhibitors waited expectantly for the Labour government's proposed Films Act of 1970 to address contemporary and historical issues of contention, including: the withdrawal of American money, the competition from television and the implications of new audiovisual technologies. Unfortunately, the Cinematograph Act of 1970 was an essentially cautious piece of legislation, providing emergency funds of £5 million to the NFFC to help stimulate production, but taking no other measures to address specific problems. Even the £5 million promised by the Board of Trade was not to materialise, becoming one of the first casualties of Conservative film policy. £1 million of this amount had been advanced before the general election, but following the Conservatives' successful return to power, the rest of the money was withheld and a change of direction in policy was announced.

Conservative film policy

In an interview in *Kinematograph Weekly* in December 1970, the newly appointed Films Minister, Nicholas Ridley, detailed the government's position:

> There is more government intervention in films, than in practically any other industry in the country. We'd like to phase out the injection of public funds [to the NFFC]...I would very much like to see the NFFC giving us a million out of successful trading instead of us giving it a million.[12]

Ridley's remarks clearly outlined the new government's approach to the industry and to the NFFC. Such an attitude is perhaps understandable when considering the chaotic state of the NFFC at the start of the 1970s, due mainly to poor investments and continued support of British Lion. In 1971, the government and the NFFC announced a new Consortium scheme to encourage city financiers to invest in the film industry. The government offered the NFFC £1 million, on the condition that every pound of government money was matched with three pounds from the private sector. The government believed that such an approach would enable the film industry to become financially viable and independent of government support.

Horrified industry figures including Michael Balcon, Richard Attenborough, Karel Reisz, John Schlesinger, Joseph Losey and Lindsay Anderson wrote an open letter to *The Times* arguing that without capital the NFFC would never be seen as a viable investment opportunity by the private sector.[13] The previous Labour Films Minister, Gwyneth

Dunwoody, who had become head of the Film Producers Association, also criticised the policy:

> In future it will become virtually impossible for the independent film-makers to attract outside finance.... It is yet another example of the total disregard for British interests displayed by a government which is rapidly becoming known for its philistine lack of appreciation for the arts.[14]

The policy was also challenged in Parliament. Roy Mason MP, roundly condemned the shift in policy in a Commons debate in July 1971, asking:

> Does the Honourable Gentleman realise where this policy is leading? He must be trying to kill British film production. His impositions on the NFFC and the reduction of its loan making powers, allied to less money from the Levy, are bound to affect production [and] employment... and to lessen confidence in the future of the British film industry.[15]

The objections of those in opposition reveal fundamental differences about how the film industry should be treated, and demonstrate how dependent the film industry was upon a sympathetic government. The Conservatives' Consortium scheme was intended to make the film industry economically viable yet denying it any kind of financial autonomy made it structurally weak. It would inevitably be larger, high-profile and financially viable projects which would attract the backing of city financiers; smaller, independent projects would be unlikely to attract finance from the private sector. But despite objections, the NFFC Consortium was established and the government's attitude towards the film industry irrevocably fixed. At a single stroke, the government had defined the NFFC as a financial institution, but had severely restricted its lending and investment capabilities by insisting that it operate on a tight budget with limited capital. In an era of spiralling costs, the funding possibilities offered by the NFFC were limited. Even the head of the Corporation, John Terry, was sceptical, noting in September 1971, 'unless we can raise a total of £3 million, we don't think the thing is worth starting... if only we could get a fund up to something like £10 million then we could really do something.'[16]

In its first six years the Consortium financed the production of only 19 feature films and city investors contributed the sum total of

£750,000. This, when added to the £1 million begrudgingly supplied by the government, offered limited opportunities. This investment sum was too small to support high-budget feature films; such films being the only type of project which would guarantee the expected significant returns.[17] One of the first film projects undertaken by the NFFC Consortium on a 'strictly commercial basis' was the 1971 production of Dylan Thomas' *Under Milk Wood* (1972) starring Richard Burton and Peter O'Toole.[18] Investment bank Samuel Hill supplied one third of the production costs, whilst the NFFC provided the remaining £200,000.[19] Despite optimistic predictions, this film failed to make any significant impact at the British box office, audiences instead preferring to see *Diamonds Are Forever* (1971), *The Godfather* (1972) and *Bedknobs and Broomsticks* (1971).[20] The success of *Under Milk Wood* would have guaranteed the investors a return on their money while also generating profit and credibility for the NFFC, but this was not to be.

The NFFC

The NFFC was the most important pillar of government support for the film industry, but it was never explicitly defined what the role of the organisation was and what kind of films it should fund. Should it fund artistic and cultural films, or those with the greatest chance of financial success? Should it act as a bank, primarily concerned with profit, or should it support creative enterprise with artistic achievement as its most important concern? Furthermore, should it support independent companies, directors and producers who had no other sources of funding, or should it only deal with established industry figures with proven records of success? With such poorly defined objectives it is perhaps unsurprising that the film projects selected for NFFC funding in the early years of the decade were neither important and artistic nor financially successful.

Films allocated production funding included, *A Touch of the Other* (1970), *Up Pompeii* (1971), *I, Monster* (1971) and *Ooh... You Are Awful* (1972), demonstrating the heavily domestic, low-budget priorities of the NFFC. Funding such films was never going to increase the credibility of the Corporation, nor generate a great deal of profit. However, in the years that followed, even this conservative, domestic policy was abandoned in favour of a range of eclectic funding choices. The NFFC's objective was to back a high-profile and financially successful film, but despite funding 68 film projects between 1969 and 1980, only four of these made it into the top 20 at the British box office.[21] The success of

Table 3.1 British film production and the NFFC

Year	Number of British films made	Number of films approved for NFFC loans	NFFC funded films as percentage of British films produced
1969–1970	97	10	10.3
1970–1971	96	15	15.6
1971–1972	104	2	1.9
1972–1973	99	4	4.0
1973–1974	88	1	1.1
1974–1975	81	9	11.1
1975–1976	80	1	1.3
1976–1977	50	5	10.0
1977–1978	54	5	9.2
1978–1979	61	10	16.4
1979–1980	31	6	19.3
Total	781	68	8.7

Source: NFFC Annual Reports 1969–1980 and www.screenonline.org.uk

Up Pompeii, Stardust (1974), *At the Earth's Core* (1976) and *Bugsy Malone* (1977) did provide an investment return for the NFFC, but also indicated their diverse funding policy.[22] In terms of broader British film production, the NFFC's influence was limited, as indicated by Table 3.1 above.

In only funding or part-funding 8.7% of films produced in the 1970s, the NFFC occupied a marginal role in British film production. While this percentage rose in the later years of the decade, fewer films were actually being made and production was sharply falling.

Back in 1971, the Corporation's annual report clearly acknowledges its confused funding policy and weak financial position:

> These unsatisfactory trading results are partly due to the very limited choice of projects available to the Corporation in recent years. This in turn derives from the fact that during this period, the most promising projects have tended to be presented for financing almost automatically to the major US companies and have generally passed the Corporation by because of its financial weakness.[23]

With the American studios pulling back from funding British films, the NFFC had an opportunity to become a major player in the British film industry, since it had first choice of all proposed film projects. Realistically, without increased investment, the Corporation could not engage in financial speculation. Increased funding from private sources had not materialised and the NFFC continued to fund films it considered to have the greatest chance of modest financial success, resulting in a strange and eclectic mixture of the popular and the lowbrow. These projects included an Agatha Christie adaptation, *Endless Night* (1972), a TV comedy sequel, *Steptoe and Son Ride Again* (1973) and a Hammer horror *Captain Kronos: Vampire Hunter* (1974).

In 1973–1974, only one film project was allocated a grant, a departure from the 15 projects funded in 1970–1971. *Stardust* was the sequel to *That'll Be the Day* (1973), which had been part-funded by EMI and been tenth at the British box office the previous year.[24] By funding only one film, albeit one that was seen as a safe bet, the NFFC was taking a risk. *Stardust* had to make money, or else be a huge financial embarrassment for all concerned. The project was funded in equal parts by EMI and the NFFC Consortium, and was chosen for funding because it was considered to be 'the only project out of 134 submitted to the corporation during the year which was ready to go into commercial production and which seemed to have an outstanding chance of commercial success.'[25]

The annual report for 1974 noted that the Consortium had resources of £1,750,000 and could easily have committed them to a variety of projects, yet this approach was felt to be 'foolhardy.'[26] Such hesitancy demonstrates a distinct lack of confidence in the film industry and can be easily understood within the context of rocketing inflation and industrial unease. By funding TV spin-offs in the early years of the decade the NFFC had been tapping into the growing audience for television in a bid to lure this audience to the cinema. By funding a sequel such as *Stardust*, the NFFC was basing their funding decision upon the straightforward belief that if the film did as well as its predecessor it would make money. Ultimately, this conservative gamble paid off, but the film ran into difficulties when its content proved troublesome for the British Board of Film Censors. It was only after the BBFC were satisfied that the film's language and content was appropriate for its teenage audience that *Stardust* was granted its AA certificate and went on to feature as one of the top films of both 1974 and 1975.[27] The success of this venture provoked a shift in NFFC policy and funding decisions began to be based around continued investment and collaboration with already successful companies and individuals.

The decision to fund established industry figures who had enjoyed recent success led to further collaboration with David Puttnam on projects including *Lisztomania* (1975) directed by Ken Russell, *Bugsy Malone* with Alan Parker and *The Duellists* (1977) directed by Ridley

Scott. These high-profile collaborations established a mutually beneficial relationship between Puttnam and Lieberson's Goodtimes Enterprises and the NFFC and provided the NFFC with much-needed artistic credibility as well as financial success. Prolonged collaboration with established partners became a standard feature of NFFC investment in the later 1970s, with established directors including Joseph Losey, Nicolas Roeg and Ken Loach also being granted funding. By 1977, this change of direction was further compounded by the NFFC's decision to become involved with more creative and artistic projects which, while not offering substantial financial returns, did allow the Corporation to become strongly associated with films of aesthetic and cultural value. After declining to part-fund *Carry On England* (1976), the annual report for 1977 proudly notes the NFFC's involvement with *Bugsy Malone*, *Black Joy* (1977), *The Shout* (1977) and *The Duellists*, all of which performed well at the Cannes film festival.[28] Involvement with such projects was a trend which continued throughout the rest of the decade, with funding of an adaptation of the Erskine Childers' novel, *The Riddle of the Sands* (1979) and the first Merchant Ivory production, *The Europeans* (1979).

Labour film policy

In 1974, Labour won the general election, and appeared to offer renewed hope to the severely depressed film industry. One of the first initiatives was a meeting of film industry representatives with Prime Minister Harold Wilson in May 1975 to discuss the future of the industry. A month later, in a statement to the House of Commons, Wilson announced that a working party would be established to 'report back on the future needs of the industry and its relationship with the Government.'[29] The working party was chaired by John Terry of the NFFC, and included Richard Attenborough, Bernard Delfont, John Woolf, Michael Deeley and Alan Sapper. The working party was hailed as a breakthrough in relations between the film industry and the Labour government; it appeared that this government recognised that film performed an important social and cultural function. It was also felt that this government believed a strong and independent British film industry could generate income from both the domestic and overseas markets. Although an excellent idea, the working party suffered from the Labour government's desire to address problems by committee. As an information-gathering exercise, surveying the views of the industry was a positive step, but it was unlikely that the disparate and polarised film industry would unanimously agree on a course of action.

The debt-ridden NFFC however, was less critical, declaring with palpable relief in 1976, 'the Corporation intends to give every support to the Interim Action Committee and to deploy its present resources as effectively as possible.'[30] The NFFC was clearly hoping for a resolution to its long-running financial predicament and it chose to believe that the problems within the industry were being taken seriously at last.

When the working party reported in January 1976, the recommendations were extensive. The report recommended that the relationship with television, the involvement of American companies in funding British films and co-production agreements all needed to be addressed. One of the most important recommendations was the establishment of a British Film Authority (BFA) which would oversee the Eady Levy and incorporate the British Film Fund Agency and the NFFC. It would also take over the role held by the Cinematograph Films Council in advising the government on film policy. This BFA would incorporate all these existing functions and operations, making it easier to administer, with the initial operating expenses to be met by the government.[31] The financial recommendations of the report included: investment in the British film industry to be £40 million per annum; one fifth of the Eady Fund yield per year to go to the NFFC; additional funds of £5 million to be provided by the government, and the right for the Films Authority to call on additional funds of £5 million in subsequent years.[32] It was also requested that the NFFC be given the residual sum of £2.3 million, which had been granted by the Board of Trade in 1970, but which had been withheld. These recommendations formed the main body of the report but there were other significant items including: finance for feature films to be provided by the British Broadcasting Corporation (BBC) and Independent Television (ITV); a three-year statutory time gap before films could be shown on television; and better prices for films offered to UK television.[33]

Meeting notes from the Cinematograph Film Council reveal widely differing responses to the recommendations of the Terry Report, highlighting once again the divisions which were tearing apart the British industry.[34] Elizabeth Ackroyd argued that there was nothing in the committee's findings or the resulting report that made a good case for government funding for the film industry or the NFFC, while Lord Brabourne shared the views of Lew Grade in believing the film industry needed to make international pictures which could be marketed abroad and recoup costs. Other committee members considered that all the problems lay with the NFFC, its organisational structure and its poor decisions in offering funding to bad films.[35] Half the committee believed that the job of deciding which films to fund belonged to a financial decision-maker, whilst others felt it was the job of an artistic director.[36] A suggestion was made that the function of the NFFC should be that of an investment bank, whilst the proposed BFA should operate like a business by securing good projects to invest in.

This range of views reveals the fundamental flaws within the industry and the differences which prevented fruitful collaboration between the industry and the government. Exhibitors and distributors disagreed with producers; small production companies argued against the well-established distribution monopoly of Rank and ABC and everyone objected to the inherent inequalities of the NFFC and the Eady Levy. These opinions also demonstrate how polarised the film industry was and how its members had little common ground. While offering pragmatic and achievable suggestions, the Terry Report inadvertently illuminated internal and industrial divisions. It is doubtful whether the implementation of the proposals could ever have lived up to the varied and wide-ranging expectations of such a fragmented industry. There was little evidence to suggest that the intransigence on the part of certain factions would ever be resolved, notably the unions and the powerful conglomerates. One of the few unequivocal supporters of the Report was Harold Wilson. In a memo to the President of the Board of Trade in January 1976, he wrote:

I should like attention directed to the main proposals for regeneration and expansion of the [film] industry. This is not a lame duck situation. It should be looked at more as a parallel... with action taken by the government to regenerate a whole series of industries... One possibility would be to provide capital comparable with what has recently been done for the wool, machine tools, textile industry and other industries.[37]

By suggesting the same provisions for the film industry as for other industries, Wilson indicated that in his opinion, the entertainment industry was crucial to Britain. Though laudable, this approach did not adequately define the industry as either commerce or art. Comparing film to other industries suggests commerce, but the call for increased government funding and subsidy, places it alongside other heavily subsided facets of culture, such as theatre or museums. However, before any of the report proposals could be realised, the political instability, which had caused so much variation in policy at the start of the decade, re-emerged.

Missed opportunities

Wilson's resignation as Prime Minister, barely three months after the publication of the Terry Report, was a catastrophe for an industry which at last stood to benefit from his support. His successor James Callaghan appointed Wilson as the chairman of an action committee to follow up on the proposals and the film industry continued to be cautiously optimistic about its future. In 1978, the Under Secretary of State for Trade made a landmark statement to the House of Commons on film policy, stating:

> We certainly intend legislation in this Parliament, in the form of a National Film Finance Corporation Bill, because we are committed to ensuring that the NFFC has enough funds for the next five years, or until it is subsumed into the British Film Authority. We are certainly committed to ensuring that its funds do not run out in this session.[38]

Unfortunately, these promised plans to secure the future of the NFFC were never realised. Labour lost the 1979 general election and the eagerly anticipated financial legislation failed to materialise. Despite assurances from the new Conservative administration which claimed to 'recognise the value to Britain of a vigorous British film industry and wish to encourage its development,' a new Films Bill was proposed which heralded the resurrection of an eerily familiar policy.[39] The bill was announced on 25 April 1980 and its change of focus was obvious. While the £13 million owed by the NFFC to the government was to be written off, the government was to make a final payment of £1 million to the NFFC to keep it afloat until 'other sources of funds are forthcoming.'[40] The bill outlined how funds would be diverted from the Eady Levy to support the NFFC, and the opportunity for the Corporation to borrow from non-governmental sources was extended from £2 million to £5 million.[41] All of these measures signalled that the government was unwilling to directly support the NFFC or the film industry any further. The bill also criticised the NFFC's failure to back a blockbuster, stating:

> If we create a climate more favourable to the creation of risk capital, private finance will be forthcoming to back more pictures. It is not an activity in which Governments can meddle with any chance of success... the government having helped to set the stage in the bill, it will be up to the industry to perform.[42]

Such statements are strikingly similar to the stance outlined by Nicholas Ridley in 1971, indicating how Conservative policy towards the film industry remained unchanged throughout the decade, with the emphasis firmly on self-funding rather than government grants. Despite criticisms of the proposed bill, one MP terming it 'an elastoplast to stop a haemorrhage,' it went ahead as planned and was unenthusiastically received by the film industry as the best deal they were likely to get.[43]

However, at the end of the 1970s, a glimmer of hope appeared for the film industry. Although production remained weak and the number of films produced was relatively small – only 31 in 1980 – the films that were being made were of high quality, often independently funded and could be sold to other markets. Figures from the Eady fund reveal shifts in distribution and production, with recently established and newly created companies taking smaller chunks of the Levy fund in later years of the decade, allowing for a greater distribution of the available money. This ensured that at least some of the money was ploughed back into the British rather than the American industry. British film production had diversified and fragmented to such an extent that small production and distribution companies proliferated, often being formed for a single film. While this ad hoc and entrepreneurial spirit of small-budget and localised film production is indicative of a lack of conventional funding opportunities, it also meant that the larger conglomerates no longer held total sway over the industry. In 1979, the tiny British company Tigon took over 1.2% of the available Levy fund (over £66,000), Rank clung on to 12% and Anglo-EMI took 5%, while the major beneficiaries from previous years had substantially reduced sums, Columbia receiving 7% and United Artists 17%.[44] Although still large sums, both of these figures are significantly lower than at the start of the decade, despite the resurgence of an American presence within British production. Perhaps this can be attributed to the cap that had been placed on the Levy which restricted the amount paid out to any single film. However, it is also important to note that the total amount available from the Levy fund had increased from the start of the decade, rising from over £3.3 million in 1970 to £5.6 million in 1979.[45] While this was partially due to rising inflation, the increase in the number of companies claiming money from the Levy indicates that the money was trickling down though smaller production and distribution outlets in the way that the fund was initially intended to function.[46]

Although the findings of the Terry Report were not acted upon, many of the suggestions and ideas proposed in the 1970s by the Annan

Report came to fruition in the decade that followed. Channel 4 was launched in 1982 and become an exhibition outlet for British films and also contributed to feature film production with the foundation of Film on Four. Film on Four contributed to many of the successes of the decades that followed, including part-funding *The Draughtsman's Contract* (1982) and *My Beautiful Laundrette* (1985). This method of film finance with a guaranteed space for exhibition helped to bridge the gap between the television and film industries and signalled the collaborative possibilities.

Conclusion

Despite the widely held belief that the film industry was destroyed by successive governments in the 1970s, the decade is notable for the myriad of opportunities proposed to aid the struggling industry. Yet, many of the governmental schemes of assistance were unsuccessful and unrealistic. The Conservatives favoured supporting film at local level, choosing to fund regional film theatres and the BFI Production Board rather than the debt-ridden NFFC, yet this did not stimulate production, and only served to illustrate that British film needed to be supported more effectively. Harold Wilson's Labour government was keen to continue funding the NFFC and to strengthen the domestic film industry, but their efforts rarely progressed beyond committees and reports, which failed to deliver practical solutions. While Labour administrations were broadly sympathetic and were seen to actively champion the film industry, in fact little was achieved by either the Working Party or the Terry Report.

Successive administrations paid lip service to cinema and film, but neither did a great deal to ensure either its survival or its demise. Neither the sympathetic inefficiency of the Labour administration nor the economic pragmatism of the Conservatives offered a real solution for the film industry in the 1970s. Many of the contentious issues visible at the beginning of the period remained unchanged at the end of the decade. However, there were positive issues to emerge from government policy towards the film industry. It was in this period that film finally came to be seen as culture and the importance of the cultural product was recognised. The Conservatives formed the Arts Council and began to make film independent of government support, paving the way for film products which performed a distinct and discrete cultural, rather than economic, function. The Conservative threat to dismantle the NFFC mooted in 1970 was not carried out until the Films Act of 1985 when it was transformed into British Screen Finance which in 2000 came under the auspices of the Film Council.

Part of the responsibility for the stagnation of the British film industry must be borne by the NFFC. By cautiously choosing to support established directors and producers (rather than fund more exciting and unpredictable projects), the NFFC limited its contribution to innovative British film. Film projects which did not benefit from NFFC funding had to seek funds elsewhere, and it was these limited funding opportunities which actively contributed to a more fluid, exciting and alternative culture of production with films including *That'll Be the Day, Tommy* (1975), *Monty Python and the Holy Grail* (1975) and *Carry On England* resulting from unconventional funding alliances.

4
Funding Innovation

While the 1960s was a prosperous era in British film production, the end of the decade saw great uncertainty in the film industry. Hollywood companies had been investing heavily in British film, creating an inflated level of economic and cultural prosperity, which could not be sustained. Estimated figures suggest that by 1968, 90% of British production capital was American, yet by the start of the next decade, economic retrenchment and new funding strategies caused American companies to withdraw much of their investment.[1]

The Anglo-American agreement of 1950 had allowed American companies to repatriate the British profits made on their films, rather than be taxed upon their earnings. Permitting the American majors to gain a financial foothold had enabled Hollywood's influence on the British industry to increase steadily. However, this relationship between the two industries was neither so straightforward nor so dependent as has been thought. As Sarah Street identifies, American production finance offered a lifeline for independent producers, particularly during the late 1960s when funding for British films was few and far between.[2] Ken Russell's *Women in Love* (1969) was made possible by United Artists, and Donald Cammell would make *Performance* (1970) with funding from Warner Brothers. Unfortunately, even the foreign investors were not infallible and at the end of the 1960s, most American studios were in financial difficulty, due in part to unsustainable overseas investment. In the light of such huge losses – Metro-Goldwyn-Mayer (MGM) lost $25 million, 20th Century Fox $36 million, United Artists $45 million and Warner Bros $52 million – Hollywood drastically reduced its activities in overseas markets and the resulting cutbacks added to the slump in British production.[3]

While this withdrawal of capital left the industry in a precarious position, it also offered a rare opportunity to restructure and rejuvenate the industry. However, for this to succeed, sympathetic and pragmatic government support was needed. As shown in the previous chapter, various governmental attitudes and initiatives had not helped to stimulate production or create alternative or effective models of funding, while the NFFC's confused policy and approach had done little to improve things. But parts of the film industry did begin to change the way it operated in order to meet the challenges offered by the decade.

Alternative arrangements

As a response to spiralling costs driven by inflation, a trend developed for filming on location to keep production costs down. The declining fortunes of Elstree Studios show that, despite involvement in important features, the studio space was heavily underused and was running at a loss. Finally, in 1975, EMI announced that Elstree would operate only three of its nine sound stages for film production, a change which had massive repercussions for technicians and studio employees.[4] Many films would still use the post-production studio space but the majority of filming would now take place elsewhere. Films had been made on location before for aesthetic reasons, but in an era of rising studio costs exacerbated by inflation, it was now a decision made through economic necessity. The types of productions which utilised filming on location film ranged from the large scale, such as *The Go-Between,* to smaller operations such as Derek Jarman's *The Tempest.* In her survey of the decade, Linda Wood noted production locations ranging from Romania and Israel to Marrakesh and Nottingham.[5] As well as the impact this had on employment at the film studios, this also created a definite shift in visual style.

One of the films of the period which encapsulates many of these stylistic changes brought about by location filming and reduced funding is *Monty Python and the Holy Grail.* It has been well documented that *Monty Python's Life of Brian* (1979) was funded by ex-Beatle George Harrison, after Bernard Delfont withdrew EMI funding due to concerns about the controversy the film would undoubtedly provoke. HandMade financed the film and, following its success became involved in other productions including *The Long Good Friday* (1979) and *Time Bandits* (1981). What is perhaps less well known is that contributions to the budget for *Monty Python and the Holy Grail* came from bands Pink Floyd and Led Zeppelin, both of whom were eager to capitalise upon the tax-break opportunities of film investment. The film also benefited from a distribution deal with EMI, thus combining independence of production with major studio support; a successful collaboration which foundered following production. *Monty Python and the Holy Grail* was filmed on location in six weeks with a tiny crew and a budget of £250,000. Instead of attempting to conceal the deficiencies in budget, the irreverent Python team incorporated them into the film, which created a home-made quality to the production making it both stylistically striking and hilariously self-aware. The animation sequences to enhance the bare locations and to interlink scenes, the coconut shells which create the clip-clopping of imaginary horses, the costumes borrowed from the dressing-up box and the low-key, high-farce action all combine to create a film which is iconic in its visual inventiveness.

At times highbrow, with its historical references to the siege of Troy and elements of Arthurian legend, and other times lowbrow with its visual comedy, ridiculous accents, expressions and mannerisms, *Monty Python and the Holy Grail* is an excellent example of a 1970s British film created in an uncertain culture of production. The film's style is also typical of many 1970s products with its 'unfinished,' occasionally uneasy, mocking, self-referential quality. Inspired by the Python's popular television series, their comedy makes a successful transition to the screen but still retains many of the elements which worked so well on television, such as the multiple roles played by the cast and the episodic narrative.

This film is perhaps one of the highlights of independent British film production in the 1970s and as well as demonstrating that production was no longer studio bound, it also revealed the possibility of making successful films on a restricted budget and with unorthodox funding. The success of this film could have signalled the way forward for British production, as it combined various industry and production trends and capitalised upon them, instead of struggling against them. But not all films were able to exploit the opportunities offered by the period. Even in popular genres, filmmakers were struggling to get films made. Horror filmmakers faced the same problems of funding, finance, exhibition and distribution that were crippling the rest of the industry. In a revealing interview with David Pirie for *Sight and Sound*, new director Stephen Weeks commented, 'now I've made a feature on budget, on schedule and good quality merchandising, hopefully I'll find it easier to get finance for my next film,'[6] The film referred to was *I, Monster* (1970), a remake of the Jekyll and Hyde story, partially funded by the NFFC. Weeks knew there was little credibility to be found in making a moderately successful horror film and that he saw the project as a means to establish himself and move away from the horror genre. Unfortunately, *I, Monster* made no discernible impact at the box office and despite the youthful director's optimism, funding for subsequent projects was not forthcoming, particularly from the NFFC.

Even national institutions such as Hammer Studios went into decline in the 1970s. Hammer's successful negotiations with American distributors had placed it in a highly enviable market position, both in the domestic and international market and it began the 1970s in a position of strength. By securing the all-important American funding and even more important distribution, Hammer was able to continue producing films when the rest of the British film industry was struggling with escalating production costs and the withdrawal of American money. Hammer films were low-budget horror and did not claim to be aesthetic or cultural, yet were enormously popular with audiences. Head of the Studio James Carreras capitalised on early film successes, spinning out many variations on well-worn themes tapping into an established market for his films.[7] The films were widely released and so did better at the box office than their smaller studio-produced counterparts. The strength of investment in the 'House of Hammer' at the beginning of the 1970s is demonstrated by the production figures for 1971, which show six films being co-financed by EMI, three by Rank and one by Warner Bros.[8] Yet even their innovative investment and distribution deals could not save the company and they made their last horror film, an adaptation of Dennis Wheatley's *To the Devil a Daughter,* in 1976.

Even films which did secure some NFFC funding also drew on unconventional funding methods, but with varying degrees of success. *Black Joy* (1977) directed by Anthony Simmons, focused on the experiences of a newly arrived immigrant in the heart of London's thriving black community. Simmons recognised that one of the most significant parts of the film was its soundtrack and set up a deal to release the songs featured in the film to accompany the film's cinematic release and to cover the production costs. Although similar to the strategy deployed by Puttnam for *That'll Be the Day*, this funding of *Black Joy* proved to be far less successful, principally because Simmons failed to acquire the relevant copyright agreements for the songs featured in the film and ran into difficulties when a number of artists protested about the unauthorised use of their material. The subsequent delay severely affected the film's performance at the box office and reveals that, although the entrepreneurial culture offered by the 1970s offered some opportunities, a certain pragmatism and understanding was required in order to fully capitalise upon them.

European opportunities

As well as innovative strategies to fund filmmaking which drew on British alliances, when Britain joined the EEC in 1973, a whole host of new European opportunities emerged. Britain had established film co-production agreements with France in 1965 and Italy in 1967 and an agreement with West Germany was finalised in 1975, yet British filmmakers were slow to take advantage of the benefits of close collaboration with European partners. Britain's co-production agreements were specifically intended to produce films which were 'capable of enhancing the reputation of the films industries of [the] two countries.'[9] In order to ensure the success of such productions in both domestic film markets, these films were granted financial concessions by the respective governments.[10] It was hoped that by allowing co-production projects to be registered as 'national films' in two markets, a climate would be created in which European film industries would be relieved of financial and artistic dependence on the American market. However, the problems in creating films which could be successful in very different national markets soon became clear. A guide to co-production published by the Film Production Association (FPA) in 1971 warned against the production of 'cultural hybrid films' and declared that 'each co-production film should be a reflection of the culture of one of the countries involved.'[11] This emphasis would appear to suggest that a French-Anglo production was to be either representative of French national cinema or British national cinema, yet paradoxically had to appeal to both markets in order to be financially successful. Despite emphasis on cultural collaboration, co-production agreements were focused on financial gain and the films produced would be the very hybrids which would be unlikely to appeal to any domestic market.

There were also deeper issues at work within the sphere of co-production, not least the issue of international collaboration itself. The FPA warned that the British were co-production amateurs when compared to the longer-standing arrangements of the French and Italian governments.[12] They cautioned, 'what has been right for a Franco-Italian film may not however be just as right for a Franco-British film,' again suggesting that the films produced under such agreements had to conform to the working practices and audience predilections of the countries which produced them. This was surely an impossible task when considering the very different industries of France, Italy and Britain?[13] Contradictorily, given the inexperience of Britain within co-production agreements, the FPA strongly advocated arrangements which established Britain as a key player, not just a junior partner.[14] Just how this was to be achieved, the FPA did not make clear.

At a conference in 1972 at the Polytechnic of Central London, F. Morris Dyson of the Department of Trade and Industry declared that Britain needed to turn to Europe in order to combat the slump in film production and to forge new ties with European countries to stand against the power of the American studios.[15] The press were also keen to highlight the benefits of closer links with the EEC; an article in *The Times* enthusiastically supported the idea of a European film funding bank which would exclude American co-productions and so curb Hollywood's influence.[16] This latter suggestion was a French proposal which found favour with countries struggling to withstand the influx of American film products, but which was not well received by the British film industry. Despite the withdrawal of American capital, the British industry remained closely linked to Hollywood through shared culture and language and could not risk alienating such a powerful ally.

While approaches to European collaboration were ambitious and potentially rewarding, there were some obvious flaws. It is difficult to see how an industry crippled financially and struggling to produce films for the domestic market was in a position to reject ties with American companies in favour of untested partnerships in Europe. Yet this is precisely what government's advocated through their support for co-production agreements throughout the 1970s.

The weaknesses of co-production became clear when the much-vaunted schemes failed to produce financially successful films. Only 29 British co-production films were made with European partners between 1970 and 1980 and only four of these – *Day of the Jackal* (1973), *Lady Caroline Lamb* (1972), *Don't Look Now* (1973) and *Moonraker* (1979) – did well at the British box office.[17] The problems associated with co-production filmmaking practices were also becoming apparent. The levels of bureaucracy in co-production filmmaking were so formidable that the FPA recommended that a British accountant should be employed on all co-production projects to avoid the possibility of legal misunderstandings arising from language difficulties. The FPA also argued that film unions should be involved before production commenced on a co-production film in order to smooth over any difficulties regarding working conditions.[18] Even established directors experienced difficulties with co-production filming; Joseph Losey's papers reveal his frustrations at being unable to cast actors of his choice for *A Doll's House* (1973), due to casting constraints imposed on this film by its co-production agreement.[19]

The obvious unease of the FPA in highlighting the importance of the unions' role is indicative of wider contemporary concerns about union power. Both the FPA and the government were acutely worried about angering the unions, while the unions' reluctance to become involved in co-production filmmaking effectively doomed the initiative. The fundamental flaws and weaknesses within the British industry, as well as the intransigence of the film unions, restricted the workability of co-production agreements and limited their levels of success.

Conclusion

By the end of the decade, the British film industry had contracted. But despite an eclectic and uneven funding policy, the NFFC had succeeded in re-establishing itself as a supporter of art house film projects by the time the decade drew to a close. But this was too little, too late. The continual confusion over funding policy and heavy pressure to back a blockbuster soured these successes and even the arrival in 1979 of Mamoun Hassan as the head of the Corporation was not enough to save the NFFC. Hassan's previous positions at the BFI Production Board and the National Film School reflected his deep involvement with the film industry and, along with his filmmaking credentials, offered a happy compromise between industrial understanding and creative flair. One of the projects chosen by Hassan for funding was Franco Rosso's *Babylon* (1980), a vivid exploration of black youth culture which was produced by Gavrik Losey. As Sally Shaw has identified, the film's consideration of racial tension as well as its use of Jamaican patois made it a contentious and awkward proposition position for film-going audiences in 1980s Britain but Hassan convinced the rest of the reluctant NFFC that the film was worthy of their support.[20] Had Hassan been allowed to steer the NFFC in the decade which followed, and capitalise on the brave funding choices of the 1970s and 1980s, the Corporation may have been in a position to usefully contribute to British film culture. But the shift in focus of the NFFC coincided with the election of a Conservative government who were keen to stop directly funding the British film industry. The NFFC was judged on its past unsuccessful commercial decisions rather than its recent cultural creativity and the new administration eventually ruled that it was extraneous to British film production and it was wound up, along with the Eady Levy in 1985. [21]

It would be easy to attribute the lack of formal funding opportunities to the NFFC's haphazard approach and incoherent internal decision-making, but external financial pressures and wider industrial uncertainty exacerbated this situation. A powerful and independent British film industry did not emerge from the 1970s but this failure cannot be attributed to one political administration or single policy. The film industry failed to grasp any of the possibilities for progress that were offered to it, however implausible some of them may have been. It was not so much that the government refused to help the film industry, but that the film industry failed to capitalise on any of the strategies which were devised to support it.

As shown here, the failure of formal methods of funding prompted new strategies and new ways of thinking in the film industry. As it became clear that many of these strategies were poorly defined and underfunded, entrepreneurial filmmakers and financiers started to find new ways of filmmaking and new sources of funding, fostering a new culture of production through their innovative and creative methods.

5
Movers and Shakers

The lack of funding for the film industry from conventional and government sources prompted parts of the industry to embark on new ventures, creating an adventurous and ad hoc culture of production. Harper and Smith have identified a range of key players in the 1970s film industry and have drawn attention to work by John Woolf, Ken Russell and John Boorman. As they note, it is significant that in this period, many of the well-established British directors from the previous decade produced only one or a few significant works or else worked solely in television. David Lean produced *Ryan's Daughter* (1970), Lindsay Anderson made *O Lucky Man!* (1973), while Ken Loach made *Family Life* (1971) and *Black Jack* (1979). The output of these filmic heavyweights was limited due to the financial shakeups in the wider industry and in their absence new directors, screenwriters and producers moved to the forefront of production. The lack of conventional funding opportunities required a particular way of thinking and working and many of the existing organisations and personnel within the industry were poorly suited to new ways of working and the unconventional alliances required. This is not to say that the output of a wide range of individuals was not crucial to the 1970s film industry but my purpose here is to link the approach of a few key players to the specific contexts of production. This chapter will highlight a number of important individuals who significantly affected the films made during the 1970s and assess what it was about the industry in this period which allowed them to make their mark.

Producers and financiers came to play a crucial role in the development of the industry in the 1970s and this shift coincided with the decline in influence of the two major players who had dominated the

British film industry for so many years: Rank and ABC. Yet despite their waning influence, a close examination of Rank and ABC's methods of working and the films they chose to make in the 1970s reveals that both these conglomerates were not entirely unaffected by wider industrial preoccupations and the fractured culture of production.

The old guard

In 1969, EMI had confirmed its ownership of ABC including its chain of 266 cinemas, the studio at Elstree and its interests in distribution.[1] Entertainment came under the control of Bernard Delfont, film production was guaranteed through Bryan Forbes, while Nat Cohen headed up Associated British Productions and Anglo-Amalgamated, which now came under the direct control of EMI.[2] In 1970, EMI announced a new collaboration with MGM; American money would be used to co-fund British film productions, which would be jointly distributed.[3] The Hollywood majors had been significantly involved in the British industry for decades, but collaborative distribution allied with direct funding was a new development. Some of these early co-productions reaped handsome profits, notably, *Villain* (1971) and *Get Carter* (1971), but by 1972 EMI/MGM co-production films tended to be wholly American projects such as *The Dove* (1974) and *The Killer Elite* (1975), in which EMI had a distribution interest and little more.[4] By 1973, the cheerful optimism had faded, MGM withdrew from the joint management arrangement and Elstree Studios suffered substantial financial losses.[5]

Despite being responsible for some of the decade's early critical and commercial hits, including *The Go-Between* (1971), *On the Buses* (1971) and *The Tales of Beatrix Potter* (1971), EMI was only able to ward off financial disaster by diverting funds to prop up film production from some of its more profitable sources of income, including electronics and radio.[6] EMI's control of Elstree, along with its entrepreneurial American collaborations ensured that film production was maintained, but at a price. Due to these financial concerns, EMI refused to commit to unorthodox or risky projects and demanded high levels of success from its productions and its staff. Director Joseph Losey's production notes for *The Go-Between* reveal his frustrations about EMI's lacklustre marketing of the film. In a telegram to Delfont, Losey raged, 'Do you totally disregard value of Cannes Award, my name and Pinter's? What is the use of making quality pictures if they are handled like shit? Expect immediate correction of situation or will publicise.'[7]

However, the fault was not solely Delfont's or even EMI's. The legal file for *The Go-Between* reveals how the head of EMI in Hollywood refused to recognise the potential of the film, considering:

> Strongly disagree with opinion that your film has any chance whatsoever at Cannes or that the reputation of Losey and Pinter enhances its potential gross. This film has been a constant problem and presents the first major breakdown in our association because of the complete lack of co-operation on the part of studio and producer. If this uncooperative and unrealistic attitude continues, I respectfully suggest that it might be better for us to disassociate ourselves with you on *The Go-Between*.[8]

The Go-Between had been part-funded by Columbia and the American investors were unhappy with the temperamental and exacting Losey, which caused tensions in the Anglo-American partnership. Much as they had in the previous decade, the American investors continued to call the financial shots. Head of Production Bryan Forbes pleaded with Delfont for the film to be recognised as an object of both creative and economic merit:

> The same care and intelligence that went into the making of this film must be carried over into the selling of it [...] here is an opportunity for us to capitalise on a very commercial property which also happens to be artistically without fault [...] *The Go-Between* represents to me the sum total of what I hoped to achieve when I first started to formulate our plans. There is a time when everybody has to stand up and be counted and I am already on my feet.[9]

Forbes left EMI a few months later, yet his tenure had not been without success; *The Tales of Beatrix Potter*, *The Railway Children* (1970) and his faith in *The Go-Between* demonstrate his commitment to quality British filmmaking at an uncertain time. After the removal of Forbes, film production at EMI was firmly concentrated in the hands of Nat Cohen, making him the most powerful man in the British film industry. In 1973, *The Guardian* dubbed him 'The arbiter of film taste' and Cohen himself admitted that he was involved in the production of around 70% of all films made in Britain, and made decisions about script, director, actors, budget and distribution.[10] The concentration of so much power in the hands of one person created a highly uncompetitive industry, a fact of which Cohen was acutely aware. He acknowledged, 'It's bad for the film industry that I am the only man making films... I need competition and it's important that there should be competition if the industry is to survive.'[11]

Cohen's approach was to make entertaining, commercial films and he believed that box office receipts were firm indications of what the public wanted. Yet he failed to recognise that audiences were changing and that popular taste could no longer be accurately mapped and predicted solely through box office figures and financial returns. Ignoring the new intricacies of popular taste and the establishment of niche audiences, Cohen continued to make films following the principles which had worked so well in earlier decades. This approach led to success with projects like the adaptation of Agatha Christie's *Murder on the Orient Express* (1974) and guaranteed the temporary expansion of EMI when the company bought British Lion. However, it was this over-extension in an uncertain time which weakened the company. British Lion had contributed to the production of important films including *The Wicker Man* (1973) and *Don't Look Now* (1973), but by the middle of the decade the company again faced bankruptcy. EMI took over in 1976, placing young entrepreneurs Michael Deeley and Barry Spikings in charge of production. One of the principal objectives of Deeley and Spikings was to produce films for the American market and in 1976 EMI funded *The Man Who Fell to Earth* (1976), a Nicolas Roeg film which was British-made but filmed entirely in the United States. Following the film's success, Spikings and Deeley concentrated their efforts on the American market, relocating to Hollywood to make *The Deer Hunter* (1978), *Convoy* (1978) and *The Driver* (1978), all part-funded by EMI and made with some British personnel, but effectively made for American audiences.

The fortunes of EMI throughout the 1970s can be mapped through its annual accounts, which highlight the company's highs and lows. The middle of the decade saw profits fall and even an ambitious £6 million programme of British production which included *To the Devil a Daughter* (1976), *The Likely Lads* (1976) and *Death on the Nile* (1978) failed to re-establish the company at the forefront of British production.[12] A subsequent series of poor investments and an ill-advised American distribution attempt which alienated the major Hollywood companies placed EMI's future in serious doubt.[13] The catastrophic fall in company profits from £65 million in 1977 to £11 million in 1978 led to the sale of EMI in 1979 to the electrical firm Thorn. This was in turn bought by the Cannon group in 1986, and this final merger signalled the end of EMI's active involvement in British film production, a sad footnote for a company which had once been at the forefront of the British film industry.[14]

The other major remaining player in British production during the 1970s was the Rank Corporation. Yet Rank had began pulling back from production in the early 1960s, preferring not to fund new projects but rather to inject money into successful franchises and organise, rather than fund, production. Even the successful *Carry On* series suffered under this retrenchment, with Rank funding their final *Carry On* in 1975. Peter Rogers and Gerard Thomas looked to the NFFC for funding for *Carry On England* (1976), and after it was denied, approached Rank's rival, EMI.[15] EMI's potential involvement was to come at a price, and included advice on casting which was not well received by Rogers and Thomas.[16] By May 1976, Rogers and Thomas were considering funding the film themselves, but eventually decided to work with a financier whose clients were keen to invest in films. These clients were the band Pink Floyd, who were heavily committed to the funding of this project and only withdrew their support at the last minute because of irresolvable problems of taxation. Finally, Rank Film Distributors offered to fund half the project and a financier stepped in with the final half of the £250,000 budget. The Rank Corporation's reluctance to fund *Carry On England* is a marked change from its previous enthusiastic, unquestioning support for the series. A letter from Peter Rogers reveals the ease and informality with which the funding for *Carry On Matron* (1972) was agreed in 1971:

> Before I become too involved in preparations for my next *Carry On* – Matron – I would very much like your approval of the subject. All the usual 'things' being equal, I would like to start shooting on October 11th. The budget will be well within our understood limit and finish up less. The cast will be the same old gang and the story is set in a maternity home with Hattie Jacques as the Matron. If there are any more details you require you have only to ask and you shall receive.[17]

Upon receiving this letter, Rank promptly agreed the usual budget of £250,000 without further negotiation. The production history of *Carry On England* is interesting as it highlights a number of key changes which had taken place in production since the late 1960s: Rank were pulling back from financing films; the NFFC were reluctant to fund projects due to their limited budget; city financiers who knew little about film began dabbling in film finance; ad hoc arrangements were becoming more frequent; and the music industry was increasingly involved in film projects. All of these changes were to have a substantial impact on the films produced throughout the 1970s. The complex production finance for *Carry On England* reveals the difficulty of securing funding, and demonstrates that even previous commercial success would not guarantee investment. EMI's influence continued throughout the decade only to fade in the 1980s, while Rank's production involvement had already begun to wane at the end of the 1960s. The decline of both of these conglomerates left space for a younger generation of directors, producers and technicians to emerge.

It is too simplistic to see the 1970s as a period in which newcomers and the old guard of the film industry faced off against one another. Often the newcomers were only newcomers to the film industry and had previously been established and successful in fields such as advertising, television or theatre. Additionally, the newcomers often had to work closely with the old guard in order to finalise production deals. When interviewed by the author, David Puttnam confirmed how crucial the support of Nat Cohen was to his early career and what a hugely influential figure Cohen was within the 1970s film industry.[18] Other alliances drew on established partnerships such as that of director John Schlesinger and producer Joseph Janni, yet also incorporated newcomers like journalist and writer Penelope Gilliatt. These unconventional collaborations drew on the music and advertising industries, art and film schools and the fields of theatre and literature to utilise a broader range of creative talents.

Newcomers

With the big conglomerates losing influence over production, British film lost much of its funding and a great deal of direction. Although the power of Delfont and Cohen at EMI and John Davis at Rank was restrictive, it was also secure and controlled, allowing projects to be funded without complex financial packages involving outside investors, all keen for a share of the profits. The decline of the conglomerates potentially offered more production opportunities, but also reflected the fall in profits exacerbated by increased filmmaking costs amid wider economic recession. New companies were founded to take control of production, some for specific types of films, such as Pete Walker's contemporary-set horror films *Frightmare* (1974) and *The House of Mortal Sin* (1976), while even the Beatles' company Apple began to be involved in film production, receiving in 1972 an estimated 100 scripts each month for possible projects.[19]

As well as new companies to fund, create and distribute films, the 1970s also saw a number of important individuals emerge and make their mark on the British industry. David Puttnam was one of a number of youthful entrepreneurs of the period who achieved great success in raising finance from unorthodox sources and who also nurtured new talents like Alan Parker and Ridley Scott. With a background in advertising, Puttnam's approach to filmmaking was pragmatic, stating when interviewed recently:

> And we really did approach this professionally – I want to be very clear here – we didn't approach the whole thing in what I'd describe in those days as a 'Ken Loach/Tony Garnett' manner, I admired them enormously for their commitment to their craft. My approach was rather more along the lines of 'here are some stories I want to tell,' and 'here is a business I want to get into'...and these are things we think we need to do to get into it.[20]

Together with Sandy Lieberson, who had worked as a theatrical agent in the 1960s for luminaries including the Rolling Stones, Puttnam formed Goodtimes Enterprises in the early 1970s to make feature films and documentaries. Lieberson remembers that their company was part-owned by Rothschild's, W.H. Smith, and Sotheby's and was run along strict business lines making and distributing films. Lieberson's comments on the roles played by himself and Puttnam within the company are revealing and suggest a great deal about the production culture of the period. He noted:

> We each had responsibilities, we had to do things, but we crossed over. Both of us were pretty adept at the finance and business side of things, because of our backgrounds. But at the same time what we also did was to find a mutual level in the creative input. In some cases it was more David's creative input because there were ideas that he felt closer to and was more involved in than me. And vice versa.[21]

Both Lieberson and Puttnam were heavily involved in their film projects and this detailed involvement suggests an understanding of all aspects of the filmmaking process from the financial to the creative. However, it was their respective backgrounds which determined their approach to filmmaking and ultimately led to such great successes. After being rejected by EMI Music for the residual funding for the rock and roll inspired *That'll Be the Day* (1973), Puttnam made a deal with Ronco Music, who agreed to part-finance the film in return for songs they could license being included on the soundtrack. Puttnam himself recognised the power of such financial arrangements, noting:

> I made a record deal which effectively underwrote, not only a third of the movie itself, but also guaranteed me a level of advertising budget which was almost unparalleled for a UK movie [...] I had come to understand that I needed to bust the existing distribution paradigm [...] I was really making a 'product', albeit the best possible product I could.[22]

This was one of the first financial arrangements of its kind in British cinema and indicated how the industry was changing. Such an innovative approach to film finance not only allowed the film to be made and for its soundtrack to generate additional profit, but also led to the production of a sequel, *Stardust* (1974). It was not only in securing financial deals which made the work of Puttnam and Lieberson unique, it was also their approach to filmmaking which involved them in all aspects of the process. Puttnam himself felt that becoming involved in film distribution during this period was crucial to understanding the business, recalling:

> I became very, very interested in distribution. When producing my first two movies I didn't know anything about distribution at all, I just made them and handed them over. By the time it came to the 3rd film I realised that didn't work, and you had to thoroughly involve yourself in the way the film was distributed, So I became very, very engaged in their distribution, and that is again where my advertising background really kicked in and became hugely beneficial [...] Because I was supplying a chunk of the money that was used in distribution, usually the money that came in from the record companies... I was able to have a real say in the way in which the money was spent.[23]

Another important figure to emerge in the period was director and producer, Don Boyd. A graduate of the London Film School and an experienced director of commercials, Boyd directed his first feature film, *Intimate Reflections*, in 1975 and remained firmly committed to British film production throughout the decade. Although a skilled producer and financier, Boyd maintains that his involvement with British cinema was motivated by his experience as a director. When interviewed recently by the author about his involvement in *Scum* (1979) and *The Tempest* (1979), Boyd stated:

> They were made because of me and my passion for a bold, innovative, political and a creative British cinema. They would not have existed without me ... I made absolutely sure that both Alan [Clarke] and Derek [Jarman] could create their work in an environment which gave them the creative control and commercial environment to make them as brilliant as I knew they could be.[24]

As Boyd recognises, it was the funding of these innovative and unorthodox projects which made such a major contribution to the film industry in the later 1970s, with his vision as a producer and financer and his experience as a director proving a winning combination. Despite wide-ranging activities, Boyd rejects the classification of his role in the period as that of an entrepreneur, claiming instead that he has always been 'a director-orientated audience-conscious film-marketing editor.'[25] Despite issues of nomenclature, Boyd's successful negotiation for bank loans for the funding of his films, coupled with his inventive financial strategy, which relied heavily on offsetting tax costs, ensured that he got films made, and such dynamic pragmatism was precisely what the 1970s film industry required.

Boyd's activities throughout the 1970s make him one of the key figures of the period. Along with Puttnam and Lieberson, he represented the new breed of entrepreneurs who specialised in getting films made by securing funding through collaborative deals. Through their production companies, Boyd's Co and Goldcrest, who supplied finance for script development and later numbered David Puttnam amongst their key personnel, these young entrepreneurs offered financial opportunities to the British film industry. In doing so they actively worked to ensure that there were other possible means of finance for film projects beyond EMI, Rank and the Americans, although they usually required more speculative and unorthodox arrangements.

Often the fortunes of these production companies were tied to the success of the projects they selected for funding. Early involvement in *Watership Down* (1978) led Goldcrest to fund the development of scripts for *Chariots of Fire* (1981), *Gandhi* (1982) and *The Ploughman's Lunch* (1983), while at the other end of the scale, after the successes of *Scum, The Tempest* and *Hussy* (1980) Boyd's Co became embroiled in one of the biggest film debacles of the 1980s.[26] In 1979, Boyd moved to America to work on a high-profile project which involved EMI, John Schlesinger, Joseph Janni, Barry Spikings, Bernard Delfont and Bryan Forbes but which ultimately proved disastrous for all concerned.[27] *Honky Tonk Freeway* (1981) was one of the final nails in the coffin for EMI and marked the last attempt by British studios, producers and directors to make high-budget films which could be sold to the Americans.[28] In this way, the entrepreneurial enthusiasm which was such a feature of the decade backfired spectacularly, with Boyd's collaborative arrangements involving a collection of people who all suffered from the film's massive failure. The failure of the film perfectly illustrates just how poorly suited the British film industry was to produce and finance a blockbuster; the risks were simply too high and failure on such a massive scale could only be absorbed by a major Hollywood corporation.

It would be easy to consider Puttnam, Lieberson and Boyd simply as money-men. Yet they all came from different backgrounds and brought with them distinct skills which impacted upon their approach to film-making. They were all intimately involved in the projects they made and fully understood the aesthetic side of the industry, as well as the production and financial side. Indeed, it was this combination of creative knowledge and financial acumen which made the young entrepreneurs such an important part of the industry. Don Boyd maintains that his work was motivated by a 'passion for cinema from a director's position' drawing on his directorial expertise, while David Puttnam considered that it was his background in advertising and his involvement in a variety of film projects, which enabled him to become 'an all round producer' by the end of the decade and his work to be that of a 'idealistic impresario.'[29]

Another impresario at work in the 1970s was producer Michael Klinger, who managed to secure funding for the *Confessions* series, which became one of the biggest commercial successes of the period and who went on to make large-budget adaptation of the Wilbur Smith novels *Gold* (1974) and *Shout at the Devil* (1976). Klinger's involvement with the *Confessions* series and with the film industry as a whole will later be examined in detail, yet he deserves mention here as another entrepreneurial figure whose innovative methods of working outside the studio system place his activities alongside those of Boyd and Puttnam.

One of the most visible directors in the British film industry and often seen as the *enfant terrible* of the period was Ken Russell. One of the few directors who was high-profile enough not to need the support of either Rank or EMI, Russell's funding was heavily dependent on the Americans in the early 1970s. *Women in Love* and *The Devils* were both funded by American studios but his later work relied on collaboration with new players in Britain, notably Puttnam on *Mahler* (1974) and *Lizstomania* (1975). Puttnam would later refer to this relationship with Russell as 'difficult' but freely acknowledged that he learnt a great deal from him about the processes of filmmaking.[30] The difficulty was always the level of excess which was a massive part of any Russell production. As Harper and Smith have pointed out, Russell required discipline to produce his best work and such restraint was desperately needed during the 1970s with declining cinema audiences impacting heavily on box office returns and inflation causing production costs to spiral.[31]

One of the decade's entrepreneurs who failed to fully understand the complexities of the industry to which he recklessly committed himself was Lew Grade. Unlike Puttnam, Boyd, Klinger or Lieberson, Grade was predominantly a salesman who had built his reputation in television and had little understanding of the film industry or the complexities of the filmmaking process. Grade was the brother of Bernard Delfront of EMI and President of the successful Associated Television (ATV) network which expanded, at his insistence, into film production. Grade created the Associated Communications Corporation (ACC) to fund film production using profits from television to make international films which would be successful in world markets. Like Nat Cohen's stubborn refusal to consider emerging markets and niche audiences, Grade firmly believed that selling big-budget international films was the only way in which the British industry could become profitable. When interviewed in 1993, Grade affirmed his fervent belief that such high-budget, international films were the only way to revitalise the British film industry, despite such productions destroying his carefully created media conglomerate. Grade stated:

> They are making too many, what we would call, local films ... anything you put on film should be for the international market ... [they] must be suitable for your transmission, or for your public, in your country, but it must be suitable for the rest of the world.[32]

After the enormous success of ACC's *Return of the Pink Panther* (1976), Grade continued to pour money into production, arranging distribution and exhibition deals with American networks. One of Grade's biggest successes was his ability to conclude distribution for films which had not yet begun production, and to negotiate separate deals for individual films.

Unfortunately, the success of *Return of the Pink Panther* and its sequels could not be replicated. Although further projects including *Voyage of the Damned* (1976) and *The Eagle Has Landed* (1976) enjoyed moderate success, Grade's American investors proved unwilling to continue to fund projects which did not attain the highest levels of success which Grade so confidently promised. Grade filled this breach by setting up his own distribution company in America and using the profits from ATV to prop up his film speculation. After the disastrous *Raise the Titanic* (1980) cost ACC $34 million, the parent company of ATV recorded its first loss of £7 million due principally to Grade's film investments. Initially Grade's losses incurred in filmmaking were offset by the tremendous profits accrued by his television empire. But eventually even these profits could not support his high-risk strategy of making large-budget films for the international market. These losses continued to escalate and made the once-profitable company vulnerable to takeover. In 1982, Grade resigned as chairman amidst fears of bankruptcy; his film speculations may not have be entirely to blame for the decline of ATV but they certainly severely damaged the company at a time of financial uncertainty.[33] Lew Grade ultimately failed to fully understand the complexities of the industry to which he wholeheartedly committed himself. Ultimately, even his characteristic impresario style and innovative business methods failed to match the technological and consumer demands of the decade and of the capricious film industry itself.

Conclusion

Following the establishment of the young, creative and ambitious in British society during the 1960s, the 1970s became a decade where pragmatism and financial acumen, coupled with youthful enthusiasm fostered by the previous decade, allowed entrepreneurs to flourish. If the 1960s was a decade of idealists, the 1970s was a time for pragmatists. Directors like Alan Parker and Ridley Scott were given opportunities in the 1970s which might have been denied to them in different periods, whilst David Puttnam, Sandy Lieberson, Michael Klinger and Don Boyd treated the film industry like a business, albeit a creative one, and reaped the rewards of their innovative financial strategies. The ad hoc nature of the deals brokered perfectly married the 1960s attitude of creative achievement with 1970s financial shrewdness and opportunism, and this can be seen in many of the films of the era. This entrepreneurial activity was to continue throughout the decade and could even be seen as early anticipation of Thatcherite ideology, which recognised and applauded the entrepreneur, allowing him to continue to operate successfully in the 1980s.

It is interesting that both Boyd and Puttnam reject the term 'entrepreneur.' Neither occupied the traditional role of the producer, and their activities within the decade demonstrate how much the industry was changing and how entrepreneurial skills were required to successfully produce films, often finding new partners in the process. The involvement of such new partners was often motivated by financial necessity rather than creative aspiration, and this combined to create a turbulent, innovative, financially weak, heavily pragmatic, highly entrepreneurial industry. These individuals fundamentally altered the way the British film industry worked, but the industry itself was tied up in a web of organisational structures which consistently failed to agree on a course of action which would allow the industry to meet the challenges of the decade.

6
Institutions and Organisations

It would be misleading to posit a cohesive British film industry in any period, but the 1970s were characterised by factionalism and polarisation. As well as internal opposing factions, the film industry faced competition not just from the Americans who were poised to take advantage of the weak domestic industry but also from television, which had become the leisure activity of choice for the British public.

The emergence of strong and vocal factions within the British film industry reveals how the power was shifting from high-profile studios and production companies and towards smaller organisations with different objectives. The marginalisation of the Cinematograph Films Council (CFC), who advised the government on film policy and the pressure group activities of the Association of Independent Producers (AIP), demonstrate the lack of industry cohesion. The splintering of the audience which was such an important characteristic of the 1970s period is also evident in the film industry itself, with increased fragmentation and division following the establishment of vocal pressure groups and the intransigence of the powerful trade unions.

Unions

The 1970s in Britain was a decade of militant trade unionism and the film industry was not exempt from the wider pattern of aggressive unionism. As already shown, the film industry unions were partially responsible for the failure of co-production agreements and their refusal to support such initiatives demonstrates their power within the industry. In the absence of effective and efficient government support, other models for the industry were proposed. In 1973, the Association of Cinema and Television Technicians (ACTT) published a pamphlet calling for public ownership of the film industry. This pamphlet claimed:

> Public ownership of vital industries and services is hardly controversial ... a publicly owned film industry promises a degree of creative competition which the existing private monopoly makes impossible. Private ownership of the film industry will fundamentally alter the financial logic of the industry.[1]

The growing power of the unions is demonstrated by this overt call to arms and the decidedly militant tone adopted by the head of the ACTT, Alan Sapper. The 1970s was a period where nationalised industries dominated headlines, yet the ACTT's proposals for a nationalised film industry were never really considered by the industry as a serious option. What the proposals highlight are the inherent divisions within an industry which could not agree on either production or policy. Although the ACTT argued that public ownership would change the 'financial logic' of the film industry, their vision of the cinema as a 'cultural and social service' was problematic, as it raised the issue of what kind of cultural product a nationalised film industry should create.[2]

In contrast to the views of the ACTT, with its focus on a strong domestic industry, both the CFC and the FPA believed that the British industry should have international objectives. The CFC declared that 'the future of the British film industry must continue to be in producing films likely to appeal to a wide audience both at home and abroad,' while the FPA considered British film to be 'an export commodity of enormous potential.'[3] By 1975, the FPA noted, 'today, more than ever before Britain needs to be sold abroad and to do this, must have a flourishing film industry.'[4] Both the CFC and the FPA believed that in order to succeed in world markets, the British industry had to produce films which would appeal to other target markets, particularly the vast American market. Yet how could an industry which was financially incapable of consistently producing successful domestic films make successful international films?

Following their success in the 1974 general election, a new Labour administration was welcomed hopefully by parts of the industry. An article in *CinemaTV Today* enthusiastically welcomed the new Films Minister Eric Deakins, but boldly queried how far the government *should* be involved in the film industry.[5] While Deakins admitted that the very mention of nationalisation 'made his hackles rise,' the contention that the film industry was of national importance was not particularly controversial.[6] Yet the intransigence of the film unions over national-isation was to become yet another issue which polarised opinion and prevented the film industry from effectively adapting in the changing social and political climate. The industry was further fragmented when another divide become apparent between high-profile successful pro-ducers of large-budget films and smaller, independent producers. There were a number of smaller companies which were successful but for many independent companies opportunities were limited. The FPA pinpointed the problem in 1975:

> Independent producers found it increasingly difficult to find finan-cial backing for their films and many who had extended all their resources on the preparation of projects had no more capital to invest in the acquisition of new properties and the preparation of scripts.[7]

The situation failed to improve, and in 1976 the more radical AIP was formed. This pressure group was created to represent the interests of those who were finding it impossible to develop their work in the British feature film industry and directly opposed the old-school composition and pro-union stance of the FPA. Founder member of the AIP, Don Boyd, recalled that the association had a radical agenda of objectives includ-ing: breaking the power of the unions, changing the way money was distributed, altering the Eady Levy, stopping the duopoly and, most importantly, ensuring that independent film producers played a pivotal role in the creation of the proposed fourth television channel.[8] Boyd remembers that the more staid FPA was horrified by such a provocative agenda and the conflict which escalated between these two industry bodies not only indicates the problems the industry faced with growing factionalism but also demonstrates through the issues raised by the AIP that the film industry faced the same problems in 1976 as it did at the start of the decade. Little had changed.

As Margaret Dickinson points out, many industry workers disillu-sioned with the state of the British film industry crossed to America to work in the better-organised environment of Hollywood.[9] Directors Ridley and Tony Scott, Alan Parker, John Boorman and John Schlesinger all chose to work in Hollywood in the period. Director Stephen Frears outlined the appeal of working in America, when he remarked, 'the Americans have an industry and it's much easier to make movies there. It makes sense. In Britain everyone is caught between thinking they are part of an industry and thinking they are independent.'[10] The relocation of key directors to Hollywood decimated an already foundering industry while important British actors fell foul of Labour's policy of increased tax on high earners. This policy caused top British stars including Michael Caine, Sean Connery and Roger Moore to become resident outside the UK, thus restricting their work in British films and in British studios. While actors could choose to film in different locations, directors and producers either left Britain to work abroad, or sought employment in a different medium. Stephan Frears and Ken Loach were two influential directors who chose to work in television, with Frears considering that unlike film, television in Britain in the 1970s was an industry which offered real opportunities.[11]

As well as the increasingly militant ACTT and the activities of the AIP, the actors' union Equity was also becoming increasingly vocal as it began to address what it saw as unacceptable practices in filmmaking. In *Carry On at Your Convenience* (1971), Peter Rogers had parodied the wildcat strikes of the trade unions but when it came to the making of *Carry On England* (1976), Rogers found himself under attack for allegedly mistreating actors by docking lunch breaks; a case of Equity flexing its union muscles.[12] Here it is clear that the actors' union was not unaffected by rising trade union power and was fully prepared to clash with powerful sections of the film industry.

As well as changes in funding, the decade also saw distinctive technological changes which altered the filmmaking process and helped contribute to a distinctive and characteristic 'look' for 1970s film. In the early 1970s, three new cameras were created – the Arriflex, the Paraflex and the Moviecam 3N – which were all lightweight, smooth running and finely balanced. The introduction of these types of cameras with their compact designs permitted filming to take place wherever there was enough light to shoot.[13] The steadicam was also invented in the decade, which permitted smooth shooting up and down and from side to side, even when walking or running. At the same time, film stocks were becoming gradually faster which, coupled with the changes in cameras, allowed camera operators increased flexibility and ease of shooting. As Petrie identifies, these technological changes allowed filmmaking to take place in a wider range of locations and gave camera operators greater ease of movement, all of which overturned many of the problems and constraints of filmmaking in earlier periods.[14] In 1975, the industry teetered hesitantly on the brink of real creative innovation, developed through financial necessity, technological developments and forced independence from the studios. However, the American investors were poised to once again alter the course of the British film industry.

The Americans

Just as the withdrawal of American money sparked a panic in 1970, the return of American money and production produced a new wave of hostility amongst sections of the British industry, a reaction easily discernible from the pages of *CinemaTV Today*. Some, including EMI, were keen to re-involve the Americans. Others, like the vocal AIP, saw their return as a resumption of 'business as usual' with the British as junior, usually silent, partners. However, the role of the Americans in Britain had changed. As British innovators continued to gain influence, the Americans had to actively negotiate new terms to collaborate with these new doyens of British cinema. Although the Americans had returned to dominate the British film industry from the middle of the decade with blockbusters such as *Jaws* (1975), *Star Wars* (1977) and *Superman* (1978), ultimately the film industry benefited from increased American production in Britain. British technicians came to be recognised as some of the best in the world and many of the special effects which were such an integral part of blockbuster films were created in British studios. This stimulated an industry which had finally begun to adapt and develop to meet wider industrial demands.

By the end of the 1970s, there was a much greater degree of cultural exchange taking place between the British and American film industries than has hitherto been acknowledged, furthered by the success already noted of some British films in America. The emergence of British entrepreneurs like Puttnam and Boyd signalled a shift in the fortunes of the British industry and indicated that co-operation between Britain and Hollywood was no longer to be solely controlled by the Americans. Perhaps this change is best located within the wider context of industry fragmentation; instead of a uniform relationship between Britain and Hollywood, there were created instead a series of varying relationships making collaboration between the two industries more innovative and speculative.

Although it is too easy to characterise the 1970s film industry as being in a state of crisis, it is undeniable that the decade saw a great deal of uncertainty and unease in response to changes in audiences and exhibition. However, the conventional narratives do not usually concern themselves with the high levels of innovation which occurred in the period; the changing role of producers, an increase in shooting on location, alliances and collaborations with the music industry and a diversification of audience tastes. It is easier to see 1970s British cinema as floundering in a morass of low-budget sex and horror than to critically evaluate the extremes of British film, from the innovative, anarchic comedy of Monty Python to the haunting beauty of *Barry Lyndon* (1975) and the popular nostalgia of *That'll Be the Day* (1973).

The levels of production in the decade must also be viewed within the context of spiralling costs and a sharp increase in inflation. Even despite these costs, it was still possible to make *The Tempest* (1979) at the end of the decade with a budget of £150,000. Despite the much vaunted and discussed production crisis, it was still possible to make films cheaply. The high levels of production identified have been consistently overlooked, negating the importance of the vast sums of money being regularly ploughed into the film industry, much of which was never recovered. Although isolated films did well, not all were backed by the vision of a Puttnam or a Boyd and many failed to recoup their costs.

Television

Even before the growth of the home video market, television continued to rival the cinema as an alternative site of film exhibition. In 1974 David Gordon commented in *Sight and Sound*:

> Television has sucked up the mass audience ... and gives precious little in return. Eventually television could kill off the feature film made for the large screen - and its audience will have to make do with those very inferior made-for-television movies.[15]

The mass audience had shifted from the cinema to the home, removing entertainment from the public to the private space and domesticising leisure and entertainment.[16] In a time when leisure was changing to suit the varied demands of its audience, cinema had to compete with a different medium. Television had not simply usurped the cinema audience, it had emerged as a powerful medium in its own right with the viewing figures to match. There were possible crossovers between television and film, and some programmes made successful transitions to the cinema, including a slew of films based on television sitcoms. Monty Python also successfully transferred to the cinema. Their films *And Now for Something Completely Different* (1971), *Monty Python and the Holy Grail* (1975) and *Monty Python's Life of Brian* (1979) transported fans of their television series to the cinema and attracted new fans along the way. Further television influences can be seen throughout the decade with films being released into cinemas despite their television roots; good examples of films of this type would be *Scum* (1979) and *The Long Good Friday* (1980).

As well as attracting the services of key directors and technicians, television expanded rapidly in the 1970s. While cinema audiences had declined from 215 to 101 million by 1980, British television ownership rose to 97%.[17] Increased television viewing figures meant more revenue from license fees and more advertising, making the newer medium much more financially secure than the film industry. Continued investment in the infrastructure of television meant that by the end of the decade almost everyone in Britain had access to good quality television, thus extending television's integral position within the British home.[18] The influx of video was also evident at the end of the decade, Linda Wood noting in 1981 that 'the availability of cheap video machines... greatly extended the choice of material for viewing in the home.'[19] Even the FPA, whose hostility to the television industry is evident from their annual reports, observed in 1971 that they would 'continue to gather all available material about audio-visual cassettes and the possibilities of the use of existing material and the production of new material for this medium.'[20]

Docherty, Morrison and Tracey suggest that the film industry believed that the principal threat of television was in its alternative technological appeal, and so devoted its energies into producing new cinematic technologies. Industry leaders were intent on showing the audience that watching films in black and white on a small screen at home was no substitute for the wonders of Cinemascope, Cinerama, Technicolor and 3D.[21] However, as the 1970s progressed, television viewing quality improved dramatically, offering direct competition with the cinematic experience. There were 18.3 million television licenses in Britain in 1980, but more significantly, the 300,000 colour sets in 1970 had grown to 12.9 million in 1980.[22] Lack of maintenance of cinema buildings was also becoming evident and the shabbiness of the auditoria contrasted with the comfort of people's own homes. It is highly significant that the decline in cinema audiences also directly corresponded with a greater commitment to the home and a steady rise in living standards.[23] Partly as a result of the consumer culture created in the 1960s, people were spending more money and time on their domestic space than ever before.

A report in *Screen Digest* in 1976 compares the film and television industries and the author notes that although it cannot compete with the cinema in terms of cinematic experience, television offered a far greater degree of choice than commercial cinema.[24] The report claims that the programming of television schedules, mainly achieved through the competition between BBC and ITV, allowed viewers a vast choice within the newer medium.[25] As well as offering choice, television audiences were also increasingly being offered cinematic products. The 1974 television premiere of *The Great Escape* (1963) garnered an audience of 21 million; a massive total when considering the total cinema admissions for that year were 138.5 million – the equivalent of just seven major films being shown on television.[26] From these figures, it is clear there was still a huge audience for films but the cinema was not necessarily the place where people wanted to see them. The issue of films on television was to become one of the most hotly debated of the decade, and it severely strained relationships between the two industries. The FPA's annual report noted angrily in 1971, 'the price paid by television companies for cinema films continues to be disgracefully low ... the film industry can no longer afford to continue to market its product at an unrealistic price.'[27] David Gordon, writing in 1974, likened the unequal relationship between film and television to the strained relationship between the British and American film industries.[28] Clearly for the film industry, television was perceived to be a far greater threat than either Hollywood product or companies.

By January 1974, questions were raised in Parliament about a possible levy on films sold to television and concerned MPs queried the current inefficient practice of selling films at such low prices.[29] Television companies could make a single payment for a film, or a collection of films and then screen them as many times as they chose. Even if the network made a payment every time the film was shown, the payment was usually a token amount and completely disproportionate to the cost of making the film. In 1974, it was the sale of six James Bond films to ITV for £850,000 that prompted questions about a film levy for television. As the average cost of making a film in this period was around £200,000 to 300,000 for a low-budget production and up to £600,000 for a more lavish production, this deal for six high-profile, high-quality and hugely popular films was a bargain for ITV, but a wasted opportunity for the film industry.[30] The five-year delay before films could be shown on television was also reduced to three years, limiting the opportunities for films to be given longer runs and to be re-booked for later releases. Despite repeated calls for the government to regulate the relationship between the two industries, successive governments refused to legislate, preferring instead to let the two industries regulate themselves.

Conclusion

Although significant, the impact of television on the film industry was not entirely negative. ABC and Rank both acquired shares and financial interests in television companies in the 1960s as a means of diversifying their interests, while films commissioned for television exhibition ensured that directors and producers remained employed and gained new skills which could be transferred back to the cinema screen. Alan Parker, Stephen Frears, Anthony Simmons, Alan Clarke and Ken Loach all worked in television as well as in film, demonstrating that journeyman directors and technicians could be successful in both industries and that the industries could co-exist and even benefit one another. Some television moguls were keen to expand into feature film making and began to use their substantial television profits to subsidise filmmaking. By 1964, Lew Grade's ATV network owned the film studios of Elstree and by the mid-1970s he was heavily involved in feature film production, in direct competition with his brother Bernard Delfont at EMI.

Despite the outward prosperity which allowed television companies to begin funding film, there were also problems in the television industry. Both industries struggled to evolve in a time of economic cut-backs; both were dominated by a strong duopoly; both frequently experienced union problems, and both owed a large debt to the keen interest and political intervention of Harold Wilson in the fields of broadcasting and filmmaking.[31] Despite emerging from the 1970s stronger than ever before, the television industry, like the beleaguered film industry, was also struggling with the varying policies adopted by the Labour and Conservative governments. Both industries would also have separate reports commissioned to consider their respective futures, the Terry Report for film in 1976 and the Annan Report for broadcasting in 1977. Yet, while the Annan Report eventually led to the creation of Channel 4 in 1982, the findings of the Terry Report were sidelined.

This exploration of the film industry in the 1970s has revealed a great deal about the range of institutions and organisations which dominated. Yet it is not enough simply to draw attention to the organisational structures and the contexts of filmmaking, it is crucial to explore how these cultures of production influenced the films themselves.

7
Production, Genre and Popular Taste

The 1970s has consistently been considered a genre-dominated decade with studies of its horror films, saucy comedies and exploitation fare contributing to popular narratives. According to Denis Gifford, the most popular genres of films produced in the period were comedy, crime and sex and between them, these three genres comprised over 40% of all British films produced in the 1970s.[1] Yet what about the other 60%? In addition to the highly visible trends already mentioned, there were some new production trends which suggest a diversity and innovation not usually associated with this period. The pie chart below (Figure 7.1)

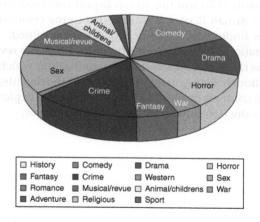

Figure 7.1 British films by genre, 1970–1979.
Source: D. Gifford, *The British Film Catalogue*, 3rd Edition (London: Fitzroy Dearborn Publishers, 2001).

is based on figures from Gifford and reveals a large range of genres, suggesting a much more interesting and diverse culture of production than usually acknowledged.

Although oversimplification of generic categories should be avoided, what this chart does reveal is the multiplicity of genres and the massive variety of films being produced in this period. However, a straightforward focus on production does not adequately address issues of popular taste. Most of the films made in the period failed to make money and so the diversity of material cannot be seen as an index of popularity and success. Rather, this production diversity demonstrates that the film industry was unsure what the audience wanted and employed a slightly haphazard approach to compensate. An examination of films produced reveals a great deal more about what the film industry believed the audience wanted. Often the gap between these perceptions of audience taste and the reality of audience taste is most interesting.

What complicates analysis of both production and reception further for this period is the large number of generic hybrids which emerged; the sex-comedy, the sex-horror, the exploitation-documentary and the experimental-historical film all feature in this era and demonstrate how unstable definitions of genre had become.

The weakness of mainstream film culture allowed products from the cultural fringes to emerge into mainstream cinema. Experimental film work by Sally Potter, Derek Jarman and Peter Greenaway, which drew its influences from art and the theatre, shifted into the mainstream, while narratives from the black British community, such as *Pressure* (1976) and *Babylon* (1980), were released into mainstream cinemas. Work by Bill Douglas, influenced by the British New Wave and documentary movements and funded by the BFI Production Board also made its way into the mainstream.

Due to the fragmented nature of film production in the 1970s and the blurring of generic categories, consideration of films in terms of their genre is limiting. For example, it has been well documented that the British sexploitation film became an established genre in this period with four *Confessions of* films and numerous imitations including *The Ups and Downs of a Handyman* (1975) and *The Adventures of a Plumber's Mate* (1978). Yet not all sexploitation films were box office hits and a much wider range of genres are evident from box office ledgers, reviews and lists of successful films.

One specific genre which became very fragmented in the 1970s is the fantasy genre. In this period, fantasy films ranged from the low-budget adventures of *The Land That Time Forgot* (1975), *At the Earth's Core* (1976) and *The Warlords of Atlantis* (1978), along with the more subversive and futuristic *Zardoz* (1974), *The Rocky Horror Picture Show* (1975) and *The Man Who Fell to Earth* and *Jubilee* (1978).[2] Again, these films fit poorly within strict generic definitions. For example, *Jubilee* could be seen as a futuristic, historical, experimental, music fantasy film, while *The Rocky Horror Picture Show* combines science fiction, fantasy, sex, horror, comedy and music. A further trend was for films to combine elements of the fantastic into their narrative structure; an excellent example of a film of this kind would be *Tommy*.

Music films were hugely popular in the 1970s, but like fantasy films, they were not a cohesive and coherent genre. *The Boyfriend* (1971), *That'll Be the Day, Stardust, Tommy* (1975), *Bugsy Malone* (1976) and *Quadrophenia* (1979) were all hits despite focusing on very different musical trends and utilising the functions of the musical films in a variety of different ways. Even the sex comedy genre tried to capitalise on the success of the music film, in the ill-advised *Confessions of a Pop Performer* (1975) and this textual and generic borrowing once again demonstrates the fluidity of notions of genre in the period. It also reinforces just how uncertain the film industry was about what kind of product to make and fund. A successful film was seen as a key indicator of popular taste and imitations and sequels seeking to quickly capitalise on its success were the inevitable result.

Following the unprecedented 1971 box office success of *On the Buses* (made by Hammer and funded by EMI) feature film versions of television sitcoms continued to be churned out throughout the decade. Adaptations of *Up Pompeii* (1971), *Dad's Army* (1971), *Please Sir!* (1971), *Bless This House* (1973), *Love Thy Neighbour* (1973) and *Porridge* (1979) all transferred to the cinema with varying degrees of success. The key objective of these films was to attract the stay-at-home television audience and in doing so brought a television aesthetic to the cinema. Yet even these family favourites failed to bring consistent success.

The presence of oddball generic hybrids as well as films inspired by existing television or musical forms can be attributed to previously successful formulae and series losing their box office appeal in this uncertain decade. Producers and directors consistently poured money into projects which flopped, while other productions made on low budgets far exceeded expectations, delighting audiences, confounding the critics and demonstrating the complexities of popular taste.

Popular taste

So how can we make sense of such a fragmented and uncertain production culture and how can we account for the inconsistencies of popular taste and box office success? Although it is difficult to study popular taste, the problems in establishing clear patterns or obtaining data should not prevent engagement in this important field of enquiry. Films cannot be simply split into the successful and the unsuccessful, the popular and the unpopular, rather the relative nature of popular taste and commercial success must be acknowledged. In 1974, *Confessions of a Window Cleaner* was popular, yet so were *Don't Look Now* (1973) and *Stardust*. The relative popularity of these films must be considered as part of the wider landscape of popular taste and audience preferences. Some people may not have chosen to see either *Confessions* or *Stardust*, yet both films were still popular. Conversely, many people would have chosen to see both films. While many flocked to see the adaptation of Agatha Christie's *Murder on the Orient Express*, which led to its becoming one of EMI most successful films of 1975, many also chose to see *The Land That Time Forgot*.[3] The popularity of one film does not prevent the popularity of another.

Due to the patchiness of the data available in documenting box office figures and popularity, it is often necessary to rely upon general sources such as compiled lists of successful films. Conclusions can still be drawn but this material should be considered alongside data from the trade press and from individual production accounts where possible. The table below shows the top films for a year at the British box office, with the figures in brackets signifying the position of the top British film when all other films are included (Table 7.1).

These data shed particular light on the British box office and, although valuable, must be viewed with caution. *Confessions of a Window Cleaner* has been widely documented as the highest grossing British film of 1974, yet it only ranked 16th after inclusion of other non-British films. This highlights its success as a British production, but is in no way comparable to the popularity of *The Sting* (1974), *The Exorcist* (1974) or *Herbie Rides Again* (1974). As director Stephen Frears recently observed about the period, 'in the end, people go and see American films.'[4] Yet, one cannot dismiss British films so hastily in the 1970s. The table reveals that far from being subordinate to Hollywood, British films were managing to hold their own at the box office in a competitive decade. The successes of the four Bond films released in this period attest to the

Table 7.1   The British box office, 1970–1980

Year	Top Grossing Film in UK	Top Grossing British Film in UK
1970	(No figures)	Battle of Britain
1971	The Aristocats	On the Buses (2nd)
1972	Diamonds Are Forever	Diamonds Are Forever (1st)
1973	Live and Let Die	Live and Let Die (1st)
1974	The Sting	Confessions of a Window Cleaner (16th)
1975	The Towering Inferno	The Man with the Golden Gun (3rd)
1976	Jaws	The Return of the Pink Panther (4th)
1977	The Spy Who Loved Me	The Spy Who Loved Me (1st)
1978	Star Wars	The Revenge of the Pink Panther (5th)
1979	Moonraker/Superman	Moonraker (1st)
1980	The Empire Strikes Back	Monty Python's Life of Brian (4th)

Source: P. Robertson, *The Guinness Book of Film Facts and Feats* (Enfield: Guinness Superlatives, 1980), p. 46.

power of the series, and are clear box office winners, even when competing with American blockbusters. One important trend which the table reveals and which has often been overlooked is the success of British comedy films. As well as the lowbrow *On the Buses*, other British comedy successes include the subversive *Monty Python's Life of Brian* and the slapstick-driven *Pink Panther* films. This diversity of comedy types suggests not only the diversification of production which led to the making of such an eclectic range of films, but also indicates the varied preferences of the audience. The relationship between popular American films and British audiences must also be considered alongside the popularity of British films with American audiences. As Sarah Street has identified, some British films had a huge impact in America, with four British films in 1975 alone taking over $50 million at the American box office. *Return of the Pink Panther* (1975) grossed $20.2 million, *Tommy* took $17.8 million, *Barry Lyndon* $9.2 million and *Monty Python and the Holy Grail* $5.2 million.[5]

The national box office picture is often very different from the regional picture and the paucity of regional data often prevents useful comparisons. A glance at the highest grossing films at the Southampton Odeon in 1973/1974 reveals that the films at this particular cinema were not the same as the top-grossing films at the UK box office (Table 7.2).

Though deliberately simplistic, this brief comparison reveals that national trends and regional trends must not be conflated within discussions of popular taste.[6] As the table reveals, the Southampton Odeon suggests a completely different regional picture to that suggested by a

Table 7.2 Local and national box office

Southampton Odeon top grossing films (1973–1974)	British Box Office top grossing films (1974)
Robin Hood	The Sting
Papillon	The Exorcist
Gold	Enter the Dragon
Zardoz	The Three Musketeers
Don't Look Now	Papillon
The Way We Were	Herbie Rides Again
Snow White and the 7 Dwarves	Robin Hood
Diamonds Are Forever/From Russia with Love	The Great Gatsby
Song of the South	Mary Poppins
Live and Let Die/On Her Majesty's Secret Service	The Way We Were

Source: Personal accounts of J. Tilmouth, Cinema Manager, Odeon Southampton, reproduced with his permission.

glance at the national box office. Regional trends include the showing of James Bond double bills, featuring films from previous years, and the absence of some of the year's biggest films.

However, the data from the Southampton cinema must also be interpreted in relation to wider distribution and exhibition patterns. As a Rank-owned cinema, products from this conglomerate would have been given precedence over other films. Statistics are of course not infallible and box office returns were open to manipulation by the film industry itself. When interviewed recently, David Puttnam recalled touring around key cinemas buying up final tickets for *That'll Be the Day* in order to ensure that the film sold out and would subsequently be booked for a further week![7] Although such small activities probably would not have affected the statistics as a whole, it is important to recognise that the picture is frequently far more complex than it first appears and it is not possible to see box office statistics as effective indicators of popular taste.

The popularity of individual films also shifts over time, making it difficult to consider films within the context of their first release. Films such as *Get Carter* (1971), *A Clockwork Orange* (1971), *Quadrophenia* (1979) and *The Long Good Friday* (1980) have all been critically acclaimed in recent years, yet not all were popular and pleasing to audiences on their first release. It would be slightly misleading to couch consideration of popular taste in terms of what we *now* revere and hold up as examples of 'quality' 1970s filmmaking. Such an approach, which separates the high-culture examples from the low, and which seeks to overlay modern notions of quality and popularity over these historical texts, avoids the comprehensive analysis which the decade needs and which the historian should aim to provide. The case studies selected for detailed scrutiny provide an opportunity to address issues of popular taste. As shall be shown, some were popular, some were not. Some aimed for big audiences and others for small. Some were successful and others were not. Some are now critically revered and technically acclaimed; others are consistently cited as low points of British 1970s cinema. Yet they are all included here to attest to the richness and diversity of the filmmaking of the period.

The case studies

The selected case studies are partially justified by the range of related archival evidence available. This evidence, which includes diaries, production notes, advertising and marketing material, profit and loss accounts and personal correspondence can be used to tease out some of the important issues highlighted by my examination of the production culture. Of course, the case studies have not simply been included because of the richness of their supporting evidence. They have been chosen mindfully, to demonstrate the different ways in which archival material can be used, as well as allowing for an interrogation of 1970s film culture. It would be a straightforward task to pick out films which fit with existing models and which 'prove' established narratives. However, as Ludmilla Jordanova reminds us, 'one of the central parts of the historian's craft is searching for and then evaluating a variety of accounts and diverse types of evidence.'[8] It is this variety of evidence which is so important in the final part of this work and which informs my approach.

Though principally drawing upon the personal papers of directors and producers, my case studies have been chosen to demonstrate the diversity of film culture of the period and not the importance of individuals. If that were the case, then the case studies should include Ken Russell, Nicolas Roeg, Stanley Kubrick and John Boorman, as well as John Schlesinger, Derek Jarman and Joseph Losey. For reasons explored earlier within this chapter, these case studies are not based upon generic definitions. Finally, although many important actors from the 1970s are included here, notably Alan Bates, Glenda Jackson, Peter Finch, Julie Christie, Robin Askwith, Ray Winstone, Phil Daniels and Toyah Willcox, absent are Sean Connery, Michael Caine, Joan Collins, Richard Burton, Malcolm McDowell, Susan George, Sid James, Barbara Windsor and Roger Moore.

The six case studies I have chosen are: *The Go-Between* (1971), *Sunday Bloody Sunday* (1971), *Confessions of a Window Cleaner, Stardust* (1974), *Scum* and *The Tempest* (1979). I have chosen these films as case studies because they offer a variety of themes, production contexts, funding details, authorial influences and creative involvement. These films are also drawn from different genres, were produced at different moments throughout the decade and involved a range of creative, professional and technical personnel. My examination of these six films will consider all aspects of their production and contributions of significant figures including costume and set designers, cinematographers, financiers, creative-producers, screenwriters and executive producers will be explored where appropriate. This examination of creative agency will also allow me to explore the important role played by actors and to analyse important visual components of these film texts including costume, performance style, body language and voice.

As well as analysing the films visually, I will also be using the archival material to consider how members of the film industry responded to both the funding crisis and the crisis in popular taste. The extensive range and variety of texts produced in this period reflect a wider uncertainty about the nature of popular taste.

The complexities of popular taste have often led to its critical neglect, but using archival information I want to examine what strategies were utilised by film producers and directors in order to maximise profits from particular films. For example, I will examine the way in which *Scum* (1979) deliberately capitalised on its X certificate, and the importance of *Confessions of a Window Cleaner* as part of a low-budget series. Such investigations into popular taste will shed new light on this important aspect of film and cinema. As shown, the balance of power in the British film industry was shifting in the period with an influx of newcomers from television, film school and advertising, and the retirement and marginalisation of some of the 'old guard.' While locating discussions about agency within this broader context, I also want to scrutinise individual creative agency within particular film texts.

Even with such a diverse and eclectic selection of films, there are crossovers. For example, Don Boyd acted as Executive Producer on both *Scum* and *The Tempest*; investors Clive Parsons and Davina Belling were involved in *Scum* and *Confessions of a Window Cleaner*; *Stardust* and *Confessions of a Window Cleaner* were released in the same year, as were *Scum* and *The Tempest*, and *The Go-Between* and *Sunday Bloody Sunday*. These are not stand-alone texts, they relate intimately to the cultures of production outlined in earlier parts of this work and also to each other. The inclusion of specific case studies and a close discussion of their individual production histories will offer an understanding of how the film industry operated in this decade. They will also provide new examples of filmmaking in this complex and fractured period as well as insights into broader trends and patterns.

8
Sunday Bloody Sunday: Authorship, Collaboration and Improvisation

Sunday Bloody Sunday (1971) was based on an original screenplay written by Penelope Gilliatt, directed by John Schlesinger and produced by Joseph Janni. The extensive John Schlesinger papers held within the BFI Special Collections will be used to examine how conflicts in agency and authorship manifested themselves within the text of the film. Set in the early 1970s, against a background of rocketing inflation and grim economic downturn, the film follows Alex Greville (Glenda Jackson) and Daniel Hirsch (Peter Finch), who are both in love with young sculptor Bob (Murray Head). All the members of the bisexual love triangle are aware of each other and both Alex and Daniel struggle to pretend that they are satisfied with the arrangement. This unhappy arrangement only ends when Bob leaves them both for a job in America.

Although not produced until 1970, the film evolved from an idea first suggested in the mid-1960s. The screenplay was also written in this period and major decisions about funding and casting also date from the late 1960s. *Sunday Bloody Sunday* sits on the cusp of two very different periods and the visual style as well as the settings and locations document this awkward transition. The cultural and social changes brought about by the 1960s are not dissected and analysed within *Sunday Bloody Sunday*, but rather the film draws upon the emotional landscape that such changes have created, especially the problems which arise when constructs such as family, marriage and love become fragmented and uncertain.

The inclusion of this film in a study of 1970s films demonstrates the fluidity of the boundaries between decades, and shows how creative ideas from one decade spill over into the next. *Sunday Bloody Sunday* revived an established working relationship between Schlesinger and Janni and incorporated the work of acclaimed writer and columnist

Penelope Gilliatt. In this way, the film was a product of 1960s film culture which relied upon American funding and utilised tried and tested creative partnerships. However, even the long-standing collaboration between Janni and Schlesinger was tested during the production of this film, while Gilliatt's contributions, though innovative, further complicated the scriptwriting and production process.

Producer Joseph Janni and director John Schlesinger first worked together on *A Kind of Loving* (1962). The success of this film prompted further collaborations on *Billy Liar* (1963), *Darling* (1965) and *Far from the Madding Crowd* (1967). It was during the filming of *Far from the Madding Crowd* that Janni and Schlesinger claimed to have come up with the premise of *Sunday Bloody Sunday*, with Janni recalling discussing ideas with Schlesinger and Penelope Gilliatt in October 1966 for 'a story with a bi-sexual theme, non-sensational and set in Brighton.'[1] Schlesinger remembered the development of the project slightly differently, recalling his and Gilliatt's conversations in spring 1967 around the proposed film, noting: 'I remember giving her the details of the bi-sexual theme, the idea of a boy who was escaping to America from an affair simultaneously between a Jewish doctor and a girl.'[2] The provenance of the project was later to become hotly contested but it is clear that in the late 1960s, as a result of discussions with Schlesinger and Janni, Penelope Gilliatt drafted the first screenplay of what was to become *Sunday Bloody Sunday*.

Following the international success of Schlesinger's *Midnight Cowboy* (1969), United Artists agreed to supply the budget of $1.25 million for the production of *Sunday Bloody Sunday*.[3] This straightforward funding contrasts with the more entrepreneurial and ad hoc arrangements that were to feature in film production in the years that followed. Despite the crisis in funding, which was to become an issue in later years, funding from major Hollywood studios remained the most usual method of film finance for established directors at the start of the decade. Due mostly to Schlesinger's reputation and recent successes, *Sunday Bloody Sunday* was seen as a good investment with even the hard-pressed National Film Finance Corporation offering to co-finance the film.[4] Ultimately, this help was not needed and United Artists championed the film, pouring money into the production and spending over £352,000 to publicise the film in America alone.[5]

The working relationship between Janni and Schlesinger was highly successful and Schlesinger acknowledged how crucial Janni was to the production process, writing in March 1968: 'I am relieved and extremely glad that Jo Janni's reaction to the script has been enormously positive... he is excited by the whole project which makes our task of continuing it much easier.'[6] However, this partnership underwent a significant shift on *Sunday Bloody Sunday*. Unlike their previous projects together, this film did not draw exclusively upon established and existing professional relationships, but rather was a complex and multifaceted arrangement which utilised the creative talents of a range of new collaborators, one of the most important being Penelope Gilliatt. One of the first problems to occur between Janni, Schlesinger and Gilliatt was during the pre-production process, when Gilliatt's absence caused difficulties. In July 1969, Janni wrote to Gilliatt:

> We definitely want to get ahead with the film but we can only do so with the writer being here with us between now and the moment we shoot, to listen to our comments and discuss every scene in great detail. This is very usual and the only way we know how to work.[7]

It is interesting that Janni stresses this point, for it suggests that it was his and Schlesinger's normal working practice for the writer to be continuously involved. On previous projects, Janni and Schlesinger had either worked with established partnerships such as Willis Hall and Keith Waterhouse on *A Kind of Loving* and *Billy Liar*, or were themselves heavily involved in the original idea, as with *Darling*. After the successful collaboration on *Darling* with Frederic Raphael – in which Janni and Schlesinger share authorship credits – the partnership was revived for *Far from the Madding Crowd*. While close collaboration with the author and reliance on established partnerships may have been a feature of their previous work, *Sunday Bloody Sunday* was only the second occasion when they were working on an original screenplay. It was also the first project in which Janni and Schlesinger collaborated with a female scriptwriter.

There were also other significant changes to the production and technical team. In *A Kind of Loving* and *Billy Liar*, the predominantly urban locations and striking cinematography was achieved through the combined efforts of art director Ray Simm whose other credits included *A Hard Day's Night* (1964) and *Help!* (1965) and cinematographer Denys Coop who photographed many of the films of the new wave including *This Sporting Life* (1963). Both Coop and Simm also worked on *Darling*, whose distinctive visual style drew on the conventions of the British New Wave but also signalled a more glamorous and stylish direction for British cinema.

The creative personnel involved on these Schlesinger and Janni film projects demonstrate a great deal about the working methods they adopted. Established teams and people were reused again and again to create distinct and specific 'looks.' But *Sunday Bloody Sunday* was the film in which methods of creative and production practice changed dramatically. Not only did the film mark the first occasion when Janni and Schlesinger collaborated with a new writer, it also signalled a break with their usual creative collaborators who had helped establish such a distinctive visual style which had been such a feature of Schlesinger's work in the 1960s.

Signs of strain within the production team appeared in July 1969, when Janni wrote to Gilliatt, informing her that they were 'perturbed and unhappy about the dialogue' in the current version of the screenplay.[8] Once shooting began more specific problems were identified. Schlesinger considered:

> The final scene with Glenda and Murray was...too long and not right...we had failed to solve the end of the weekend and the Hodsons' return. The bar mitzvah ceremony remained an idea rather than a fact...the first scene in the film with the neurotic patient, when we started to shoot it, did not work at all.[9]

Scriptwriters David Sherwin and Ken Levinson, both of whom had previously worked with Janni, were drafted in to help resolve many of the problems with the screenplay. It is indicative of the deteriorating working relationship with Gilliatt that she was not informed of the involvement of Sherwin and Levinson. Schlesinger recalled, 'we did not tell Penelope...as we didn't want extra problems developing at this stage.'[10] It is also significant that both Levinson and Sherwin were brought in to work on *Sunday Bloody Sunday* at Janni's suggestion, indicating that Janni was heavily involved in the pre-production process as well as occupying the more usual role of the producer.

Further problems arose in 1971 when Gilliatt began claiming sole authorship of the finished project. After such extensive collaboration, both Janni and Schlesinger took exception to the proposed cover of the screenplay, which declared, '*Sunday Bloody Sunday* by Penelope Gilliatt, the script of the film directed by John Schlesinger. A Joe Janni production for United Artists.'[11] Worse still was the dedication, which read 'John Schlesinger and Joseph Janni worked through subsequent drafts of this screenplay and I am in their debt as well as the actors and crew.'[12]

Instead of attempting to judge the credibility of opposing claims, it is far more helpful to use the material contained in the Schlesinger papers to dissect the processes of authorship. The tormented protagonists within the film and their uneasy relationship with one another can be seen as a distorted reflection of the awkward, often confrontational relationship between the production team. Gilliatt's extensive screenplay contains remarkably detailed character descriptions, suggesting she had firm ideas about character. Gilliatt describes Alex Greville, who would ultimately be played by Glenda Jackson, as 'thirty four, pretty, disorganised, separated from her husband for two years, doing the wrong job in a public relations firm and writing out her resignation every few days.'[13] In Gilliatt's screenplay it is difficult to discern what came first; the character of Alex Greville or the casting of Glenda Jackson, so perfect is the match between them. One script note reads 'though she looks a bit got-down physically, walking with the classic upper-class flamingo gait, she attacks life with exuberance and tough-mindedness.'[14] The characteristic 'flamingo gait' and the discernible physical awkwardness are both crucial parts of Jackson's performance. Whilst the pragmatic vulnerability of Glenda Jackson's performance would ultimately win critical accolades, the character is also heavily invested with Gilliatt's own witty, unpredictable personality.

Schlesinger also felt a personal involvement with the characters, claiming when interviewed in 1978, 'the story was very personal to me. I knew all those people extremely well.'[15] Himself the son of a doctor, the Jewish, homosexual Schlesinger evidently saw a great deal of himself within the character of Daniel. Although Janni differs distinctly from Bob, his role as a mediator between the artistic personalities of Gilliatt and Schlesinger, his established collaborative relationship with Schlesinger and his help solving some of the films problems, such as drafting in Levinson and Sherwin, position him as a definite third party in this creative relationship. The film's fragmented, complex and uneasy emotional landscape reflects these struggles for creative control, but also draws on the influence of the cast.

The subtlety required for the three central parts made casting the film crucial. As Schlesinger conceded, 'it's got to be very carefully made or otherwise it will be a disaster.'[16] By January 1969, Schlesinger firmly believed 'Vanessa Redgrave is the only actress who can fill the range of the part and make the film we want,' while Janni agreed 'I think she will be absolutely perfect.'[17] Other actresses, including Jean Simmons and Billie Whitelaw, are mentioned in the archives as possibilities, but Redgrave was the clear favourite until August 1969. A lengthy letter from Schlesinger explains the sudden *volte-face*:

> Joe and I saw *Women in Love* last night and were absolutely bowled over by a great deal of it, particularly Alan and Glenda Jackson's

performances. The hardness that I was frightened of has mellowed now and although she comes across as pretty tough it is still utterly feminine and I think the whole personality might work in a strangely marvellous way to our advantage.[18]

Jackson herself felt that she had been typecast following *Women in Love* (1969), stating when interviewed recently by the author:

Producers are very unimaginative. So I was constantly being sent scripts of the same thing. Then I did *The Music Lovers, Sunday Bloody Sunday*, and I was in that kind of category of love star, probably neurotic, all that highly dramatic kind of thing.[19]

It is significant that Jackson considers her role in *Sunday Bloody Sunday* to be one of the 'neurotic... highly dramatic' parts, for within the film her character is a glorious paradox of confidence, insecurity, conformity and rebellion. Alex is certainly neurotic but is also pragmatic, appealing and articulate. Her awkwardness of manner contrasts with the directness of her gaze, suggesting a woman not quite at ease with herself or with the world she inhabits. As one of the character notations reveals, 'the outer self works efficiently enough, but the inner self has mysteriously stalled.'[20] Alex epitomises an intriguing aspect of 1970s femininity; an intelligent, well-educated, successful, independent woman who actively questions her life and its purpose and finds none of the answers.

Some years later, Alexander Walker wrote, 'Just as Julie Christie's "golden girl" had given a characteristic burnish to the 60s, Jackson's articulate, pragmatic rebarbative nature seemed in tune with the raw new decade.'[21] Again, this pragmatism, intelligence and prickly yet vulnerable persona perfectly encapsulated a woman attempting to ignore the social conventions of her class and prevailing dictates about marriage, sex and love while yearning for that same conformity. Jackson's personal image fits perfectly with the depiction she offers of the character and this is perhaps unsurprising when considering the amount of input the cast had into the development of their characters.

The Schlesinger papers reveal how the cast were involved in helping to shape their roles as well as developing the storylines and amending the script and specific scenes. Many of these improvisations and changes grew from Gilliatt not being present for much of the shooting. Schlesinger remembered 'during rehearsals... the actors and I still felt that certain scenes did not work and during a process of improvisation, we found new ways of dealing with certain scenes, which she

[Gilliatt] then re-wrote before shooting commenced.'[22] A later file note reads, 'certain scenes were discovered not to work' while other notes detail a scene with Peggy Ashcroft which was found not to work and had to be 'drastically altered' during rehearsals.[23] Again, this suggests an evolving process in which the actors played a significant part and it was their improvisations which led to a number of the rewrites and changes being made to the script and the screenplay. The fact that many of the scenes were found not to work at rehearsals rather than in the scriptwriting stage suggest the relative inexperience of Gilliatt in writing for the screen. However, it also indicates an important opportunity for the performers to make their own suggestions about character and motivation and, most of all, demonstrates Schlesinger's directorial approach which allowed and encouraged such suggestions and input.

Just as Glenda Jackson perfectly encapsulates the angst-ridden Alex, Peter Finch's moving performance as the steady, reliable, though emotionally unsatisfied Daniel provides the film with much needed pathos. Despite the strength and quality of Finch's performance, he was not the original choice for the role. When casting was being considered in 1969, Schlesinger's casting agent noted that the part of Daniel 'needs something really very special and in general, actors are not called upon to reveal their delicate layers of character and personality and emotion that [we] need for him.'[24] Certain casting suggestions, while recognised as highly appropriate, were rejected due to their obviousness, namely Harold Pinter and Dirk Bogarde. Schlesinger agreed 'the casting of Dirk is terribly on the nose. He is marvellous at playing long-suffering lovers and indeed has already done so for us' (a reference to *Darling*).[25] But he ultimately felt 'the casting is so obvious I think it would seriously rob the film of some of its originality. The character, after all, needs to be played with a great deal of self-awareness and a certain bitter humour about his predicament.'[26] Another actor felt to be unsuitable for the role was Albert Finney, whom Schlesinger wrote to, apologising, 'although I know you could act the part of Daniel, practically off the screen, we feel that there would be an element of cheat-casting in it which could be difficult to get round.'[27]

The part demanded great emotional depth and sincerity and sometime between March and August 1970, Ian Bannen was replaced by Peter Finch who had worked with Janni and Schlesinger on *Far from the Madding Crowd*. This re-casting appeared to rejuvenate the film with Schlesinger believing that 'Peter Finch is really finding the measure of Daniel.'[28] Murray Head remembered, 'Peter was the easiest person in the world to get on with' and the working relationship which developed between the actors allowed for the intimacy of the physical and emotional relationship to be explored on screen.[29] Schlesinger recalled, 'Peter plunged right into his part and there was no time to talk it over with him. He knew the character in some way without, I think, ever having experienced any of it.'[30] Finch's sensitive and thoughtful portrayal of Daniel allowed the character to extend far beyond a caricature of the middle-aged homosexual doctor and confirmed to Schlesinger that he had found the right actor. Elaine Dundy writes in her biography of Finch that this part is his most skilful performance and in particular, the careful portrayal of the character as an ordinary person, neither as a paragon nor as an object of pity.[31]

Casting the role of Bob was less problematic because, according to Gilliatt's acerbic synopsis, the character is 'almost described in describing the other two.'[32] Janni and Schlesinger felt that they could easily find 'a number of people who may be right' and their casting suggestions included, at various times, Anthony Andrews, Timothy Dalton, Robert Powell and Ian McKellen.[33] Pop singer and actor Murray Head was finally cast and although Schlesinger rather disparagingly considered him to be 'more of a personality than an actor' he did acknowledge 'he was very uptight when playing opposite Ian, but I think he feels freer and given stronger support by Peter.'[34] The pairing of Bob and Daniel is as important within the film as that of Bob and Alex, yet Bob is the character who, despite his youth, suggests the transition between the 1960s and the 1970s. Bob's role is that of a catalyst, he moves between Daniel and Alex and as the *Sight and Sound* review noted, '[he] is the nearest of the three principals to a free soul, 1970s style... he feels no guilt, because no sense of duty towards either.'[35] For Murray Head the experience of playing Bob was disconcerting. Head remembered:

> I was twenty at the time... and having all sorts of conflicting feelings about responsibility on the one hand and doing my own thing on the other and I was beginning to hate the character I was playing. Things were being pulled out of me that were like him, I didn't like it a bit. It was getting very claustrophobic.[36]

Once filming was completed, Janni wrote to Schlesinger, 'I know you don't think Murray comes out very well, but now that I see the film as a whole, I think he's perfect. He seems to personify youth and the lack of responsibility and all those other things which seem today to go with that word in respect of relationships.'[37] Schlesinger remained unhappy with Head's performance, suggesting in an interview in 1978 that 'the film would have been improved by a more vital force in the centre of it...it would have been better if there had been a glimmer that he was really a quite interesting person.'[38] However, Janni's convictions demonstrate his clear understanding of the importance of the character. As well as representing the positives of youth: possibility, optimism, hedonism and freedom, Bob also represents selfishness, self-absorption and unreliability.

Bob is one of the youthful, transient male figures who emerge in a diverse and eclectic range of British films of the period. This is an important aspect of 1970s British cinema with Malcolm McDowell's coffee salesman in *O Lucky Man!* (1973) and even the eponymous opportunistic hero of *Barry Lyndon* (1975), examples of the rootless, classless Picaro who moves easily between and within classes, generations and social groups. These transient characters suggest a period of flux in which barriers of class, gender, occupation and privilege are challenged and occasionally overcome. Bob represents a new classlessness which allows greater social freedom and movement; he moves easily between Alex and Daniel's middle-class friends, yet appears to have no fixed family or class roots of his own. Class is a social construct which the 1960s aimed to dispense with, but within *Sunday Bloody Sunday*, it is the characters and their emotional landscape which is the principle focus of the narrative, rather than overt discussions of class. Unlike Joseph Losey who saw class as a critical and integral aspect of the British psyche, Schlesinger implies class difference through the varying presentations of Alex, Daniel and the Hodson family but does not structure the film around the issue.

Within *Sunday Bloody Sunday* love, sex, marriage, home and family are all in a state of disorder and this confusion and lack of clarity is effectively communicated through visual style and sets. Director of photography Billy Williams, designer Luciana Arrighi and set decorator Harry Cordwell were drafted in to create *Sunday Bloody Sunday*'s visual style. The trio had worked together on *Women in Love* and were responsible for the film's exquisite lighting, stunning photography and most importantly of all, the visual depiction of Glenda Jackson. In choosing a creative team who had already worked with Jackson and whose work was critically acclaimed, Janni and Schlesinger hoped to utilise the successfully working partnership for their own project, in the absence of erstwhile collaborators. Although the cinematography of *Sunday Bloody Sunday* bears little resemblance to the visceral vibrancy of the Lawrence adaptation, this film's visual style is just as striking as that of *Women in Love*. Lawrence's preoccupation with nature perfectly complemented the artistic vision of Russell, yet in *Sunday Bloody Sunday*, the settings are pre-dominantly urban and the locations and interiors created suggest drab, faded modernity. Billy Williams later recalled that the film was delib-erately under-photographed so that the visuals would not come into conflict with the story.[39] The disordered set decoration is a direct con-trast to the modernity of the visual style with its sharp, clinical lighting. Through its visual style, the film suggests that the exuberant excesses of the 1960s had faded and what remains in the early 1970s is slightly worn, threadbare and dated.

Many of the interior locations within the film evoke a transience, particularly Alex's flat with its half-built kitchen, jumble of furniture and crockery, and the empty spaces on the bookshelves where Alex's husband has removed his possessions. The character's personal confu-sion is reflected in this space which we see with renewed clarity when she returns home alone after her stay at the Hodsons. The half-filled coffee cup and the upturned ashtray, the mess of papers and the dust sheets thrown carelessly over furniture all reflect her disordered, lonely and shattered emotional state. Unlike the slovenly hollowness of Alex's flat, Daniel's home and surgery are both austerely tidy and meticu-lously ordered, yet still possess the same quality of emptiness. His heavy wooden furniture sits awkwardly alongside Bob's plastic inventions, while the cold perfection of the living space deliberately calls atten-tion to the character's loneliness and isolation. Most of the homes in the film are contained within Victorian buildings, not yet dilapidated, but characterised by a faded grandeur which bears traces of the colour and richness of an earlier time. The uncertainty of the period and of the characters is also evident within the set design and locations. Even the cheerful business of the Hodson's home is shown to be awkward and uncomfortable for Bob and Alex. Just as the characters are awk-ward within the setting, the mise-en-scène conspires to reinforce this uneasiness, with the breast milk in the fridge, the children in the adults' bed, the posters about starvation in Africa in the family kitchen all deliberately creating jarring and discordant notes.

The issues of transience and unease identified within the set design and the visual style are also evident elsewhere within the film, partic-ularly within the costumes. Alex's clothes also reiterate awkwardness and disjuncture. The modernity of her work attire contrasts with the enveloping Victorian nightdress she wears at the Hodson's, suggesting a conventionality and a slightly prudish streak. In a similar way, Daniel's neatly pressed cardigans and deliberately casual shirts suggest another character who is awkward when not defined by the drab, yet well-fitting anonymity of his work clothes. This awkwardness is rendered even more interesting as costume designer Jocelyn Rickards remembered, 'there wasn't time to do a wardrobe for Peter...most of the clothes he wore in the film were his own.'[40] It is a testament to the performance of Peter Finch that although predominantly wearing his own clothes, the character of Daniel is uneasy and unsure and appears to be awkwardly dressed throughout the film. Rickards had recently worked on *Ryan's Daughter* (1970) with David Lean, and although the dramatic scarlet petticoat of Sarah Miles is absent here, the costumes of the characters are highly significant. In her autobiography, Rickards outlined her approach to costume which fitted in so perfectly to *Sunday Bloody Sunday*:

> If the clothes are well designed, they are probably unnoticeable, but they should carry with them a number of messages, like what kind of school the character went to, what newspapers he or she reads, what political affiliation he has, what his sexual inclinations are.[41]

Within the film, Rickard's costumes do exactly this. Jackson's voluminous nightdress, Finch's awkwardly youthful cardigans and meticulously ironed slacks suggest important details about character while also deliberately reinforcing the unease and notion of transition which permeates the rest of the film.

For Schlesinger, the emotions of the characters were central to the film, and he firmly maintained, 'the one thing I didn't want to make...was a problem film. This had to be a story of relationships, in which the characters are complex people in a difficult emotional situation.'[42] Peter Finch agreed about the importance of the characters, conceding 'there's hardly any plot, it's all character...this is the first script I have ever seen in which homosexuality is just a fact about a character, not presented at all as an issue in itself.'[43] In a recent interview with the author, Glenda Jackson felt that the film was not just about character and that it did deal with the 'issues' that Schlesinger was so anxious to avoid. Jackson observed:

> It was probably one of the first films that dealt with homosexuality as though it was a perfectly normal thing to be and...it was actually more about love than about sex. And that was the big thing in that film I think, rather more than my character.[44]

Perhaps the combination of detailed characterisation and the subordination of issues of sexuality within the characters' own personalities, makes the potentially controversial sexuality normal and even commonplace. In this way, *Sunday Bloody Sunday* proved that is was possible for homosexuality to feature in a film without that film becoming solely about homosexuality. Picking up where *Darling* left off, *Sunday Bloody Sunday* allows the emotional unease of the characters to reflect the fleeting nature of sexual and emotional pleasure. Love and sex have become commodities and, whilst free love and readily available sex offer pleasure, they offer no lasting fulfilment and leave only bitterness and emotional unease. Here it is not just the principal protagonists who highlight the emptiness of the free love ideals; a woman at Daniel's party publicly and drunkenly berates her husband for his infidelity with the au pair, Alex herself has an unsatisfactory affair with one of her clients, whilst her ghastly friends the Hodsons see her relationship with Bob as an opportunity for sociological debate.

More so than in *Darling*, age is also a critical theme in *Sunday Bloody Sunday*. Both Alex and Daniel are older, sadder and wiser than Bob, yet both gladly enter into a relationship with him knowing what he is and how much of himself he withholds. While Bob is full of the optimism of youth, Daniel and Alex carry the experience of their years. Daniel attends his nephew's Bar Mitzvah and is pestered about his unmarried status and deliberately seated next to an attractive middle-aged woman, while Alex visits her parents, who encourage her to reconcile with her ex-husband. A client of Alex's is unable to get a job because of his age and resorts to temporary facelifts for job interviews in a sad attempt to turn back the years. The bitterness of aging is compounded in the film through the clever use of flashbacks of both Alex's and Daniel's childhoods. Alex remembers herself as a little girl, desperately craving her father's attention, while Daniel remembers his own acceptance into the Jewish faith as a time of unquestioned and easy belonging. Paradoxically, the film does not idealise childhood. The precocious Hodson children experience the death of the family pet, and Daniel's concluding lines in the film contradict the notion of childhood as a carefree and happy time:

> When you're at school and want to quit, people say you're going to hate being out in the world. Well, I didn't believe them and I was right. When I was a kid, I couldn't wait to be a grown up and they said childhood was the best time of my life and it wasn't.[45]

Adulthood is no more an idealised and happy place than childhood and the film carefully reveals the empty and deliberately constructed nature of both these states. Unlike other 1970s films, *Sunday Bloody Sunday* is not nostalgic about the past, but rather draws parallels between the fixed certainties of the past and the uncertainty and unease of the present.

This depiction of marriage as essentially empty again focuses the narrative on the uneven transition between the 1960s and the 1970s and the difficulties of living in such a period. The 1970s is shown to be an era where you cannot have it all, and everyone is making do; a contrast to the hedonism, accessibility and availability of the previous decade. Motherhood is also a case of 'making do.' Children are shown to be demanding, tiring, chaotic and unrewarding and this pragmatic presentation avoids sentiment and nostalgia. This avoidance of sentiment successfully prevents family life being idealised when contrasted with the unconventional existences of both Alex and Daniel. Alex's attempts to look after the Hodson children for a weekend prove disastrous and demonstrate her awkwardness in this milieu. Penelope Gilliatt's notes suggest it is the 'enlightened modern upbringing' that has made the children 'rather more revolting to be with than other children,' and reveal yet another remnant of the 1960s counterculture which is found to be unsatisfactory – that of creative childrearing.[46] In eschewing the alternative methods of childrearing and the earnest intellectualism offered by the Hodsons, Alex is shown to be no serene earth mother. She is completely out of her depth and unable to cope with the demands of motherhood even for a weekend.

Although she is smart, educated and professional, Alex is emotionally, sexually and professionally unsatisfied. She outwardly despises conformity and security yet her deliberate attempts to prove her independence only reveal how inadequately equipped she is for a carefree, sexually liberated, unconventional life. In her final conversation with Bob, Alex's frustrations are obvious:

> All this fitting in and shutting up and making do. Me being careful not to ask you about Daniel, Daniel not getting any answers from you because you're here . . . I don't want us to live like this. I don't want to live like this anymore . . . . We've got to pack this in and I don't know what else to say.[47]

The bitterness of *Sunday Bloody Sunday* successfully evokes the loss of 1960s exuberance, optimism and possibility. Images of domestic bliss such as walking in the park, lying in front of the fire or relaxing in bed are subverted by reality; the walk in the park ends with the death of the family pet, the lack of heat caused by industrial action ensures the lovers cannot linger by the fire, while Sunday morning in bed is disturbed by precocious children smoking pot. This uncompromising reality of character and scenario was entirely deliberate and was achieved through painstaking rewriting of the script and extensive improvisations by the central performers. As Janni wrote to Schlesinger 'I have never, never seen a film before when one has felt one has known these people for ever and that, I'm sure is because they are so real.'[48] The presentation of modern life without sentimentality, the preoccupation with aging and the pointed rejection of the unsuccessful experiments of the 1960s suggest a film dealing with the present brought about by the past, but with occasional glances towards the future. The visual style of the film reinforces notions of unease and uncertainty whilst also offering glimpses of modernity.

The *Monthly Film Bulletin* highlighted the drab modernity of *Sunday Bloody Sunday*, noting the subdued cinematography and 'the muddle of multi-living... a subterranean entanglement of telephone cables coldly representing a token of communication, radios speaking of economic gloom, drug dependent drop-outs standing sadly in a nocturnal chemist's shop.'[49]

Sunday Bloody Sunday's visual style suggests uncomfortable modernity, social isolation and loneliness as well as a period of disorder and transition. America is consistently presented as a place of desirable possibility, yet the land of opportunity never seemed so close and, paradoxically, so far away. Consistently contrasted to Britain with its faltering economy, plummeting sterling and industrial shutdowns, America symbolises prosperity, consumption, success and, most of all, youth. America is only ever associated with the character of Bob and Penelope Gilliatt's early screenplay clearly links Bob with America, stating '[he] will probably suddenly become famous and lionised, if not in this country, then certainly in the US.'[50] Bob's work is artistic and unnecessary; a fusion of art and technology which manages to be neither one nor the other. An early notation in the script presciently observes: 'Bob is a Londoner of about 25 who makes a living out of designing plastic furniture, kinetic sculpture and various bits of paraphernalia. He has so far escaped being famous for it.'[51] The American market with its consumer culture is shown to be the perfect location in which to sell such impractical and unnecessary modern items.

America is contrasted not only with the drabness of Britain but also with the place that Daniel longs to visit. He envisages a long trip to Italy; a romantic and cultural exploration of a country much associated with the refinement and sophistication lacking in both Britain and America.

The high-culture associations of Italy are part of the character of Daniel and the deliberate linking of the middle-aged character with the age-old sophistication and heritage of Italy contrasts with Bob and the brash modernity of America. This deliberately juxtaposes the past and the future in uneasy accord and is perfectly encapsulated by the scene in Daniel's garden; as Daniel's recording of *Cosi Fan Tutti* plays, Bob's plastic fountain bursts into life. The modernity of the invention contrasts with the high cultural and artistic associations of the music and once again highlights the differences between Daniel and Bob, reinforcing the improbability of their relationship and acknowledging its likely failure.

Bob's departure at the end of the film is conceived not only as a move which will benefit his career but also as a way in which to extricate himself from his complex relationships with both Alex and Daniel. In this way, *Sunday Bloody Sunday* constructs America not so much as the land of opportunity, but as a place of new beginnings. Both Schlesinger and Gilliatt lived and worked in the United States in this period and Gilliatt in particular left Britain in the late 1960s with the deliberate aim of creating a new life for herself in America.[52]

The loneliness of the characters and the role of technology in all the relationships was another deliberate thematic focus within the film, with early script notes detailing:

> Emphasis on solace through mechanisms as in the electronic details of the telephone system... receiver on the side of his head that faces camera, obscuring a lot of his profile – a stylistic device used throughout the film wherever one of the characters fails to get through on a call.[53]

The telephone is a constant interruption and plays an active role in the relationships in the film. The telephonist at the message service also becomes a mediator in the relationships between Bob and Alex and Bob and Daniel and this actively illustrates the frustrations of modern life; the business and the loneliness along with technology's now central and pivotal role in people's lives. The radio news also forms part of the background diagesis and offers regular updates and commentary on the current economic situation. This intrusion of technology runs throughout the course of the film and perfectly suggests many of the anxieties of transition in the period of the late 1960s and early 1970s.

Sunday Bloody Sunday is considered to be amongst Schlesinger's finest work and is also held up as the high point of Gilliatt's.[54] However, despite winning five British Academy of Film and Television Arts

(BAFTA) awards in 1972 for Best Actress, Best Actor, Best Film, Best Editing and Best Direction, the film failed to match critical approbation with contemporary popular success. After its premiere in July 1971, the film was released throughout the UK, opening in 43 Odeon cinemas across the country and in 57 Rank cinemas in London.[55] In London, the film did significantly better in the cinemas of North London, taking £31,000 in the first weeks of release, compared to £17,000 in South London, while the *Evening Standard* was considering serialising the screenplay to capitalise on the film's success.[56]

Marketing material from the Schlesinger papers document the 'enthusiastic reaction' and 'encouraging' turnout for the film in London, yet the film failed to reach the popular heights that the marketing and advertising departments confidently predicted.[57] American publicity agents Guttman and Pam were hired to bring the film to the attention of Academy Award voters and the subsequent promotional campaign focused on creating a 'mystique' around the film and developing the profiles of the central actors and of the creative team of Schlesinger, Janni and Gilliatt.[58] However, much of the advertising campaign focused on the relationships between the three protagonists, but placed Jackson at the centre, as if to suggest a woman torn between two lovers. This inaccuracy of presentation may well have baffled an audience as the subsequent film bore little resemblance to what is suggested by the posters and publicity stills. The marketing material also emphasised domesticity and the family, with images of tea cups, the Hodson children and the family dog being presented alongside Jackson, Finch and Head, as if to suggest a gentle, domestic comedy. This confusion of marketing coupled with a slump in cinema audiences had a devastating impact on the success of the film.

The intense detailed collaboration between Gilliatt, Schlesinger and Janni created a text which benefited immensely from such detailed, often conflicting input. The reliance upon improvisation, the detailed consideration given to casting and the frequent rewrites following rehearsals all suggest the involvement of the cast in creating the realistic and touching relationships between characters, whilst preventing any descent into melodrama or farce.

The autonomy given to the cast as well as the ad hoc improvisation of production and the involvement of 'problem solvers' such as scriptwriters Sherwin and Levinson suggest a text which is not only multi-authored but which owes its evolution to a range of interventions; some creative, some practical. The range of creative talents brought to bear on the production indicated a huge break in practice for the

Janni/Schlesinger working relationship but indicated a move towards highly collaborative and experimental production which came to characterise 1970s British film. What must also be remembered is that the film itself would not have been made possible without generous funding from a major Hollywood studio and the freedom given to Schlesinger and Janni. *Sunday Bloody Sunday* is inevitably a product of this financial and economic base, but its organic evolution owes much more to the fusion of conflicting creative agencies than to any financial constraints or freedoms.

In critiquing so much that was central to the 1960s – free love, consumption, social mobility and creative childrearing – the film would appear to be a text which looks back. Yet it adopts a Janus-faced approach by focusing on the uneasy modernity of the early 1970s. The past *is* important in *Sunday Bloody Sunday*, but only in explaining the present. Within the film, the changes which had arisen from the 1960s are presented as an uncomfortable and ultimately unsatisfying way of dealing with the demands of the previous decade. *Sunday Bloody Sunday* allows an insight into the early 1970s taken from a 1960s perspective. The film thus manages to balance itself precariously between the different decades and its unhappy and uneasy narrative, visual style and characters further accentuate this awkward perspective.

9
The Go-Between: The Past, the Present and the 1970s

Directed by Joseph Losey, *The Go-Between* (1971) is based on the L.P. Hartley novel first published in 1953, and was adapted for the screen by Harold Pinter. However, this film is much more than a traditional literary adaptation and combines a modernity of manner and performance with an exploration of a range of contemporary issues within the relative safety of the past. The film rejects a nostalgic evocation of the past in favour of an insight into a life destroyed by the past. Young Leo Colston (Dominic Guard) visits Brandham Hall, home of his school friend Marcus Maudsley, and is received by Marcus' wealthy family with flattering attention. Leo's devotion to Marian (Julie Christie), Marcus's beautiful and vivacious older sister, leads him into becoming a go-between, carrying her love letters to local farmer Ted Burgess (Alan Bates). It is the public discovery of their affair, combined with Ted's subsequent suicide, which blights Leo's life. For him, passion and the past will always be linked with pain, loss and shame.

The Go-Between is not a typical period piece firmly rooted in a historical past, but is instead an innovative adaptation with deep contemporary social and cultural significance. Like *Sunday Bloody Sunday*, the film spent many years in development, predominantly due to copyright issues, and was the final filmed collaboration between Pinter and Losey following their work on *The Servant* (1963) and *Accident* (1967). The extensive Joseph Losey papers housed within the Special Collections at the BFI offer a unique insight into the production of the film, documenting the involvement of key creative personnel. This material will be used to consider how the film adaptation reinforces or subverts Hartley's original novel, while analysis of the film's visual and cultural codes will explore how this technically innovative film deliberately constructed an historical past to critique contemporary concerns of class, gender and childhood.

The range of material in the 1970s which was adapted for British cinema ranged from the literary heights of Ibsen, Chekhov and Murdoch, to the more middlebrow fare of Lawrence, Kipling, Dickens and Shakespeare. The period is also notable for the high number of literary adaptations which drew upon popular novels such as *Jane Eyre* (1970), *Wuthering Heights* (1970), *Black Beauty* (1971), *Kidnapped* (1972), *Treasure Island* (1973), *Gulliver's Travels* (1977), *The 39 Steps* (1978) and *Riddle of the Sands* (1979). Yet, as shall be shown in the next chapter, it was not only high and middlebrow literature which was transformed into film in the 1970s; one of the most popular texts to be adapted for the screen was the pulp sex novel, *Confessions of a Window Cleaner* (1974).

The adaptation of *The Go-Between* drew heavily on the creative input of screenwriter Harold Pinter and author L.P Hartley. Hartley was extensively involved in the filming of his novel and offered his own ideas about casting and suitable shooting location. He enthused over Pinter's screenplay:

> It is absolutely splendid and more faithful to the letter and spirit of the book than I could have believed possible seeing that there are bound to be changes in translating work from one medium to another. You needn't have said 'based' on *The Go-Between*, for it IS *The Go-Between* – the essence of it.[1]

Yet, what exactly is the essence that Hartley refers to, and how have Losey and Pinter managed successfully to capture and communicate it? While the film is a standalone text, it does draw upon the narrative and characters created within the source novel. There are subtle yet significant differences between the novel and the film, one of the most important being the absence of Leo's voiceover. As the narrator of the novel, Leo's thoughts and ideas permeate all aspects of the novel, yet in the film this effect is achieved much more subtly. Instead of lengthy prose, Leo's confusion, excitement or unhappiness is communicated through performance, visual style, costume, setting and music. This allows for a greater exploration of the thematic issues within the text, rather than a straightforward replication of everything included in the novel.

There are also important thematic concerns which the film explores in a different way to the novel; these predominantly relate to money, class and the role of women, suggesting some interesting contemporary preoccupations. Within the novel, Leo's middle-class family background is revealed in detail, but the film locates him more awkwardly between manual worker Ted and the wealthy Maudsleys. He does not belong in either world; he is not eligible by birth or fortune to be part of the Maudsley's social sphere and yet his education places him far above Burgess, and he considers himself superior to the farmer. As the narrative develops and as Leo becomes trapped by the intrigues of Ted and Marian, his discomfort, awkwardness and social inadequacy is reiterated through the mise-en-scène of the film, with its beautiful, ornate and decoratively cluttered interior locations.

Money is another important feature of Losey's adaptation, just as it was for Hartley, yet the film and the novel present the wealthy Maudsleys in different ways. The novel explicitly details that the family are wealthy but are renting Brandham Hall from Lord Trimmingham, an impoverished aristocrat who cannot afford to live in his ancestral home. Hartley refers to 'Mr Maudsley of Princes Gate and Threadneedle Street,' implying Maudsley is a wealthy city banker, not part of the landed aristocracy.[2] This positioning of the Maudsleys as wealthy but not well born is one of the film's most careful constructions and is achieved through the complexity of the mise-en-scène and the deliberate awkwardness of the performances. Harold Pinter remembered that although the film script had begun as 'a straight dramatization of the central story about the young boy and the lovers,' gradually he became more interested in 'the role of time; the annihilation of time by the man's return to the scene of his childhood experience,' suggesting contemporary concerns which went beyond the scope of the original novel.[3]

The Go-Between presents the past in a unique and technically innovative way, subverting conventional uses of history within the costume film. The traditional cultural task of the past is to reinforce stability, recall past victories, or, as frequently within horror films, to allow contemporary concerns to be played out in foreign lands and in the distant past. The historical film has often been seen as a vehicle for presenting historical 'fact,' although the 'fact' that films choose to present is highly deliberate and subjective. For example, the successful adaptation of Henry Fielding's *Tom Jones* (1963) recreated the past as a bawdy romp through the dressing up-box and in doing so successfully captured the exuberance and hedonism of the 1960s, thus guaranteeing the film's success.

The fluctuations in film finance identified by Sue Harper gave the costume film greater opportunities to experiment in the 1970s and move beyond predictable uses of the past.[4] Although some films, including

Monty Python and the Holy Grail (1975), *Royal Flash* (1975) and *Joseph Andrews* (1977) challenged traditional historical discourses by deploying the past in a heavily ironic and comedic way, conventional uses of the past prevailed. Biopics such as *Cromwell* (1970), *Mary, Queen of Scots* (1971) and *Young Winston* (1972) were intended for world markets and these films recreate the past as lush and extravagant, peopled with worthy leaders and glamorous scoundrels. Later in the decade, the popular Agatha Christie adaptations *Murder on the Orient Express* (1974) and *Death on the Nile* (1978) effectively utilised the 1920s as a backdrop for exciting and out-of the-ordinary events, thereby deploying the past in a traditional manner. Yet there were also a number of historical films of the period which were not easy to classify such as *Ryan's Daughter* (1970) or *Barry Lyndon* (1975). Although they are historical, they have very different thematic preoccupations from some of the more traditional historical narratives identified above. Such pluralism within 1970s historical films suggests an increasingly complex preoccupation with the past.

In *The Go-Between,* Losey creates a complicated past, inter-cutting the historical setting with modern sequences which links the past inextricably with the present. Losey believed it was the juxtaposition of past and present which made the text so fascinating:

> What interested me primarily was the possibility of representing 1900 using shots from the present, not in chronological order but in an almost subliminal sequence, superimposing voices from the present on the past and voices from the past on the present, so that threads which started off parallel gradually intertwine and in the end the past and present are one and the same.[5]

This construction of past and present signalled a real innovation for the period and one which Hartley himself came to admire, writing to Pinter, 'I am quite overwhelmed by the beauty of your script and incidentally by the ingenuity and convincingness with which you interweave the young Leo and the young Marian with the old Leo and the old Marian. That was a feat.'[6] Through its interweaving narratives and its overlapping flashback sequences, the film suggests that the past is never very far away. The flashbacks reoccur throughout the film, disrupting the completeness of the past and dislocating the textual and pictorial field. These flashbacks also allow an innovative structure; the historical narrative forms the central part of the film yet the text begins and ends with modern sequences. The opening sequence visually constructs the period setting but then undercuts it with a modern voiceover which posits the narrative as a constructed memory. It is the adult Leo who constructs the historical past; it is his memories of childhood events which propel the narrative, yet he is not remembering as a child but as an old man. This subjectivity filters the narrative through the eyes of the child, while simultaneously reinforcing how the adult Leo is looking back to this period with bitterness.

Flashback, voiceover and narrative structure are deliberately used to affirm the importance and accessibility of the past yet also to prevent the audience from indulging in nostalgic escapism. The way in which Losey anchors the historical past to the present prevents critical issues of class and gender from being relegated to 'another place, another time.' Losey felt that despite the Edwardian setting, the film had important resonance for the 1970s, claiming, 'I believe there are many traces of the society of that time remaining in society today – things haven't changed that much.'[7] Losey's principal concerns within *The Go-Between*, as they had been in *The Servant* and *Accident*, were class, wealth and privilege and he addressed these issues through all the visual aspects of the film.

The beauty of *The Go-Between* was praised by the critics. *Film Review* declared it; 'a finely sculpted piece, visually stunning,' while Radio 4 programme *Film Time* praised the atmosphere the film deliberately evoked, commenting how 'an illicit passion smoulders and erupts during a long Edwardian summer.'[8] The visual style was a result of the combined talents of art director Carmen Dillon and cinematographer Gerry Fisher. Both Dillon and Fisher had previously collaborated with Losey and had worked together on *Accident*. Dillon was responsible for finding the location of Melton Constable, which became the central shooting location as Brandham Hall. Initially considered to be 'a large fine house, beginning to get very dilapidated,' Dillon cleverly redecorated the house to reflect the status, position and wealth of the family.[9] When interviewed during shooting, Dillon commented that she disliked the house intensely but felt that its 'rather elaborate vulgarity' was just right for the story.[10] This elaborate vulgarity is one of the critical aspects of Brandham Hall and the wider Maudsley family as the location deliberately positions the socially aspirational family within a grandiose setting. This elaborates on the social unease detailed in the novel in a visual way. The colour palette used to evoke the wealthy yet unexceptional lifestyle of the family is also important and Dillon remembered, 'we've kept the colour to an absolute minimum, nearly all in the fawn-brown-grey range so that it makes a neutral background for the characters.'[11]

In a similar way to the character-driven *Sunday Bloody Sunday*, the visual style of *The Go-Between* was deliberately intended to be as unremarkable as possible in order not to draw the attention away from the narrative. The unremarkable quality of Dillon's work is deliberately utilised for *The Go-Between* yet, while the film's mise-en-scène does not stand out, other elements of the production are visually arresting. The cinematography of Gerry Fisher builds upon the deliberately unremarkable mise-en-scène by lighting the internal locations naturalistically but by bathing the external locations in 'a slightly sour sunlight' to highlight Leo's growing disillusionment and the progression of the summer.[12] In contrast, the modern sequences are rainy, grey and grainy, forcing the attention of the audience away from the golden summer into the dreary present. One review commented that these sequences 'strip the buildings of both sunlight and splendour [to reveal] that the story itself has been embellished by memory.'[13] The idealistic sunny summer is shown to be a deliberately crafted sham underscoring both the seductive allure of the past and the inaccuracies of memory.

Losey's use of Fisher and Dillon suggests he was keen to work with technical staff with whom he had already established an effective working relationship. However, by choosing Dillon and Fisher over other collaborators, Losey demonstrated that he had definite ideas about the visual style he wanted to achieve for this particular film. *The Servant* had combined the art direction of Ted Clements with a production design by Richard MacDonald. Despite MacDonald's previous work including the sumptuous period detail on *Far from the Madding Crowd* (1967), his contribution to *The Go-Between* was limited to designing the title sequence. The lavish richness delivered by MacDonald in *Far from the Madding Crowd* did not fit in with the uneasy image of the past that Losey wanted to recreate in *The Go-Between*. For this purpose Dillon's pragmatic, detailed set design which is neither flamboyant nor visually stunning is much more suitable for the film; it suits the textual narrative perfectly and presents Brandham Hall as nothing more than a beautiful backdrop filled with rich yet inconsequential objects. These objects create a sense of wealth and prestige, but are part of the overall mise-en-scène, rather than invested with significance or importance. Their function is purely decorative, a sharp contrast to the clutter of workaday items in Ted's cottage, where the emphasis is on the practical and the functional. Such contrasts suggest not only differences in class and wealth but also distinguish the languid, leisurely life of the Maudsley's with the more physical, working world of the farmer.

The almost continuous focus on the location of Brandham Hall, with sweeping shots of the house and its ornate staircases, beautiful façade and uniformed servants, all suggest consistency and constancy. The Hall and the Trimmingham line will continue, regardless of the incursions of Ted or Leo. The irony is that everything Trimmingham and Brandham Hall represent will be decimated in a few short years by war. The film does not labour this point, but in the novel, Marian tells Leo that both her brothers were killed in World War I, leaving the Maudsley family without a male heir, while Leo himself discovers the memorial stones of Hugh and his son and daughter-in-law in the parish church.[14] Films such as *The Shooting Party* (1985) and *Remains of the Day* (1993) focused on the decline of the aristocracy, but *The Go-Between* only hinted at the massive social changes which would be brought about by war.

Losey considered Carmen Dillon's contribution to the film to be critical and wrote to her once production was completed: 'I cannot imagine anyone doing *The Go-Between* better than you have done. I hope you are as pleased with the film as I am and if you are, it is largely attributable to your talents.'[15] Yet while the locations, settings and visual style of the film create a backdrop for the narrative, other important factors allow the narrative to develop further, specifically, the costumes and music.

As well as reflecting wealth and status, the costumes, particularly the dresses worn by Marian and Mrs Maudsley eloquently demonstrate the constraints of society through the constraints of costume. Marian frequently finds her clothes impractical and suffocating. Even her clothes for swimming are highly elaborate and constricting, with layer upon layer of material covering all of her body. Her clothes are also without pockets and openings, despite the ample space for them in the yards of material, which makes clear that her role is to be decorative and beautiful rather than functional or practical. As well as reinforcing the depiction of Marian as a demure Edwardian virgin who has no need for pockets in which to secrete love letters, the lack of openings and pockets is also a symbolic 'lack.' There is no access to her body through her clothes, or openings which could be read as inviting such access. Her clothes are predominantly white and pale yellow to reflect her unmarried status, whilst her mother wears richer greens and mauves, colours which in the late 19th and early 20th centuries were associated with the women's suffrage movement. This important association is cleverly utilised by costume designer John Furniss, who also visualised Leo's important Lincoln green suit, which features heavily in the novel. Leo is, of course, literally green due to his naiveté, innocence and candour, yet he is also visually out of place. His bright green suit, comprising short trousers and smart jacket with a bow contrasts with the pale colours worn by the women and the suited elegance of the men. Green of course also represents the colour of envy; an emotion that the young Leo experiences when he falls hopeless in love with the glamorous Marian, only to be rebuffed by her.

The detailed costumes, as well as allowing for character implications, also serve another important function. While period is carefully recreated, Furniss' clever touches allow for modern influences to creep into the designs, once again preventing submersion in an entirely historical world. Modern touches like the colours of Mrs Maudsleys' gowns, Marian's elaborate and deliberately contrived hairstyles and bathing costume of coral pink, which does not suit Christie's colouring, all reveal that the past is more than simply a beautiful picture. Although entirely accurate, the textures, styles and colours create jarring notes within the film and problematise notions of the past being easy, enjoyable and pleasant.

The musical score by Michel LeGrand adds to this sense of unease and uncertainty. It crashes through scenes, frequently intruding at pivotal moments, loudly shattering images of bucolic bliss. The thundering bass notes and sudden disjointed interjections into the text are indicative of Leo's emotional state, which is carefully detailed throughout the novel. The emotions of the child are effectively captured and communicated through the music, removing the need for the lengthy introspection which occupies much of the novel. The absence of diegetic sound again deliberately subverts the period and country setting, once again rejecting the conventions of the historical costume film and drawing attention to the modernity of what little music is included in the text. The choice of LeGrand, a modern composer who had recently won an Oscar for 'The Windmills of Your Mind' in *The Thomas Crown Affair* (1968), over a more traditional classical arrangement of suitable period music reinforces the modernity of the film and once again prevents it from remaining solely a period piece. Much of the music seems overloud and slightly discordant. Even the celebration following the cricket match strikes the same slightly off-key note, with the awkward vocal performances of Ted and Leo. Leo's high vocal range emphasises his youth, whilst the uncertainty of his performance as he strains for the highest notes suggests his burgeoning adolescence.

Both the music and costumes enhance and complement the visual style of the film, yet also draw attention to the ways in which the past does not entirely fit. Through this use of textual detail, Losey is drawing attention to the ruptures between past and present; the past may be easy to access but it is not always a pleasant and easy place to be.

As well as addressing issues of the past, *The Go-Between* develops and furthers issues from the original novel, notably the presentation of childhood. As Alan Bates noted in his autobiography, the character of Leo is 'exploited by these people and in this superficially proper society this innocent is thrown among them all and becomes the victim of their selfishness.'[16] Losey also saw the importance of the character and unpublished script notes reveal that he considered the film to be 'the story of the destruction of a little boy and his life by unthinking, but not necessarily malicious use of him by a variety of adults, propelled by their self interest and their passions.'[17]

Unlike other 1970s films such as *The Railway Children* (1970), *Swallows and Amazons* (1974) and *The Water Babies* (1978), which sentimentalised childhood, in *The Go-Between*, Losey utilised the adult concept of nostalgia to show how memories of the past are constructed by adults not by children. The loss of childhood innocence is one of the principal thematic concerns of the film, and the position of the child at the centre of the text placed massive importance on the casting of Leo. The Losey papers reveal both Losey and Pinter knew exactly what they were looking for; a young boy with an air of maturity, yet innocent, or as Losey put it 'on the edge of innocence but not entirely innocent.... caught at a time of delicate balance.'[18] In casting this pivotal part, Losey felt that the boy's age was vital, for 'it really was a story of very young lovers who were using a little boy who was only slightly younger than they were.'[19] The background of the young actor was also taken into consideration; Losey held auditions for young boys between 11 and 14, who attended private school and who spoke in a certain way. The mannered performance of Leo is not as overstated as that of Marcus or Denys Maudsley, yet it was important to suggest within the film that Leo was well-educated and attended the same school as the other boys. Out of the numerous boys who auditioned, Losey and Pinter finally cast Dominic Guard as Leo.[20] After production was completed, Losey wrote to Guard:

> Many thanks again for your enormous contribution to the film. If you finally decide to become an actor, I would suggest that you get a print of *The Go-Between* and run it at least once a year for the rest of your life to remind yourself how pure your art was when you were fourteen.[21]

This purity, of both art and character, is crucial to the character of Leo. In the novel Leo is aware of Marian's intended engagement to Hugh Trimmingham *before* he meets Ted, while within the film this is only made clear to Leo after several days operating as the go-between for Marian and Ted. By preventing the child in the film from having this knowledge, Losey is ensuring that the childish innocence of the character is maintained. Within both texts, Leo hovers on the cusp of adolescence; he is no longer a child, but not yet an adult, and he is acutely aware of his position as an outsider. Within the film, he comments wistfully to Ted, 'nobody talks to me, they are all grown ups you see.' This neglect of the child was deliberate, for Losey wanted the audience to experience the film through the eyes of the child: 'All children are voyeurs, this one is more that most because he is forced into it, nobody speaks to him, his friend is ill, he is in a strange world, the others speak openly in front of him because they see him as a piece of furniture with no feelings.'[22]

Throughout the novel and film Leo gradually matures; innocent games have been replaced by more subtle and exciting pastimes which are part of his rite of passage. One of the strongest scenes in the film shows how Leo's innocence is shattered when he reads an unsealed message he is carrying from Marian to Ted. When the newly enlightened, yet visibly confused child hands over the letter to Ted, the farmer smears the paper with the blood of the rabbits he has been shooting, much to the boy's horror. His growing understanding of the relationship between Marian and Ted is perfectly captured in this sequence, which combines the furtive secrecy of the letters with the sexual, visceral reality of Burgess.

As the summer progresses, Leo begins to understand the rules of society, realising why Marian and Hugh are to marry and the importance of the match for the Maudsley family, 'by getting him [Hugh]... Marian would also get his house. Married to her, he could afford to live there.'[23] The summer is full of slow steps towards maturity; his successes on the cricket pitch and in the concert hall are greeted with approval from the adult world and he feels that he has been 'called upon to exchange the immunities of childhood for the responsibilities of the grown up world.'[24] Yet, Leo's constant questions and desire for information are dangerous and the knowledge he gains propels him irrevocably from childhood into adulthood.

On the cricket pitch, some evidence of Leo's anxieties about adulthood emerge; after he 'catches out' Ted, he feels torn between loyalty to Ted and loyalty to Hugh. Importantly, he also reflects that he had managed to usurp Ted's position with Marian, fantasising in the novel, 'I had killed him. He was dead.'[25] This metaphorical slaying of the 'father' figure of Ted, coupled with Leo's slavish devotion to Marian and his later positioning of her as 'the mother' suggests a visual and verbal Oedipal complex which is reiterated throughout the film. A *Films and Filming* review highlighted this most important aspect of the film, observing Leo 'has a bad case of puppy love for Marian and he begins subconsciously to regard the farmer as a replacement for his dead father.'[26]

Although in the novel Leo remembers, 'I think I was more mystified than horrified,' it is clear in both texts his attitude towards love and sex has become irrevocably associated with Marian and Ted.[27] The novel describes his growing view of Marian and Ted's relationship as 'a parasite of the emotions' and something which, as the film makes clear, he has deliberately and consistently avoided.[28] Leo's desire to know about 'spooning' was catastrophic, 'Ted hadn't told what it was, but he had shown me, he had paid with his life for showing me and after that I never felt like it.'[29] Although these revelations and sequences are more detailed in the book than they are in the film, the haunted look of betrayal in the child's eyes and the rigid, empty and immobile face of the old man perfectly reflect the trauma that Leo has experienced and how he has closed himself off since that eventful summer. The final scene between Leo and Marian reveals just how little she understands. She still believes, 'You came out of the blue to make us happy, and we made you happy didn't we? We trusted you with our greatest treasure. You might never have known what it was, have gone through life without knowing.'[30] The end of the film is ambiguous: the audience are never sure if Leo resumes his role once again as Marian's go-between or if in refusing to take her final message he will finally be free of Brandham Hall and of his past.

Within the film, performance is crucial. Many of the performers manifest a hesitant awkwardness which can tentatively be identified as a characteristic of 1970s British cinema. In complete contrast to the performance of Guard as Leo, the performances of Marcus Maudsley (Richard Gibson) and his older brother Denys (Simon Hume-Kendall) are awkward, forced and stilted. Both the Maudsley boys consistently attempt to adopt an ease of manner which sits awkwardly alongside their naïve and unwary observations. Denys observes about Ted Burgess; 'We don't know him socially of course, but I think I'd better be nice to him,' then after a stilted exchange with Ted, 'I think I put him at his ease, don't you?' Marcus copies Denys' behaviour and both boys are often reproved by their more socially adept mother for their lapses. The performances by both the young actors perfectly capture social inadequacy and discomfort. Unlike the strong and assured performances of Margaret Leighton (Mrs Maudsley) and Julie Christie, the younger Maudsleys are not comfortable within their social space and are frequently betrayed into statements and actions which do not befit their social position. Such deliberately stilted performances actively reinforce one of the film's central preoccupations – position and class cannot be bought for the season but instead are the privileges of birth. The film is not solely preoccupied with class in the 1890s, it also implicitly highlights the uncertainties which surrounded social class in the 1970s and the blurring of social boundaries. By the end of the 1960s, privilege, wealth and position no longer belonged exclusively to the well born; footballers, models, rock stars and actors could, and did, live in a manner which consciously aped the lifestyles of the aristocracy. Losey's film critiques these social changes, drawing attention to them through clever deployment of performance and manner.

The uncertainty and awkwardness of performance is not discernible anywhere in the portrayals of Marian and Mrs Maudsley. In the novel, the parallels between Marian and Mrs Maudsley are clearly drawn and Hartley likens conversations between the two women to 'two steel threads crossing each other,' a tension which is played out throughout the film.[31] A contemporary review from *Sight and Sound* highlighted this aspect of the film, describing the narrative as a 'battle of wills between mother and daughter.'[32] Although the text is preoccupied with class and childhood, this review foregrounds female power over notions of troubled masculinity, indicating that the text is offering something more than accepted depictions of gender relations within a historical setting. Margaret Leighton's hard smile, guarded body language and penetrating glance suggest not only the power with which Mrs Maudsley dominates her family, but also her astute intelligence. Leighton's polished performance encapsulates this will of iron hidden behind the silk flounces of the elaborate costumes. It is easy to read in her performance her prior knowledge of Marian's behaviour and it is this which makes her treatment of Leo so cruel when she demands he accompany her to discover the lovers.[33] She knows exactly what she may find, she is fully aware of what has been taking place and yet she insists the child accompany her, thus punishing him for his involvement. It is a chilling yet masterful performance by Leighton who combines the mouthed social platitudes of the Edwardian hostess with a modern awareness of manner. However, the fate of Mrs Maudsley within the novel is not what is suggested by Leighton's performance within the film. Marian tells Leo that her mother could not cope and had to go away.[34] It is difficult to reconcile this image of a hysterical, broken mother with the final film visualisation of Mrs Maudsley dripping wet and rigidly furious. Hartley's final presentation of Mrs Maudsley does not accord with Leighton's strong performance within the film and this is an interesting divergence. There had certainly been a shift in the perception of women between the publication of the novel in 1953 and the production of the film in 1970. Perhaps Losey felt that the removal of the hysterical older woman no longer fitted with newer models of stronger, sexually liberated femininity which had emerged in the intervening years? It is these new models of femininity which provide important context for the film performances of both Leighton and Christie.

Julie Christie had been Losey's actress of choice back in 1964 when he originally planned to make the film, but by 1970 Losey had serious doubts whether the internationally acclaimed 30-year-old Christie could successfully play seventeen-year-old Marian. Losey later commented that, in response to demands from EMI, he accepted that he needed a 'name' in the film and so 'conceded Julie Christie,' yet the BFI papers reveal that Christie was not the first choice for the part.[35] Charlotte Rampling was suggested by Dirk Bogarde, Georgina Hale by Harold Pinter, while Lynn Redgrave was favoured by Losey himself, with Jane Asher, Mia Farrow, Sarah Miles and Marianne Faithfull also being considered.[36] Christie's *tour de force* performance lends an air of arch sexuality to Marian, which deliberately subverts her visual presentation of innocent Edwardian virginity and brings believability and depth to the character. The obvious sexual maturity which she brings to her portrayal of Marian strongly suggests that Christie is far too old to play the virgin but, paradoxically, it is this air of sexuality which perfectly suits the character. Her deliberate and assured manner and the candour which she brings to the performance suggest a level of experience, knowledge and sexual maturity which go far beyond the limited scope of Marian's character. Christie's responses to innocuous questions in the film, 'Am I?' 'Was I?' 'Did I?' reflect this worldly knowledge which she makes no effort to conceal. As Christie herself would later note, 'Marian was quite ruthless and incapable of thinking of anyone but herself.'[37]

Christie's sexuality might seem out of place in a period piece, but it is critical to the *The Go-Between*. Losey uses Christie's sexuality and allure to highlight contemporary anxieties about sexually aware women. Period adaptations such as *Far from the Madding Crowd* and *Women in Love* (1969) had dealt with the sexually liberated female and her pursuit of sexual pleasure, brought to the fore by the changes of the 1960s. However, Marian is far more sexually pragmatic than either Bathsheba Everdene or Gudrun Brangwen. She chooses her sexual partner with scant regard for convention or class; she is sexually discerning and has deliberately chosen Ted over Hugh in her conscious pursuit of pleasure.

Colin Gardner sees Edward Fox's Hugh Trimmingham as acquiescing to the period's rules of 'patriarchal gallantry.'[38] Nowhere is this more evident than in his conversation with Leo in which he declares, 'nothing is ever a lady's fault.' However, this exchange also suggests that Hugh knows exactly how the game is played and how society works. The scene in the smoking room between Trimmingham and Mr Maudsley, in which they discuss Ted Burgess and his reputation as a ladykiller, is pregnant with meaning and in both the book and the film, it is clear that both men have firm suspicions about the relationship between Marian and Ted. What the film significantly achieves with this sequence is that without saying so explicitly, each man understands the other perfectly, communicating a great deal with long silences and significant glances, to the obvious mystification of Leo.

As the novel makes clear, Marian was partially reconciled to her marriage to Hugh and the whole family looked upon it as a suitable match, yet the film is more ambiguous. Fox manages to convey with complete ease and naturalness of performance that no vulgar scandal involving money or sex could ever intrude into his carefully ordered world. His kindness to Leo and his assured captaincy of the cricket team would seem to place him within the film as the naive, rather insipid hero, but in the novel he is shown to be far more subtle.[39] Here, it is Hugh who speaks to Ted about joining the army; he knows about Marian and Ted and sees this as the easiest way of separating them. It is also significant that, unlike in the novel, where Hugh's unappealing appearance is described in detail, Fox sports a dashing scar which in no way renders his appearance hideous. Presenting Trimmingham as handsome and desirable places yet more importance on Marian's deliberate choice of Ted as her sexual partner. Trimmingham is not a hideous, wealthy man that Marian is being forced to marry, he is both attractive and aristocratic, yet Marian's choice of Ted over Hugh serves only to confirm female sexual choice.

The final male character who contributes significantly to the film is Ted Burgess. The substantial notes from the Losey papers which debate this casting decision include suggestions of Albert Finney, Tom Courtenay, Malcolm McDowell, Ian McShane and David Warner.[40] The eventual choice of Alan Bates revived a partnership with Christie first established in *Far from the Madding Crowd*, yet the relationship between Ted and Marian is unusual in that it shapes the film, but is for the most part absent. They are in very few scenes together and their interaction is minimal, providing little understanding of the depth or intensity of their relationship; it is all constructed through the languorous delivery of Christie and the suppressed tension of Bates as they interact with Leo.

Once production was completed, Losey wrote to Bates, thanking him for his contribution to the film, which he termed, 'absolutely first rate' and to Christie, enthusing, 'The picture looks good and you look superb.'[41] Whilst Christie herself felt, '[It is a] lovely, lovely picture... such a soft, sad, spell-like film.'[42] Losey tried to revive their partnership for *The Romantic Englishwoman* but Christie declined, believing, 'I think specific people together can create their own electricity and I can't say that Alan and I have ever done that.'[43] The lack of chemistry that Christie perceived between herself and Bates is vital to *The Go-Between*. It allows the audience – through the eyes of Leo – to suspend their disbelief in Marian and Ted's relationship, partially because it is visibly absent, but also because the audience sees through the eyes of child how impossible it is to associate the accomplished Marian with the earthy Ted.

The self-consciousness and awkward delivery of the children, the deliberately deployed irony and sexual awareness of the women and the quiet control and comfortable self-assuredness of the male characters all combine to create a paradoxical combination of naturalness and unease. This style of performance is characterised by a self-awareness of manner which again prevents the film remaining solely as a period piece.

Despite winning the Grand Prix at Cannes in 1971 and critical success in West Germany, Spain, Italy and France, the film only enjoyed moderate financial success in Britain, taking a total of £233,000 in three years – a meagre amount compared to its substantial budget of £1 million.[44] With mainstream appeal but art-house sensibilities, high-culture associations but box office stars, the film was indeed a conundrum. *The Go-Between* did not fit into the British mainstream when it was released, and was seen as a possible crossover text from the mainstream into more independent and alternative spheres of exhibition. The BFI papers reveal how Losey was unexpectedly offered help with the distribution of the film from the independent distributor, The Other Cinema. Director Peter Sainsbury wrote to Losey, 'I am wondering what problems you will have with the distribution. Perhaps presumptuously, I would like to show the film in London if it should turn out that no preferable exhibition is likely.'[45] Although the offer was not accepted, it is interesting that a collaboration between mainstream and minority film organisations was considered as a viable option, even for a film backed by EMI. It was rare for a commercial film to be deemed potentially viable and desirable for a fringe audience, and again demonstrates the uncertain and permeable nature of film culture in this period.

While *The Go-Between* is an important literary adaptation, the film is much more than a period piece or straightforward costume drama. Despite the high level of textual detail used to render the past historically accurate, the film does not strive to create a truthful rendition of the past. Any notion of an accurate historical past is deliberately subverted by the manner and style of performance adopted by the cast, particularly the knowingness of Margaret Leighton and Julie Christie. This modernity of manner is furthered through the deliberately unremarkable mise-en-scène and the cleverly intricate costumes which do not entirely fit within the period surroundings. All of these subtle hints of modernity reinforce the position of *The Go-Between* as a modern text with contemporary preoccupations. Losey uses Hartley's novel to visualise the world he so painstakingly described, yet through Pinter's innovative screenplay he manages to structure the film in a completely different way, thus altering the text's preoccupations. While the film of *The Go-Between* remains concerned with class and gender, Losey and Pinter foreground a range of other issues including the loss of innocence, the role of time and the accessibility of the past.

The Go-Between is a film about modern, aware, liberated characters within a period setting. The performance style allows the characters to be presented as outsiders or interlopers into a world whose rules, conventions and structures are no longer relevant. Losey uses the past to discuss the present and in doing so offers a reading of a number of historical periods which he interweaves with great skill and ambiguity. The Edwardian era, the 1950s when the book was published and the 1970s when the film was made, all come together in the film. This allows scrutiny of, as Losey intended, 'the span of a whole life in a setting which changes in 70 years, not so very much.'[46] Perhaps Losey considered that Hartley was wrong; the past may be a foreign country but things were not so very different there.

10
Confessions of a Window Cleaner: Sex, Class and Popular Taste

Confessions of a Window Cleaner (1974) was one of the most popular films of the sexploitation genre, and its backing by a major studio ensured that it became part of the commercial mainstream, rather than remaining on the grubby fringes more commonly associated with films of this genre. Loathed by critics, the film was dismissed as tawdry and vulgar, yet its massive popular appeal makes it an important indicator of popular taste. As Hunter has recognised, such films offered 'valuable insights into the tastes, values and frustrated desires of ordinary filmgoers.'[1] The film cannot be dismissed on the grounds of its quality, for as Andy Medhurst has recently pointed out in relation to the *Carry On* films, 'texts which are abysmal by most conventional aesthetic standards can nonetheless have significant importance when considering the complicated dynamics of identity and belonging.'[2] The massive popularity of the film makes it significant in terms of audience preferences and reveals the uncertain and complicated nature of popular taste in the period, with a particularly acute contradiction between popular taste and notions of 'quality' and critical approbation.

The British sexploitation film has recently received recognition as an important genre, and has subsequently been the focus of increased critical attention. Sweet, McGillivray and Conrich have all recognised the importance of this frequently neglected genre and helped reposition it within British cinema.[3] Hunter has examined the variety of the genre and the number of sub-genres which can be categorised as sexploitation, while Leon Hunt has authoritatively demonstrated the fluidity of the genre and suggested how sexploitation began to spill into horror films such as *House of Whipcord* (1974) and *Killer's Moon* (1978).[4] However, more remains to be done in order to fully understand the appeal and potency of the sexploitation genre and of its significant texts.

In contrast to the box office success of *Confessions of a Window Cleaner*, the film industry failed to recognise the appeal of the material, with *Films and Filming* complaining, '*Confessions of a Window Cleaner* might well be re-titled *Confessions of the British; what they don't know about making films, making erotic images, making people laugh and making love. We probably don't clean windows too well either.*'[5] In a recent interview, Robin Askwith recalled that the film industry was 'totally negative about films like *Confessions*... [they were] totally ignoring the fact that people were going to see them in droves.'[6]

Upon its release, the film ran for nine weeks in one West End cinema, with 29 performances each week, finally taking over £30,000.[7] By January 1975 – 14 months after its release – the film had earned £200,000 from the Eady Levy fund and by 1979, profits had topped £800,000.[8] The film's popularity was matched by its profitability, a rare feat for any British film in the period. What the film was selling, the audience was certainly buying. Leon Hunt has recognised that the *Confessions* series was a combination of 'adult entertainment and good clean fun,' which drew upon its cast, the source novels and the series' traditional aspects to help market itself.[9] Yet who was being targeted by the film and what aspects of the film's narrative and aesthetics were helping to ensure this popularity?

The provenance of *Confessions of a Window Cleaner* is made clear through the extensive Michael Klinger papers; first-time producer Greg Smith became interested in using Christopher Wood's best-selling 'Timmy Lea' paperback novels as the basis for a series of films. The *Confessions* novels were one of the first examples of extremely low-brow popular literature crossing over into a visual medium. Author and scriptwriter Christopher Wood was not in any way like the fictional 'Timmy Lea,' but by presenting the texts as first-hand accounts, Wood accessed a mass readership by drawing upon literary conventions which position the audience as the privileged recipients of private information. The attempt to locate Timmy Lea as a real person was maintained in the films by the screen credit to 'Timmy Lea' as the author of the source material, lending notions of authenticity to the material presented, while at the same time allowing the sexual 'real-life' antics to emerge as fantasy to titillate an audience.

Michael Klinger came to the project with the responsibility of raising the £100,000 budget, and his papers document his negotiations with a number of British financiers, including independent investors Caroline Enterprises and Lington Holdings. Despite his best efforts to secure funding, the various finance deals fell apart and Klinger had to approach a major studio to secure the necessary funds. After lengthy negotiations, Columbia agreed to fund the film, seeing in *Window Cleaner* the start of a successful series which could be distributed within world markets. Columbia recognised the potential of the series and agreed to help fund the project. This contrasts with other potential investors such as the Star Group, who declined to become involved in a 'titillating sex film.'[10] Columbia's backing of the project appears risky but demonstrates the prevailing uncertain, haphazard and occasionally adventurous film culture of the period. The deal that they brokered for the sequel, allowing them 50% of all profits from subsequent films suggests that whilst the studio was keen to invest in *Window Cleaner*, they used their investment opportunity to capitalise on any future successes, driving a very hard bargain in the process.

As the films were always designed to be a series, it is useful to briefly consider the different cultural tasks undertaken by each of the films; *Confessions of a Window Cleaner* is perhaps the most straightforward with its combination of sexploitation, comedy and conventional narrative. Early critiques of the screenplay referred to it as 'breezy and bawdy ... an amiable little script with no style of its own,' whilst the ordinary characters, locations and scenarios proved popular with audiences seeking to be diverted by the film's content but reassured by its familiar setting and milieu.[11] *Confessions of a Pop Performer* (1975) swapped the solid domesticity of *Confessions of a Window Cleaner* for the more glamorous world of pop stardom with unsatisfactory results. As Klinger himself acknowledged, 'in *Pop Performer* we allowed ourselves to be deviated from the original successful formula and there is no question that it was not so successful.'[12] Despite costing nearly twice as much as *Confessions of a Window Cleaner*, and with an album distribution deal with Polydor, the film's attempt to elevate the ordinary Timmy Lea to extra-ordinary pop star proved unsuccessful, with audiences preferring instead to see real music stars Roger Daltrey and David Essex on film in *Tommy* (1975) and *That'll Be the Day* (1973).

Confessions of a Driving Instructor (1976) was an attempt to recapture the successful formula of 'a believable hero who the audience could relate to, in a believable family background that everyone could understand.'[13] This film successfully tapped into the narrative of the young transient male, and was seen by the production team to be the most successful after *Confessions of a Window Cleaner*. The final film in the series, *Confessions from a Holiday Camp* (1977) again moved away from the domestic setting which had made *Confessions of a Window Cleaner* so successful, preferring instead to focus on the holiday camp as a location for typical British comedy, in the vein of *Carry On Camping* (1969). Michael Klinger objected to this shift in focus, complaining:

> The script is a carefully contrived series of funny incidents but is totally without an acceptable storyline. Despite various meetings at which we all agreed that it was essential to maintain the family background and the relationship between our principal and permanent characters, this has now been totally ignored.[14]

Ultimately Klinger was proved right: the film did not match *Confessions of a Window Cleaner*'s success and failed to convince Columbia to finance a fifth *Confessions* film, effectively ending the series.

Confessions of a Window Cleaner is a product of the precarious economic conditions of the early 1970s, yet its phenomenal success far outstripped expectations of such a small-budget film. *Confessions of a Window Cleaner*'s £100,000 budget places it firmly within the low-budget spectrum and the film's aesthetic reflects these financial limitations. The involvement of a major studio in the production of the film – despite the best efforts of the production team to secure independent funding – demonstrates that in this period, parts of the British film industry was still dependent on the Americans. Yet where was the film drawing its inspiration from and to whom was it trying to appeal?

Sexploitation comedy was made possible through a changing culture of permission and relaxation of some aspects of censorship. However, the aesthetics, themes and characters of this new genre drew upon an established film trend; the TV sitcom. The films of *Dad's Army* (1971), *Up Pompeii* (1971), *On the Buses* (1971) and *Steptoe and Son* (1972) performed well at the box office, and the *Confessions* films looked to this successful formula for inspiration. Timmy's working-class family of Tony Booth, Doris Hare, Dandy Nicholls and Bill Maynard could have been lifted directly from *Bless This House* (1972) or *On the Buses*, while guest stars in *Window Cleaner* included John Le Mesurier and Joan Hickson. Casting familiar faces from television was a deliberate strategy deployed by the production team who sought 'useful UK names' to boost the profile of the film and to deliberately target the television audience.[15]

There are other aspects of *Confessions of a Window Cleaner* that owe a great deal to the TV sitcom; Timmy's father works on the railways and brings home junk in a manner reminiscent of Albert Steptoe, whilst his mother's fondness for consumer items on credit recalls Stan's mother in *On the Buses* – perhaps unsurprising as they were both played at one time by Doris Hare. However, *Confessions of a Window Cleaner* utilises social class in an unusual way. The film's deployment of working class stereotypes, from the philandering Sid, to pregnant Rosie in her curlers and the kleptomaniac father offers a less than flattering depiction of a class usually treated more affectionately within British cinema and within the TV sitcom. So just what are the audience being encouraged to laugh at? Sociologist Simon Frith argued that:

> The book is written in the form of a yob's autobiography but the author is clearly a writer of some skill and the resulting tone of class condescension feeds my suspicion that the prejudices to which the books are finally appealing are those of the middle classes against the great unwashed. This best seller reflects its reader's longing for a Britain in which everything the way it's supposed to be – women in bed or at the cooker, the workers in their slum, the bourgeoisie in their smart houses on the common.[16]

Frith suggests that the books were deliberately produced for the amusement of the middle classes by successfully parodying the working-class family. However, within the novels, it is not the respectable working class that is being presented: the Lea family are bordering on the criminal. In the original text, Timmy has just been released from prison after being caught stealing lead from the church roof, a scenario which is omitted from the film in order to make the young hero sympathetic and hapless rather than criminal. The Klinger material supports this positioning of Timmy as the sympathetic hero, with an early suggestion of *Confessions from the Clink* as a possible sequel to *Confessions of a Window Cleaner* never being mentioned again after February 1974, and the more conventional choices of *Pop Performer*, *Plumber's Mate* and *Holiday Camp* being advocated instead.[17]

Window Cleaner accentuates class divisions with both the working-class Lea family and the family of Timmy's girlfriend Elizabeth, operating on the margins of their respective classes. The Leas occupy the space at the bottom of the working class, whilst the Radletts have been elevated to the top of the middle class, a shift designed to position Timmy and Elizabeth's relationship across a wide class divide. The focus on class marginality within the films allows working-class viewers to distance themselves from the lowly Leas, and middle-class viewers to aspire to the socially superior Radletts. The antics of Timmy's family at his aborted wedding reinforce their placement as ridiculous characters. His mother wears an over-trimmed, home-made dress, his father in his top hat 'borrowed' from the railway Lost Property Office becomes roaringly drunk, while his brother-in-law Sid attempts to seduce the bride. Such actions and character presentation emphasise the family's vulgarity and allows the lower working class to be parodied for the amusement of a socially superior audience.

The importance of class in the *Confessions of a Window Cleaner* is always combined with sex. Timmy clearly has a penchant for upper-class girls, or as Sid puts it in *Driving Instructor*, 'It's the voice, isn't it? A touch of the Barbara Cartlands and you're anybody's.' From Elizabeth, the policewoman in *Confessions of a Window Cleaner* to Mary, the archery enthusiast in *Driving Instructor*, these unobtainable girls use language and mannerisms with which he is not familiar; their speech is sprinkled with 'Mummy,' 'Daddy,' 'tiddly' and 'rugger.' Elizabeth cooks spaghetti bolognaise and they watch a televised classical music concert, while Mary invites him to her parents' wine-tasting and enrols him in a rugby match. Timmy attempts to be upwardly mobile and circumnavigate class barriers, while simultaneously remaining firmly rooted in his working-class background.

The importance of social class in these films echoes a heavily residual theme in British cinema. From *Room at the Top* (1959) and *Saturday Night and Sunday Morning* (1960), class-consciousness permeates British cinema and is very much evident in *Confessions of a Window Cleaner*. After the success of the film, scriptwriter Christopher Wood noted features which should be continued in subsequent films, including: maintaining the characters of Timmy as an endearing innocent and Sid as an incompetent schemer; continuing the family involvement; and providing Timmy with a potential marriage partner.[18] These strengths not only reiterate the importance of the films as a series, but also suggest the great conventionality of the texts, with their reliance on family and the importance of marriage.

Within the films, Timmy is to be provided with a nice, respectable girl to marry, suggesting that, despite the liberalisation of sex which the film presents, the ideal objective in this film is still marriage. In this way the series is entirely conventional; most of the women are married and, despite the frequent infidelity and constant bed-hopping, marriage is imagined as the ultimate goal. This focus on marriage in *Confessions of a Window Cleaner* was queried by director Val Guest when he reviewed the screenplay. He complained, 'in practically every case the woman is married, which I feel is a mistake. Engaged, divorced, steady boyfriend, carefully chaperoned etc – but why all married?'[19] Clearly Guest felt the conventionality of the screenplay was not fitting in an era of increased sexual permission, and yet married females dominate the film. This implies a great deal about the ideals and mores of the audience and suggests a deliberate targeting of thoroughly conventional middle-class and working-class audiences.

The material from the Klinger archive continuously reiterates the focus on the 'unobtainable girl' from a higher class as well as on the working-class family dynamic. The production team were fully aware of the potency and importance of class within the film, and how it could be successfully utilised to maximise the film's appeal to the widest of audiences.[20] A fan letter from *Film and Filming* claimed *Confessions of a Window Cleaner* was, 'a truly great *people's film* – an accurate and inspiring picture of the life of the average British working lad, his dreams and aspirations.'[21] The presentation of Timmy as an average working lad was central to the film's popular appeal, just as notions of class and social mobility are central to the film's narrative. Combining the emphasis on class difference with the established narrative of the labourer or salesman, the film allows a high level of sexual interaction to take place between social classes. Social class is shown to be less firmly defined and fixed than in previous periods and sex is shown as a means to overcome class distinctions. Incidentally, Michael Klinger found the idea of *Confessions of a Window Cleaner* as a great people's film hilarious and suggested using the enthusiastic praise in the film's publicity.[22] Clearly the production team recognised what the film offered to audiences but fully appreciated that the series would never win critical accolades.

As identified, the use of class as a means of identification for the audience is a heavily residual theme in British cinema, but the increased sexual content was something new. The British attitude to sex has been always been presented on film as a combination of round-eyed prurience and deep-rooted embarrassment. Building on the easily traced trajectory of the *Carry On* series, *Confessions of a Window Cleaner* offered increased sexual content and titillation. Initial reviews of the screenplay noted, 'it is somewhere in the class of those *Carry On* pictures, it could be called *Carry on Window Cleaner.*'[23] Yet the *Confessions* series went further than *Carry On*, deliberately progressing from the 'look but don't touch' attitude propagated by the earlier series. A guest star of *Carry On Girls* (1973), Robin Askwith believes that the success of the *Confessions* series was due to its racy content, which surpassed that of the *Carry On* series. He recalls, 'they [Peter Rogers and Gerald Thomas] never forgave me for the success of the *Confessions* films. It was where they should have gone, but they couldn't. They eventually tried it with *Carry On Emmannuelle* (1978). But it failed.'[24] As a new series, the *Confessions* films could attempt things which an established series could not, and this innovation and break with convention helped create the British sex film. This established the British sex film as a new genre and allowed it to become self-referential, often alluding to the stereotypical attitudes towards sex previously deployed throughout British cinema. *Confessions of a Window Cleaner* offers none of the exotic sensuality or eroticism of films such as *Emmanuelle* (1975) and settles instead for being comical; effectively combining comedy and sex in an accessible way.

Michael Klinger referred to *Confessions of a Window Cleaner* as 'a good, saucy, sexy comedy,' implying that sex was only part of the formula and the comedy was just as important.[25] Christopher Wood noted in an early synopsis of *Pop Performer* that they should 'keep the sex content jokey and not too heavy,' reinforcing the idea of a tried and tested formula.[26] By allowing the audience to laugh at the antics on screen, the films effectively undercut the residual embarrassment for an audience presented with sexual material. The humour and irony which is being deployed diffuses possible discomfort by actively utilising this awkwardness as a deliberate comedic and filmic device. This allows for shared embarrassment and collusion on the part of the audience. It permits them to actively engage with the pantomime sexual behaviour being shown, while at the same time distancing themselves from the material and its potential to embarrass.

The awkwardness of Timmy's sexual behaviour is frequently contrasted throughout the film by his innuendo-laced accompanying voiceover. However, phrases like 'retracting your ladder' and 'squeezing out your chamois' are greeted on screen with pained glances rather than appreciative laughter. The innuendo and double entendres are shown to be even more tired than they are in the *Carry On* films. The difference here is that all the lines are delivered and received with a world-weary, cynical and jaundiced air; an air of having seen it all before and wondering, 'What else is new?' The use of deliberately tired innuendo which does not evoke the usual responses – the dirty chuckle of Sid James or Barbara Windsor's appreciative giggle of 'saucy' – suggests that *Confessions of a Window Cleaner* is mocking the familiar British humour of the seaside postcard and the rude joke, whilst also building on the cultural capital they provide. This allows the audience a brief snigger at the innuendo but the film does not rely upon it as the principal source of comedy. The awkwardness and embarrassment of the characters in the delivery of the dialogue permeates the text and reaches the audience, encouraging complicity and allowing for shared embarrassment, whilst at the same time offering reassurance in the conventionality of its sexual themes.

It is ironic that, as a sex film, *Confessions of a Window Cleaner* is not so much about sex but about the problems and anxieties associated with sex. Timmy's failure to perform, his embarrassment at his sexual inexperience, his ineptitude, his fear of the female body and his acute suspicion of his own body all combine to offer a film which is thoroughly British in its attitudes towards sex and the body. Anxiety about male performance is combined with the more overt elements of comedy: slapstick and pratfalls, endless spilled drinks and being caught without clothes. Again, complicity plays an important part here, for whilst the audience is being encouraged to sympathise with Timmy, they are also encouraged to laugh at his ineptitude. Embarrassment and awkwardness is further deployed in the film, through constant representation of the sexual act as confusing, difficult and troublesome. Throughout the course of his sexual encounters, Timmy is constantly dirtied, either floundering into a puddle of washing up liquid, or tumbling around in a coal cellar and being referred to as a 'dirty little boy' by the lady of the house. Such episodes reinforce the notion of sex being dirty, shameful and shabby. Despite his occupation as a cleaner, Timmy's experiences often reflect the rumpled, the soiled and the dirty; the physical actuality of sex. The scene in which Timmy is seduced in a sea of washing up bubbles perfectly encapsulates the duality of newly increased permission and deep-seated residual fear. Although a scene of sexual fantasy, the entire experience takes place on the kitchen floor – a location both domestically mundane and depressingly ordinary – with the lovers wrestling enthusiastically in detergent surrounded by saucepans and accompanied by Wurlitzer-style music, which perfectly matches the high-tempo sexual parody. The awkwardness of the text, propagated through its attitude to sex and its deliberate deployment of embarrassment as a filmic device, is furthered by the performance style and the visual aesthetics.

The visual style of *Confessions of a Window Cleaner* is located firmly in the world of the TV sitcom. The interior of the Lea family home is brightly lit and overly full of quirky, useless items such as a gorilla suit, flippers and a moose's head. This cluttered and eclectic set dressing creates a deliberately cramped space which restricts movement and keeps the characters firmly within the confines of the domestic comedy; the front room within the terraced house. The characters are awkwardly situated within the frame, and the claustrophobic settings are furthered through other interior locations; Timmy's bedroom in the attic and the tiny hallway. Identification with Timmy's family was a crucial part of the film's appeal, but emphasis on working-class domestic life was initially seen as drab and uninteresting. In his detailed comments on the screenplay, Val Guest complained:

> We seem to be in everyone's kitchen at some time or another and a kitchen is dreary at the best of times unless there's a reason – like the thunderstorm sequence. The screenplay has a downbeat flavour because everything is described as working class – streets, semi-detached, kitchens, pubs, British Legion Hall etc.[27]

However, it was this ordinariness that was crucial to the film's success. Simon Frith noted about the novel of *Confessions of a Window Cleaner,* 'the enjoyment in such reading lies in having one's values and wishes confirmed without effort, in moving at ease in a familiar world.'[28] The familiarity of the characters and the attention given to 'the minutiae of everyday life' is clearly part of the text's popular appeal, and these details are successfully utilised within the film adaptation with emphasis remaining firmly on the everyday, the ordinary and the conventional.

The claustrophobic settings, predominantly studio-bound filming and brightly lit interiors all intimate the television sitcom aesthetic, but the film is also drawing on other contemporary trends in British cinema. Leon Hunt acknowledges that the horror films of the 1970s began to borrow freely from the sexploitation genre for their narratives, but there is also a crossover in terms of aesthetics.[29] The budgetary limitations of horror and sexploitation comedy, and the personnel engaged on and in films which ranged across the low-budget spectrum indicate an interesting convergence.

Most of those who worked on *Confessions of a Window Cleaner* had experience of the low-budget end of British cinema. Director of photography Norman Warwick worked on *The Abominable Dr Phibes* (1971), *Dr Jekyll and Sister Hyde* (1971) and *Tales from the Crypt* (1972) while production designer Robert Jones' film credits include *Dr Jekyll and Sister Hyde, Carry On Girls* (1973), *Captain Kronos: Vampire Hunter* (1974) and later *The Likely Lads* (1976) and *Are You Being Served?* (1977). Assistant director Bert Betts worked on *Frankenstein Must Be Destroyed* (1969), *Dr Jekyll and Sister Hyde* and *The Legend of Hell House* (1973), whilst production supervisor Frank Bevis worked on contemporary-set thrillers *Psychomania* (1973) and *Dark Places* (1973). Casting ideas for *Confessions* also reflected this crossover from other low-budget genres with those suggested including horror favourites Veronica Carlson, Kate O' Mara, Adrienne Corri and Martine Beswick and *Carry On* regulars Maggie Nolan, Valerie Leon and Barbara Windsor.

Although this crossover may seem incidental, there are discernible stylistic similarities in the mise-en-scène of many of these low-budget films. Contemporary-set horror films like *Dracula AD 1972* (1972), *Asylum* (1972), *Frightmare* (1974) and *House of Mortal Sin* (1976) feature the cramped locations, gaudy scenery and costumes and the recycled studio sets which all indicate the low-budget production. The locations for contemporary-set horror tended to be urban with a focus on everyday settings including a funfair (*Frightmare*), an antique shop (*House of Mortal Sin*), a modelling agency (*House of Whipcord, Virgin Witch*), a nightclub (*Frightmare, Dracula AD 1972*), a 'swinging' house party (*Dracula AD 1972, House of Whipcord*) plus a wide range of flats, houses and shops, which all combine to create an aesthetic of easily identifiable urban Britain.

By relocating horror to the present day, removing the period trappings and careful class distinctions, 1970s horror films became peopled with rootless, socially mobile characters decked out in gaudy patterns, unrestricted by notions of class, age, gender and location. These characters are models, photographers, writers and make-up artists, a series of occupations which not only cashed in on the glamour the swinging 1960s had accorded them but which also allowed for social mobility. In contemporary-set horror, these characters operate in the same way as Timmy Lea; by bridging the gap between classes and allowing interaction to take place between people from a variety of backgrounds and in a variety of locations. The visual representation of the transient worker on the fringes of the traditional workplace is an important feature in films of the period, from long-distance lorry driver in *Alfie Darling* (1975) to Malcolm McDowell's coffee salesman in *O Lucky Man!* (1973). Unlike the *Carry On* films, which parody easily identifiable institutions and occupations, Timmy Lea operates on the fringes of the workplace, allowing for a greater degree of social mobility and variety of location.

The style of performance deployed by the actors furthers the awkwardness and discomfort already noted. Robin Askwith's Timmy is ungainly and awkward, with slightly hunched shoulders, spindly legs and long arms, clenched nervously at his sides. The mannerisms of the character suggest an uncertainty of masculinity manifested in the nervous laugh, verbal hesitancy and constant clumsiness. Askwith remembers that many of these mannerisms were the result of his own suggestions for the character and that he was given free rein to make the character of Timmy Lea as comical as possible.[30] Askwith's weedy frame is emphasised by his snugly fitting denims, tight white T-shirt and his small, decidedly non-erotic, underwear which all suggest the child –

a boy in a man's world, far out of his depth. When Timmy changes into his smart clothes for his dates with Elizabeth, his awkward posture and nervous mannerisms remain, but the jacket he wears appears too big for him, suggesting once again the boy, still growing into his smart clothes.

The women in the film, from Elizabeth and sister Rosie to the cleanliness-obsessed Mrs Villiers and her Swedish au pair, are shown as being much more comfortable with their own bodies, their confidence and assurance contrasting with Timmy's terror and ineptitude. However, the ease with which they are divested of their clothes suggests a real lack of control. The female body is far easier to access than the male's, with fewer zips and buckles in the clothing and easy entry through seams, sides and openings. Female clothing is also fallible; skirts get ripped off, while the lack of underwear and low décolletages reveal the female body as a site of obvious consumption for Timmy's lascivious gaze.

The exception to this ease of access is Elizabeth, whose clothing constantly frustrates Timmy. The struggle with Elizabeth's clothing is, of course, mirrored by Timmy's struggle with her body. She wears short skirts, with her legs on display inviting easy access, yet she continually rebuffs Timmy's fumblings, underlining her position within the text as the 'nice girl,' the one he can look at but not touch. As shown, this identification of Elizabeth as unobtainable was seen as one of the most important aspects of the film. Additionally, it locates her as a provocative tease, through the deliberate display of her body she arouses sexual feelings in Timmy but then refuses to allow him to touch her; everything is accessible but not available. Timmy's attempts to reconcile his desire for her with her desire to prevent him is suggestive of a wider struggle taking place within masculinity as men attempted to come to terms with newly accessible, liberated women who were sexualised beings with a sexual agenda of their own.

The awkwardness of much of the performance style, the settings, costumes and presentation of the characters reinforces notions of embarrassment, whilst at the same time acting as a point of identification for the audience and focusing on issues of class. The film also addresses wider notions of gender, specifically in its positioning of Timmy as a typical example of 1970s British masculinity. But is this really as straightforward as it appears?

Leon Hunt considers that characters like Timmy Lea offer a 'nostalgic evocation of the masculine presence' and present 'an almost unprecedented empowering of the male gaze.'[31] However, if we momentarily ignore Timmy's raging libido, the character that remains is kindly, clumsy and inept. What subverts this image is not so much Timmy's lascivious behaviour – which only occurs quite late in the film – but rather his inner commentary; his voiceover dialogue is full of 'phwoar' and 'cor,' much in the manner of a boy leering at dirty magazines. The dichotomy between the rabid sexual aggression of Timmy's dialogue and his physically inept and inexpert fumbling could not be more marked. His series of sexual encounters are either interrupted, inexpert grappling or a sequence of events through which he is seduced, victimised or bullied into bed.

His sexual education is undertaken by Sid, who attempts to get him laid. In finally reaching sexual maturity, he becomes empowered, but also recognizes and represents complex anxieties about sexual performance and sexual satisfaction from a male perspective; concerns which do not entirely fit with notions of traditional masculinity. Anxieties about masculinity and performance run throughout the narrative and the character of Timmy is not the only character presented as a site to address these concerns. In an early scene, his sister Rosie threatens Sid with her embroidery scissors over his constant philandering and threatens to 'chop it off' if he strays again. At the end of the film, Timmy hospitalises his cheating brother-in-law with a deluge from a hosepipe; he has literally castrated Sid, once with the hosepipe and also in the following scene when Sid is tied to the hospital bed and Timmy looms over him, enthusiastically consuming a banana with eager gulps.

The frequent undercutting of innuendo previously noted, again demonstrates the extent to which the male characters are being challenged by their female counterparts; suggesting that the aggressive male gaze and masculine authority of the central protagonists are not as fixed as conventional readings of the text initially suggest. Elizabeth and Rosie are both presented as assertive, knowing females who are fully aware of male sexual behaviour and boldly challenge the masculinity of the gaze and often return it with indulgent interest. Many of the older women take charge in their sexual encounters, suggesting a predatory enthusiasm which reinforces Timmy's naiveté and inexperience. The patterns of speech, tone of voice, body language and the frequent infantilising of Timmy demonstrate how females within the text are enthusiastic and proactive sexual partners. As Val Guest complained of the screenplay, 'Timmy never "makes" any female – they ALL "make" him. He's attacked, undressed, led to bed by forceful, hunting women. If ever Women's Lib had a case, this is it.'[32]

Unlike in *Carry On Girls*, where the chief role of women's liberation is to oppose the sexual display of the beauty pageant, the assertive, 'hunting' females in *Confessions of a Window Cleaner* are keen to participate fully and enthusiastically in the sexual experience, not object to it. This female enthusiasm for sex is being configured as 'Women's Lib,' as if this is the only possible reason for women's appropriation of the sexual experience. These anxieties about women and their position within the text are articulating deeper anxieties about the growing independence of women.

However, the main function of the women in *Confessions of a Window Cleaner* is as objects of consumption. Val Guest felt dubious about the screenplay because, 'Too many of the birds are described as being unattractive. If you're putting over other people's fantasies it must be bad film-wise – getting involved with so many unattractive or sleazy females.'[33] A range of female 'types' are included within the text from the mother to the virgin, to the whore and the lesbian, but overall, the women are physically attractive, sexually demanding, cynically pragmatic, faithless and suspicious. There are few dutiful wives here, and promiscuity is rife in a modern climate of sexual permission which was now applied to women as well as men. However, as demonstrated, the films are highly conventional, separating encounters into those which allow pleasure and those which lead to marriage. In this way, the range of sexual encounters that Timmy experiences both propels the narrative and propels him towards Elizabeth, the ideal wife. What prevents this union is her faithlessness, not his, again positioning Timmy as the hapless innocent who had a lucky escape. More pragmatically, it also enabled the film to remain open-ended with none of the narrative resolution which would have prevented a sequel.

In a decade of extreme gender instability, Timmy Lea is a traditional and conventional figure who operates in his own work environment, unaffected by strikes, unemployment or recession and whose position as a manual worker makes him highly desirable. *Confessions of a Window Cleaner*'s success and appeal must be seen within this context of changing masculine roles as perhaps offering a male-focused text in which the central character is a manual worker, a typical everyman. The theme of the handyman or casual worker and his sexual adventures is a popular one in the 1970s and strongly links manual labour and sex. Films including *Confessions of a Window Cleaner* strengthened this link in a period which saw a decline in traditional industries such as mining and manufacturing – all occupations heavily redolent with masculine associations. *Confessions of a Window Cleaner* allows the persona of the dominant male to continue unchallenged by economics or feminism. This nostalgic and backward-looking evocation bears no resemblance to the realities of 1970s Britain but it clearly struck a chord with audiences, as the success of the film corroborates.

Michael Klinger's papers document his determination to make the *Confessions* films profitable and to maintain the formula of sex, comedy and working-class life, which he felt was central to the series. Such tenacity demonstrates how Klinger believed that the film's winning formula could be replicated again and again. Indeed, his desire to make further films continued throughout the decade and beyond with plans for another *Confessions* film being suggested as late as 1986.[34] The films were not critically acclaimed, yet they appealed to audiences and made a great deal of money. As Klinger himself wrote to David Puttnam when he attempted to resuscitate the series in the 1980s, 'the *Confessions* films will never win awards but did cause Columbia British to pay corporation tax for the first time.'[35] Klinger's obituary in *The Times* recognised his skill in bringing popular, commercial projects to fruition, noting, 'film-making to him was the business of finding subjects with wide popular appeal and making them as economically as possible.'[36] Such an epitaph perfectly encapsulates the *Confessions* films: a combination of sex and comedy with audience appeal, made on a strict budget to maximise profits. The combination of financial acumen and acute cultural perspicacity provided by the production team of Klinger, Smith, Cohen, Guest and Wood created a popular, nostalgic comedy which addressed important and relevant issues of class, sex and gender.

While maintaining the elements of titillation and high comedy which characterise sexploitation films of the period, *Confessions of a Window Cleaner* foregrounds the narrative of the itinerant tradesman and combines it with a great deal of social comment which is carefully disguised through the conventions of the TV sitcom and the low-budget aesthetics. As well as providing British cinema with one of its most unlikely successes of the period, *Confessions of a Window Cleaner* spawned a raft of imitations, which all capitalised on sex, titillation and farce and demonstrated the possibilities of the British sexploitation film.

11
Stardust: Stardom, Performance and Masculinity

As the sequel to the popular *That'll Be the Day* (1973), *Stardust* (1974) documents the rise and fall of the pop star through school dropout Jim Maclaine. The film reunited producers David Puttnam and Sandy Lieberson with writer Ray Connolly, art director Brian Morris and stars David Essex, Keith Moon and Rosalind Ayres. But there were some important changes; Tony Richmond joined the project as cinematographer, replacing Peter Suschitsky and director Claude Whatham was replaced by Michael Apted. Sandy Lieberson remembers that Apted was chosen to direct *Stardust* because, 'we wanted a very different feel and look to the movie. Apted came from a background of documentaries that fit into the style we wanted.'[1] Although *Stardust* does not have a typical documentary style, it is interesting that the project was initially conceived with this intention. Perhaps the biggest change was the refusal of Ringo Starr to reprise his role as Mike which led to the part being offered to 1960s pop star Adam Faith.

Andy Medhurst confidently proclaims that after the mid-1960s the pop film was only marginal to what remained of British cinema, but this is perhaps an over-simplification, for throughout the 1970s there were distinct trends for films which drew upon the popular music industry.[2] Linda Wood lists 30 British films in the category of 'pop music' made between 1971 and 1981 whilst Denis Gifford places the figure of 'musical' films closer to 60.[3]

Many of the films which are listed in the categories defined by Wood and Gifford have few similarities of style, form, narrative or content. Gifford's categories are particularly wide-ranging and include the ballet *Tales of Beatrix Potter* (1971), sexploitation *Groupie Girl* (1970), musicals *The Boyfriend* (1971), *Scrooge* (1970), *The Rocky Horror Picture Show* (1975) and *The Slipper and the Rose* (1976), as well as a number of films which do not appear to fit at all including *The Little Prince* (1974), *Black Joy* (1977) and *Babylon* (1980). Strange omissions also occur with punk-inspired *Jubilee* (1978) and music-infused *Quadrophenia* (1979) being classed as dramas and *Melody* (1971), which features the music of the Bee Gees, labelled a comedy.

In addition to straightforward musicals and music-based films, the decade also saw a number of rock documentaries such as *Let It Be* (1970), documenting the making of The Beatles album, and *Glastonbury Fayre* (1972), which featured performances from the festival, as well as films which captured live musical concert performances such as *Born to Boogie* (1972). Finally, there were a number of films which used pop stars and bands in narrative roles. *That'll Be the Day, Stardust, Slade in Flame* (1974) and *The Kids Are Alright* (1979) drew on an established British cinematic tradition of pop stars on film which had begun with Cliff Richard in *Expresso Bongo* (1959) and *Summer Holiday* (1963) and had led to the hugely successful Beatles films, *A Hard Day's Night* (1964) and *Help!* (1965). These films linked pop music and cinema and paved the way for future films to extend, develop and capitalise upon these crossovers. Perhaps, as Mark Kermode suggests, filmmakers discovered the potency and possibility of popular music and recognised it as, 'a disposable, transient product which reflects, mimics and occasionally shapes the Zeitgeist.'[4] Kevin Donnelly suggests that the establishment of pop music as an increasingly respectable medium coincided with its inclusion in most mainstream dramatic films by the end of the 1970s, but this oversimplifies the developments within the music film in the period.[5] The 1970s were the first time that the pop film began to critique its own past and become self-reflective, a wider change which was also evident within popular music. Pop films were no longer the straightforward star vehicles they had been in the 1960s; the films of the 1970s offered an insight into a post-1960s world.

Andrew Higson suggests that in the 1970s, the ailing British film industry looked to the music industry as a means of renewing itself by 'strategic alignment,' or as Medhurst more bluntly recognises, 'two cultural industries seeking an uneasy alliance.'[6] This would imply that both industries needed the support of the other, yet the 1970s music industry was booming whilst the film industry floundered. Donnelly posits that there were two distinct ways in which music was utilised in film during the decade: in excessive, spectacular rock operas, such as those typically made by Ken Russell, and the cheaply-made British films which used pop music by capitalising on contemporary music trends.[7] However, this view does not leave adequate space for films such as *Stardust*. This film does not fit comfortably in either the budget or the spectacular category; it is not a music documentary, nor is it a filmed concert performance. *Stardust* cannot be characterised as a musical, yet undeniably music is a defining feature of the narrative. *Stardust* utilises most of the musical forms identified above and combines them in a way which is picaresque and episodic, and entirely typical of a great deal of 1970s British cinema of the period. Through its scathing critique of the music industry and its deliberate evocation of powerful star images from earlier periods, *Stardust* offered access to both past and present.

The film was criticised by some reviewers, who considered that the narrative was overly bitter and critical of 1960s hedonism. The *Monthly Film Bulletin* believed that this cynicism could be traced to screenwriter Ray Connolly:

> The greater part of this film can be seen as an answer to the counterfeit felicities of *A Hard Day's Night*... a more cynical variant on the I-told-you-so platitudes of the Hollywood biopic... Connolly seems bent on so predictably squeezing every last drop from the sour fruits of his own disillusion.[8]

Connolly wrote the screenplays for both *That'll Be the Day* and *Stardust*, drawing on his extensive experience as a journalist working for the *Evening Standard* in the 1960s. Throughout this period, Connolly interviewed celebrities, models and photographers as well as stars from the film and music industries. The potent combination of pop stars and film actors demonstrates the crossover between these two industries and the celebrity status accorded to stars of both industries. When interviewed by the author, Connolly remembered:

> The inspiration for *That'll Be The Day* came from David Puttnam, the film's producer. He and I had become friendly and I'd gone to his house to borrow an American book on Elvis one Saturday afternoon in Spring 1972, and we got talking about films... We had a little help in shaping the film from the director Claude Whatham, but the story was a Connolly/Puttnam creation. David should have taken more credit for his involvement in that. While I was writing he would come around for his breakfast most mornings to see what I'd written the night before.[9]

Although Puttnam considers that Connolly gives him, 'rather too much credit' for his involvement in *That'll Be the Day* and *Stardust*, he does assert that, 'both films were a collaboration between myself and Ray with the director in each case (Claude and Michael) brought in to shoot the script and work with the music and the artists that we had selected.'[10] The involvement of Puttnam was critical to the film and much of what he achieved on *That'll Be the Day*, particularly the release of the film's soundtrack, helped guarantee the film both profit and success. On the back of this success, funding was elicited from the National Film Finance Corporation to supply half the production finance for *Stardust*. Puttnam's negotiation for the release of soundtracks from both films was one of the first arrangements of its type within British cinema, and demonstrated the entrepreneurial skills gleaned from his advertising career. Puttnam himself recognises what he achieved on *Stardust*, suggesting when interviewed, 'I think I was as creative with the deal for the film, as I was for the film.'[11] This creativity extended to the use of current pop stars within the film and the charisma and stage presence which they brought to the production.

The performances of cast members including David Essex as Jim Maclaine, Keith Moon as drummer J.D. and Adam Faith as manager Mike cannot simply be viewed in terms of film stardom and film star performance but must be critiqued in terms of their previously existing pop star personas. In this way, David Essex's performance in *Stardust* cannot be understood as David Essex playing Jim Maclaine, but rather David Essex *presenting himself* as David Essex playing Jim Maclaine. In his autobiography, Essex wrote about *Stardust*:

> So much of the make-believe in the film was being mirrored by me in real life... if there was ever a time when I was vulnerable, I feel, it was around this period, when if you like, David Essex almost got lost in an alter ego called Jim Maclaine.[12]

Essex's burgeoning fame and star persona reinforced the crossover between fiction and reality. It is this notion of fluid performativity and intertextuality, which allowed one industry to capitalise upon the success achieved by a performer in another. Drawing on the pop star personas of the 1960s and 1970s – many of whom were still high-profile contemporary figures, such as Mick Jagger, David Bowie, James Bolan and John Lennon – *Stardust* successfully engages with the hedonism, visual excess, male-dominated performance and flamboyance of the period. However, in eschewing the nostalgia of *That'll Be the Day*, *Stardust* refuses to remain in the past; as the *Monthly Film Bulletin* noted presciently, 'from *That'll Be The Day* to those *were* the days.'[13] *Stardust* presents its anti-hero as a contemporary pop icon and successfully blurs the lines between fantasy and reality, as well as past and present. Essex's performance does not imitate any single figure but rather features episodes and images culled from the lives of a range of stars. As the *Films and Filming* reviewer noted:

> The story of the rise and fall of pop star Jim Maclaine seems like an amalgam of various incidents in the lives of various real pop-stars of the 1960s, only the artificial compound lacks the strength of any one of its real elements... it's all too predictable, too superficial.[14]

As the reviewer highlights, the performance of Essex as pop star Maclaine fails to convince. Despite drawing on explosive and charismatic personalities, what Maclaine offers is bland and vacuous, with little evidence of charisma or star persona. Although this could be seen as a deficiency in Essex's acting, the *quality* of the performance delivered is itself consistent and convincing. This suggests that it is Jim Maclaine (rather than David Essex) who is the star found wanting. Essex is a performer and is successfully demonstrating the distance between his own star persona and that of Jim Maclaine. It is this slippage and distance which makes the performance so interesting and offers an intriguing insight into the 'real' pop star persona.

Connolly remembers that Essex was cast in *That'll Be the Day* 'almost by accident' and that crucially, 'he wasn't a pop star, but wanted to be one.'[15] Significantly, at the time of his performance in *Stardust*, Essex had become a successful pop star and was enjoying the early heady days of his fame. Film footage of his early music performances demonstrate that Essex undoubtedly possessed the charismatic qualities that Jim Maclaine singularly lacks.[16] Perhaps as Charles Lindholm believes, charisma cannot be attained but rather must be possessed as part of one's character; in this way Jim Maclaine can never have the charisma of David Essex.[17] While acknowledging that stars are principally figures of identification, Richard Dyer suggests that it is the occasions in which star persona and characterisation conflict and oppose rather than accord which offer the most distinct breaks between star persona and actor.[18] Again, we see this crucial idea of *slippage* between performances – the pop star hiding behind an image but occasionally revealing flashes of the 'real person' rather than the carefully constructed façade.

In his work on interactionism, Goffman suggests that social interaction should be interpreted as a set of rules and codes and in the maintaining of these coded rules, some verbal and some visual, an individual tends to become, 'committed to a particular image of self.'[19] Can we consider then, that in presenting Jim Maclaine, David Essex is offering a coded interpretation, not of a rock star but of his interpretation of a rock star which fits in with established codes of behaviour *for* rock stars? This would help to further understand the intentions behind Essex's performance, and reveal once again the deliberate slippage between image and reality. This could be a useful way of considering the use of star personas within the film, particularly if we also consider, as Goffman posits, that: 'rules of conduct transform both action and inaction into expression and whether the individual abides by the rules or breaks them, something significant is likely to be communicated.'[20]

The deliberate construction of the central character within *Stardust* as empty and devoid of personality subverts not only the charisma of Essex's own personality but also that of the music stars upon which the character is loosely based. The construction of Maclaine is further problematised by the fact that not only must Essex's pop persona be taken into account when analysing the character, but also his theatrical persona. Can it really be coincidental that the messiah-like figure he presents in *Stardust* followed closely on his own prolonged stage performance in the musical 'Godspell' as Jesus Christ? The *NME* review of *Stardust* commented on, 'the pop-messiah status' of Essex as Maclaine and reinforced the connection between pop icons and their mythical status as heroes and idols.[21] So how then can we understand the character of Jim Maclaine? Is he truly 'a morality tale of Sixties/Seventies rock self-indulgence' or can he be positioned more carefully within historical traditions of British cinema?[22]

Within his study of British masculinity, Andrew Spicer identifies some key 'types' which recur, re-emerge and reform within popular British cinema. One of these identified masculine types offers parallels with the character of Jim Maclaine. The 'angry young men' emerged from social realism in the late 1950s but Spicer believes that, in the period that followed, this type fragmented to reveal, 'an alienated young man – vulnerable, disillusioned and unsure of his identity and direction in life.'[23] Spicer sees the development of this particular character type as a product of a fragmented youth culture.[24] The character of the alienated young man has particular resonance in the late 1960s and early 1970s and could include Mick Travis in *If...* (1968), Turner in *Performance* (1970) and the eponymous hero of *Tommy* (1975), along with Jim Maclaine. The youthful, uncertain male signals the difficult transition from the fixed certainties and exciting possibilities of the 1960s to the awkward unease of the 1970s. Within *Stardust*, even stardom, frequently represented as the apogee of success and prosperity, is shown to be empty, unsatisfying and unforgiving.

Stardust focused on the coming of age of the post-war generation and successfully captured the lost dreams of that generation. The tagline for the film challenged: 'Show me a boy who doesn't want to be a rock star and I'll show you a liar,' and Ray Connolly confirms that both films were based on his own and David Puttnam's youthful dreams. He recalled:

Basically I was writing about what he and I might like to have done-that is, follow our teenage dreams. In the film Jim Maclaine has a best friend who does what I did, which is go to university and be a goody-goody. The dropping out idea was David's.[25]

Here, the personal histories of Connolly and Puttnam intersect with the experiences and memories of a particular generation who had lived through the possibilities of the 1960s. Jim Maclaine personifies these youthful dreams and his story is told with an exuberance and nostalgia, but also with a bitterness and cynicism. Jim is located as part of the 1960s generation of young men for whom stardom, fame and success were tantalising possibilities. As Connolly suggests, both That'll Be the Day and Stardust were about, 'a boy finding what he wanted to do and pursuing it,' an idea which resonated with audiences and managed to effectively locate the desires of Jim Maclaine alongside the desires of Puttnam and Connolly and, most importantly, alongside the desires of a generation. As reviewer Derek Malcolm identified, 'it's a film that appeals for its memories and music but also has the power and skill to make us think a bit about the negative side of instant stardom. If you've opted into this sort of world, can you ever opt out again?'[26] Even Essex would later acknowledge that the subject matter for Stardust was much more serious and made making the film much less enjoyable than the previous film.[27]

There are a range of star personas at work within the film, including wild-man drummer Keith Moon, 1960s pop star Adam Faith and musical theatre actor Paul Nicholas as well as emerging star Essex. Each actor/star performs a distinct role and cultural task as masculine 'types'; Keith Moon brings his own charismatic chaos to the role of JD, tapping into his extrovert stage persona as drummer with The Who, while Adam Faith lends a weary and jaded cynicism to the role of Mike, drawing perhaps on his own experiences as a pop star in the 1960s, as well as his more recent performance as an ex-convict in the television series Budgie. Despite his scheming machinations, it is Mike who emerges as a sympathetic character; a man who has the self-awareness and honesty that Jim lacks, who sums up their mutually destructive relationship with the bitter, 'we deserve each other, don't we?'

While an integral part of the film, Mike manages to retain an objectivity and humanity which contrasts with Jim's self-absorption, drug addiction and mental fragility. Mike also recognises Jim for what he really is, a character who, as Connelly pointed out, 'hardly does a decent thing in the entire film.'[28] The deliberate softness of the Maclaine character is a deliberate contrast to Adam Faith's strong, cynical and vivid portrayal of Mike. Yet as Connelly remembers, Faith was not first choice for the part and was cast because, 'Ringo didn't want to do it... David had liked Adam in *Budgie*. I didn't want him, but David insisted I at least meet Adam, and Adam proved me wrong. He was very good.'[29]

While the key characters in the film are male, women fall into two categories within *Stardust*: anonymous groupies and significant others. The three significant females who, despite occupying marginal roles within the narrative, are important, are Jim's forgotten wife Jeanette – played by Rosalind Ayres representing other left-behind wives such as Cynthia Lennon – his French girlfriend, Danielle and his mother. Jeanette is shown to have rebuilt her life following his abandonment and is in no way interested in rekindling their relationship. Crucially, she is shown as the mother of Jim's child, and the cosy domesticity of the family unit demonstrates what Jim has lost while pursuing his rock star dreams. Ironically, it was this stifling and unbearable domesticity which drove Jim from home in *That'll Be the Day*. Whilst Jeanette is a reminder of his past, the influence of his mother is ever-present. His *magnum opus* 'Dea Sancta' is a celebration of woman yet, like Jim's pop star persona, it ultimately fails to convince. Instead of being a sincere and moving tribute, the opera seems hollow, false and over-laden with its orchestral score, backing singers and streaming lights. Ken Russell's *Tommy* would also satirise false idols using rock stars Eric Clapton and Pete Townshend to explore similar ideas, but in a way which privileged the fantastic over a realist aesthetic.

The vocal which accompanies the visual of Jim's performance is also important and reinforces the notion of androgyny and femininity, which is an integral part of Essex's persona. The musical pitch is very high and the more masculine bass notes are absent. The combination of the high awkward notes and the overblown performance of his opera signify Jim's guilt and anxiety; he knows that in throwing away his schoolbooks and abandoning his family he disappointed his mother. His opera is a way of atoning for this guilt, and is one of the most obvious and visible reference to femininity within the film. However, the film also refers extensively to motherhood and in doing so reveals high levels of anxiety about shifting gender roles and responsibilities within the period, notably the frequent references to abortion and avoidance of motherhood. Mike comments laconically to Jim, 'all my mistakes got flushed away. Just like yours,' whilst Jim deliberately feeds drugs to the dog, which induces a messy miscarriage. Such casual references to abortion sit awkwardly with the celebration of the mother which Jim constructs through his opera. With the sole exception of Jeanette and his mother, women within the film are not mothers. Their purpose is not reproduction and stability but sexual entertainment and pleasure, reflecting the casual availability and free love ethos of the 1960s.

The sexual encounters which take place throughout the film border on fantasy; exotic women, multiple partners and a range of readily available females. However, such aggressive promiscuity is also shown to be dangerous and problematic; Johnny's (Paul Nicholas) raging libido is harmful to the group's image and he is distracted by sex and subsequently evicted from the band. Such representations of easy promiscuity for men in the period could suggest a nostalgic undercurrent which has already been identified in a number of other important 1970s British film texts such as *Confessions of a Window Cleaner* and *Alfie Darling* (1975). The aggressive, assured masculinity of earlier periods can be traced back to the angry young men of social realism, but the depiction of masculinity in *Stardust* is neither confidently assured nor firmly authoritative. Instead, *Stardust* again represents the anxieties associated with changing masculine roles and the irreconcilable differences between facets of masculine identity; despite his pop icon status, Jim is repeatedly shown as powerless and insubstantial. He cannot successfully control his business or his personal affairs; he is unable to prevent his mother from dying, he cannot take his child back from Jeannette, and is at the mercy of Mike and his American record producers. This uncertain and impaired masculinity can not only be seen throughout the characters within the film but also through the mise-en-scéne created.

The visual style of the film was created by photographer Tony Richmond and art director Brian Morris. Richmond brought experience to the project gained from documentary music films including work on *Sympathy for the Devil* (1968), *Let It Be* and *Glastonbury Fayre*, whilst Morris was familiar with working with pop stars, having recently completed *Flame* with glam rockers Slade. In *Stardust*, a distinctive and different visual style emerges, which juxtaposes elements of the music documentary with a focus on established stars. It is this fusing together of visual modes and music film sub-genres which make *Stardust* so unusual and visually innovative. The fly-on-the-wall mode favoured by backstage documentaries is apparent throughout the film, notably in the scenes in hotel rooms whose confined spaces, muted lighting, shaky camerawork and deliberately confused audio of overlapping voices and background music combine to create a documentary mode and aesthetic. The documentaries of the Maysles brothers in this period, such as *Gimme Shelter* (1970), also offer a behind-the-scenes look at the music industry and *Stardust* deliberately utilises many of the techniques created in these films. The notion of the documentary-maker as voyeur, offering an insight into the lives of the famous, is also furthered by the use of television clips within the film, specifically when the band members watch Jim being interviewed on television. The cuts between the television images, the desultory hotel room commentary and the interview itself reinforce the documentary aesthetic and position the audience as both voyeur and privileged insider. The duality of the role of voyeur and insider is crucial to understanding the film's appeal. The presentation of rock icons as charismatic, messiah-like figures who are also 'ordinary' people reinforces star personas and popular appeal, whilst combining it with the notion of the everyman.

The visual style of the later stages of the film is reminiscent of the stylistic excesses of Ken Russell within *The Music Lovers* (1970) and *The Boyfriend*, yet the first half of the film draws upon the inexpensive pop music films of the 1960s, with their over-bright costumes, cheap sets and myriad of extras.

Designer Ruth Myers styled Maclaine as he morphs from grubby denim-wearing pop band member to satin-clad, avant-garde musical icon with his clothes reflecting the shift from the 1960s to the 1970s. Moya Luckett suggests a direct link between the confusion surrounding national identity in the 1960s and 1970s and the use of costume and dress in helping to foreground and explore male identities.[30] Luckett argues:

> The sartorial extremes of men's fashion revivals seem, to require support from other cultural phenomenon like film and popular music suggesting that breaking with conventions of male dress is far more radical than transformations in female style.[31]

This renders the visual transformation of Maclaine highly significant. The transformation is filtered through the medium of popular music and draws on the cultural capital provided by Bowie, Lennon, Dylan and Bolan. Jim's transformation through clothing further demonstrates his radical yet uneasy evolution and underscores his inability to ever return to his roots; he can never return to the band or return home, any more than he can adopt the fashions of previous years. In this way, his sartorial transformation mirrors his psychological one; his career begins to reflect the unpredictable, transient and unfixed nature of the clothing styles he adopts. His dress reinforces the uncertainties of masculinity already noted within glam rock music and the accompanying androgyny of both vocal and visual performance.

While the early images of The Stray Cats performing in velvet collar suits with mop top haircuts offers an easy reference to the heyday of The Beatles, the flared trousers, satin shirts and fur-trimmed waistcoats suggest the hippy-inspired and drug-fuelled transformations many stars underwent in the late 1960s. The final shift from the garish and ostentatious world of glam, to the simplicity of the white tunic and Indian trousers again evokes images of the musical stars of the period who turned to Eastern mysticism and religion. Leon Hunt suggests that the flamboyance of glam was the most obvious popular articulation of the codes of masculinity in a limited state of flux within the 1970s, yet within *Stardust*, a wide range of male fashions are deployed, each signifying unease within contemporary masculinity.[32] The range of masculine extremes of fashion visually suggests the extremely fluid role for all men in the period, even iconic rock stars. However, the star persona and performative nature of the character must be recognised. As Noel McLaughlin points out, 'the meanings of dress will be inflected, altered, amplified or contradicted by the musical and performing conventions and associations within which they are placed.'[33] The changes which are manifest in the costumes within the film signal the different stages of performativity which Jim undertakes; he is a performer and his clothes always reflect this. The bland uniformity of his suit for his role as band member, the satin, chiffon and glitter for his overblown operetta, the stark blankness of the final white suit he wears for the televised interview. Each costume signals a different stage of performance and the clothes themselves can be read as yet another layer to Essex's presentation of the doomed rock star.

Andrew Hill and Pamela Church Gibson see some films of the 1970s, including *A Clockwork Orange* (1971) and *Get Carter* (1971) as also containing an element of visual excess in terms of style and costume and it is possible to also view *Stardust* in this way.[34] Hill and Church Gibson also posit that this excess is a response to a society in turmoil and breakdown, but I would argue that *Stardust* demonstrates a more cynical awareness of the period through its critique of stardom and masculinity.[35]

It is easy to trace the evolution of Jim and The Stray Cats from working class heroes to affluent rock stars. As Luckett suggests, 'different clothes for different events testified to the new affluence that made fashion possible for working class youths' and it is this variety of costume and diversity of dress which mark the band's transformation.[36] In a late scene when The Stray Cats ask Jim to leave the band, they have adopted the hippy-inspired fashions and flamboyant dress which Jim has also been wearing. As well as signalling that the band members are also wealthy and prosperous, the costumes also signify the move from their cohesive existence as a band through a deliberate rejection of uniformity of dress.

The shifts in class can also be seen in the frequent changes of location. The working-class clubs and dance halls of northern England give way to the sunny, modern anonymity of America via the country house showcase arranged by their management. This location and setting positions the band within a rural, aristocratic setting and underlines their awkwardness and unease within this milieu. The setting here does not simply represent the country but also a class and its associated wealth and breeding with which none of the band is familiar. The awkwardness is further highlighted by the way the band members behave; chasing girls and attempting to ride the donkeys instead of mingling with the important and influential guests. In this period it was rock stars who became the new aristocracy; money could now buy lifestyle. Mike demonstrates how age-old conventions and class codes can be easily manipulated; while his accent jars in the aristocratic setting, he moves with confidence, ease and assurance, refusing to remain in his 'place' and physically representing the fragmentation of class and status brought about by the social changes of the 1960s.

The function of America as the classless land of opportunity is also crucial. Like Bob in *Sunday Bloody Sunday*, Jim is keen to embrace everything that America has to offer. The size of America is shown through the wide shots and open spaces, whilst the opulent hotel rooms, packed stadiums and huge freeways suggest a scale which cannot be matched by anything in Britain. This 'othering' of America is at first exciting and exotic, but quickly becomes mundane and dull both visually and narratively. The hotel rooms become full of strangers, the character exchanges increasingly take place in moving vehicles highlighting the frenetic, transient life of music stars on the road, places become less specific, with cities merging together to become anonymous locations. The opportunities of America soon become overshadowed by the pace of life and the constant demands. Jim has become a success and a commodity; his face adorns the cover of *Time* magazine, yet he sits in a hotel room surrounded by strangers.

Jim's retreat from the modernity of America results in his purchase of the hilltop castle in Spain. Ray Connolly remembered that when he and director Michael Apted found this location, they recognised how essential such a setting was to the film and how much it added to the overall 'look' of the film.[37] In rejecting new world modernity for old world heritage, Jim is positioning himself between the drabness of Britain in the 1970s and the hyper-modernity of America. Here, new money buys faded-grandeur, class, position and style, for, as Mike estimates, 'a few million pesetas.' In the consumption-driven world of the pop star, everything is for sale. In its locations and within the second half of the film, *Stardust* offers an international depiction of the successful pop star, removing him from the confines of Britain and making him a world-wide phenomenon. The film offers none of the domestic reassurance of *That'll Be the Day*, but instead positions the hero within a world context without the safety and security of friends, home and family. None of these signifiers fit into the world of the pop star and in his final moments, Jim is surrounded by strangers. Asked by a journalist if it was all worth it, Jim replies baldly, 'no, not really,' a sobering verdict on the life of a rock star.

While *That'll Be the Day* drew heavily on nostalgia, aspiration and social mobility, *Stardust* showcased fame and stardom. The film revealed that the possibilities of the 1960s with their promise of success to be empty, fickle and ultimately destructive; a salutary lesson on the deficiencies of stardom. Leon Hunt claimed that much of the film product of the early years of the decade displayed 'a sense of not noticing that the 1960s were over' yet *Stardust* starkly revealed that the 1960s *were* over and can never be revisited.[38] Through the use of former pop stars from the previous decade, as well as young stars at the height of their fame, *Stardust* capitalised on the success stories of the 1960s whilst simultaneously revealing them to be precarious and unstable. The film's message seems clear; regardless of charisma, talent and success, fame cannot be sustained and is ultimately destructive. There is no other possible outcome for Jim Maclaine and his 'harrowing finale' is merely the inevitable outcome of his journey as a pop star and signals the end of yet another potent version of popular masculinity which had manifested itself in the 1960s.[39]

The costume and visual style of the film underscore this failure of masculinity by revealing how icons who achieve success and fame ultimately remain flawed and lacking. The rise and fall of a pop star is deliberately depicted in unapologetic graphic detail and it was this level of detail that caused problems when the film came to be classified for exhibition. The film was submitted to the British Board of Film Censors in July 1974 and it quickly became apparent that the film's content was not suitable for the 'AA' category desired by the production company. Following a meeting with the BBFC, David Puttnam and production company, Goodtimes Enterprises, decided to conduct some audience research to see how audiences responded to the material in the film which dealt with the problematic issues the BBFC had identified: bad language, drugs and sex.

The file on *Stardust* from the BBFC offers new and intriguing information into how audiences responded to the film and this material offers a rare insight into the notoriously difficult world of popular taste. Documents from the file reveal how the audience research was carried out as well as detailing the responses of the carefully selected audience to the film itself.[40] Such material is rare and adds greatly to understanding of audience, popular taste and issues of contention within the period. The survey was placed in the care of independent researchers to specifically focus upon the 14–18 age group, who were seen as the target audience for the film. The researchers sought to target two distinct groups to comment on the film; those who worked with children in this age bracket and parents of teenagers. The size of the sample was small, with only 70 respondents of whom only 27% were women, but the study points out:

> The experiment did receive good coverage in the local press and it must be assumed that a large proportion of those seriously concerned about media content for young people were present. If the sample over-represents certain points of view the fault must lie partly with those of a different opinion who failed to appear to give expression to their views.[41]

While the research carried out was by no means perfect and has some serious flaws, some of the conclusions drawn from the data effectively illustrate exactly what the concerns were about the film's content and how those who saw the film responded to it. The raw data is missing from the BBFC archives but a detailed analysis of the responses survives, which details the findings of the study and highlights some of the key observations.

The results showed overwhelmingly that most concerns were about sex. The analysis notes, 'when asked whether there were any scenes or dialogue that they thought were unsuitable for teenagers, 32 mentioned sex (although 11 of these were tentative in their comments with much use of "perhaps," "might" and "for some 14 year olds")' while only eight mentioned bad language and four referred to drug use.[42] The report highlights that specific objections were made to the *ménage à trois* scenes and that five respondents felt the whole of the last part of the film 'might be unsuitable for some' whilst a further three thought that the dog's miscarriage was censorable.[43]

The second half of the research asked the respondents if they agreed with a series of statements. The results recorded only include those who agreed with these statements, those who disagreed or were not sure were omitted from the overall results. However, despite the paucity of data, some general trends can be noted. Approximately two thirds of all respondents agreed with the following statements: 'The film presents a realistic picture of the pop world,' 'The theme and moral of the film outweigh any tendency to glamorise,' 'Young people are not naïve: nothing in this film will surprise or shock them.'[44]

Revealingly, less that 10% of the respondents agreed with the statements: 'The film's treatment of marijuana smoking is likely to encourage its use by young people' and 'The film over-glamorises the pop world.'[45] The indication here is that the realism and the morality of the narrative outweighed any of the negative aspects of the story. The only statement that remained divisive supported the earlier findings about the sexual content of the film with nearly 30% of respondents agreeing that, 'The treatment of sex in *Stardust* is too explicit for some 14–15 year olds.'[46]

Finally, the respondents were asked about rating the film and if they would encourage young people to go and see it. The results are illuminating, with a clear majority of two thirds of respondents in favour of the 'AA' (over 14) category. Tellingly, a third of all respondents said that they would discourage young people from going to see the film, whilst the vast majority said that they would take no action to encourage or discourage. The report's author believes that this 'no doubt reflect[s] the extent to which adults feel they are likely to be able to influence their young in any way.'[47]

The concerns over the sexual content of the film reveal that this was the issue which audiences felt to be most harmful, the language and the drug references were not seen to be as potentially damaging. The consideration of the film as moral rather than glamorous also confirms the desires of the production company for the film to be 'a realistic portrayal of a pop-star's life rather than a glamorised version of it.'[48]

Once the findings were fed back to the BBFC, Secretary Stephen Murphy issued a press release, which stated:

> We all felt that this film, made with integrity, represented a current social problem with which adolescents are involved...we have considered the evidence given by experts in this field and by members of the general public. Overwhelmingly, that evidence leads us to the award of an 'AA' certificate to *Stardust*.[49]

The lack of glamour identified by the test audience is commented upon extensively in the critical reviews. Derek Malcolm believed; 'the film is in deadly earnest about its subject – the pop phenomenon of the 60s – and the picture painted is by no means a pretty one,' whilst *Variety* considered, 'Though pic[ture] is never preachy there should be some sobering subliminal lessons to be learned from this item about coping with sudden riches and fame, the value of solid relationships (both private and business) and especially about drugs.'[50] Other reviewers disagreed on the realism of the narrative, *Films and Filming* averring that '*Stardust* doesn't quite get it: it has a synthetic taste to it.'[51] Interestingly, the perceived educational and informative aspects of *Stardust* led the *Variety* reviewer to suggest that 'youngsters should not only be free to see the pic[ture] but should be urged to do so.'[52] *Stardust* successfully captures the teenage audience with its narrative and vicarious pop star appeal, whilst at the same time carrying a strongly moral message which appealed to teachers and parents. The pleasures of the narrative are therefore tempered; the morality of the film ensures that the text can be enjoyed, but the underlying message cannot be ignored.

Despite some negative reviews, *Stardust* went on to become one of the most successful British films of 1974, taking over £135,000 at the box office in its first week.[53] The success of the film must take into account its position as a sequel, the successful tie-ins and funding negotiations arranged by David Puttnam, the importance of pop star David Essex and the film's pedigree as part of a tradition of pop music films.

The film effectively polices the boundaries of pleasure; it allows the teenage audience to revel in the star persona of Essex and the constructed narrative of rock star hedonism and excess, whilst simultaneously and deliberately articulating dominant social and cultural norms about the consequences of such behaviour. *Stardust* allows the viewer access into the text, suggesting a variety of open interpretations and readings, whilst at the same time clearly reinforcing conservative and functional ideologies within the moral landscape. Excessive behaviour is punished and, despite his rock star lifestyle and flamboyant appearance, Jim is shown to be an empty vessel who cannot fulfil the role of superstardom which is offered to him. His physical surroundings come to signify this barrenness; his white, sterile room in the rooftop castle in Spain, located in rough terrain, accessed only by helicopter. Jim has withdrawn to these surroundings in order to retreat and to find himself, but as his white room illustrates, he is a blank canvas; there is nothing left to be found. *Stardust* articulates these anxieties about false heroes in a more explicit and unforgiving way than *Tommy* would later do, drawing a clear line between the outward performance and inner emptiness.

Stardust occupies a transitional place within 1970s popular culture. Its subject matter addresses the period between the 1960s and 1970s and critiques it with a frankness and cynicism unusual within the music film. With *Stardust*, the music film was transformed as the powerful interrelation between music, pop stardom and film was fully realised and the pop music star was successfully packaged and represented for an audience. No longer would the music film have to rely upon constructed songs and personas; it could function as a serious narrative addressing contemporary issues, while drawing upon the very conventions and personalities that it set out to critique. In this way, *Stardust* is perhaps one of the first post-modern texts of the period which samples and borrows from other texts across a range of media both within the music film genre and beyond. Such borrowing indicates not only the possibilities of crossover between the film and music genres, but also demonstrates, through its effective and memorable use of David Essex, how stars and star personas could be deliberately deployed and utilised to deliberate effect. Through this clever positioning, *Stardust* really was able to have it both ways.

12
Scum: Institutional Control and Patriarchy

In 1976, the BBC commissioned a television drama, *Scum*, about a borstal, from a script by Roy Minton, to be directed by Alan Clarke. However, the completed film was deemed too shocking by the BBC and was subsequently shelved. In 1979, a new version of *Scum*, again written by Minton and directed by Clarke, was released as a feature film which followed the incarceration of young offenders including Carlin (Ray Winstone), Banks (John Blundell) and Richards (Phil Daniels) within a borstal.

Institutional life is a dominant theme within British cinema in the 1940s and the 1950s, it is notably absent in the 1960s and reappears strongly in the 1970s. Although *Scum* is not a documentary, the film draws upon cinematic modes of social realism and documentary to present this insight into institutional life. While these two modes are important strands within British cinema, they are not greatly in evidence in the 1970s. They can, however, be found in the television of the period. As *Scum* was originally commissioned for television, it is important to consider how this influenced the feature film's production and visual style. Director Alan Clarke and writer Roy Minton had worked together on a number of television dramas for the BBC including *Funny Farm* (1975) and *Fast Hands* (1976) as well as a number of *Play for Today* subjects. Initially envisaged as part of a trilogy, with other segments focusing on army and police training, Minton began working on *Scum* in 1976 following extensive research into the institutional life of the borstal. The completed script was selected by Margaret Matheson, producer of *Play for Today*, as a stand-alone project to be directed by Clarke, and production began.

Despite commissioning the project, the BBC refused to show the film once it was completed. The later years of the 1970s saw the BBC begin to shy away from provocative or controversial television drama. Its role in showcasing social realist material was partially assumed by Channel 4 after its launch in 1982 and the feature film version of *Scum* was first shown on this channel in 1983. One of the reasons given by Alasdair Milne of the BBC to justify the rejection of the television film was because it was a 'drama-documentary,' an assertion vigorously contested by Alan Clarke.[1]

Clarke himself drew a sharp distinction between drama and documentary, and asserted that *Scum* was a play, not a documentary, and that the actors were playing characters, not re-enacting past events. Clarke did agree that the subject matter was something he felt strongly about and highlighted his and Minton's feelings, stating when interviewed, 'The main thesis of the film is that borstal doesn't work and it's something that society has to think about.'[2] Such beliefs are evident within *Scum* and are articulated by the character of Archer. White-collar criminal Archer expounds his own, and possibly Clarke's and Minton's beliefs when he states, 'the punitive system does not work... my own experience of borstal convinces me that more criminal acts are imposed on criminals than by criminals on society.' Such overt political statements locate the film as social realism, yet the debate as to whether it was fiction, documentary or a combination of both continued to plague the film and its creators. In utilising documentary filmmaking techniques, selecting political subject matter and frequently creating a social realist aesthetic, Clarke's work has frequently been classed as 'documentary-style,' an assessment which can be usefully explored by considering his approach to *Scum*.

Considered by both the cast and production team of *Scum* to be very much 'an actor's director,' part of Clarke's skill was in eliciting captivatingly real performances from his predominantly youthful cast.[3] David Threlfall, who played Archer in the television film, remembers real fights breaking out between the actors and the youth-club extras, during the filming of the sports hall scene. Following this uncoordinated fracas, Alan Clarke suggested to his battered cast that the scene looked 'a bit Mickey Mouse' and could they try it again![4] Threlfall felt that this approach was part of Clarke's method of working, while his insistence on numerous takes was to make sure he captured the scenes as realistically as possible. Phil Daniels, who played Richards in both versions of *Scum* agreed, believing 'that was his style... put you in amongst it, see how you coped and then film it.'[5]

Scum is not a documentary, yet during its production as a cinematic feature film the issues of documentary style, mode and narrative continued to arise. Archival material from the Don Boyd papers document the uneasy transformation of *Scum* from a television drama into a feature film and reveal the involvement of financiers Clive Parsons and Davina Belling.

Following a screening of the television film, Parsons and Belling began working to secure investment for the feature film project and after rejections from Rank, EMI and the National Film Finance Corporation, independent producer Don Boyd agreed to finance the film, putting up a budget of £250,000.[6] In a recent interview Boyd confirmed that he joined the project, 'because of Alan and [...] I believed him when he showed me the TV film and told me how he would make movie from the new script.'[7]

Roy Minton was unhappy about changes that were made to his script for the television film, particularly the removal of a homosexual relationship between 'the Daddy' Carlin and another inmate. In a letter to Boyd, he complained, 'virtually all of Alan's alterations are extremely detrimental to the project,' while in a letter to Clarke himself, his erstwhile collaborator and friend, he raged, 'your text is a travesty of the final script... it is sometimes coarse, vulgar and gratuitous. *Scum* is not a commercial piece written for desperate money, it is something I care passionately for and I will fight for it.'[8] Minton did not see *Scum* as a commercial piece, but this was precisely what Parsons considered it to be. Minton wrote scathingly to Parsons:

> You have not only betrayed my work, but you, more importantly, betrayed all those boys for whom I wrote. They shared themselves with me and I took on the responsibility and gave them my word I would not sell out... you are squandering the opportunity of making a very important film that is also successful.[9]

The desire of Minton to make a film which stayed true to the purity of his original research conflicted with the wishes of Parsons to make a commercial film. Parsons believed:

> Our film is not a documentary or a so-called drama documentary, but a story with a strong narrative [...] I am convinced that we have got to get across that our film works on the level of an exciting story which will appeal to a wide-range of audiences – and we need to play down the more serious aspects of the work, such as its

disturbing indictment of the system [...] I don't think that we will get distributors to buy *Scum* or the public to see it if we emphasise the more serious levels of the film.[10]

By clearly stipulating that the film was in no way a dramatised documentary and was instead an 'exciting story,' Parsons would appear to be directly contradicting Minton's desire to critique the borstal system using careful research. The shift from television drama to commercial feature film saw Minton unwilling to compromise on the initial premise and Parsons insistent that the film needed to be more cinematic. The feature film was to be very similar to the television drama yet executive producer Don Boyd considers that Alan Clarke saw the project as entirely separate, believing, 'Alan never saw it as a remake... he saw it as a feature film based on the same material.'[11] Boyd also considers that 'the TV drama has historical value but not much else,' clearly affirming the importance of the film version.[12]

The BBFC also considered the film to be different from the television version, stating in their monthly bulletin, 'if the film was like the TV version it could get an "AA," but we were forced to go to "X" because of the far more brutal style.'[13] Despite being extensively involved in the classification process, the BBFC remained concerned about the content within the film.[14] Both female examiners had concerns about the graphic rape scene, yet the Board as a whole felt, 'there is not sufficient justification to cut' and so the scene remained in the film.[15] Although the rape in *Scum* is neither gratuitous nor excessively graphic, its inclusion within the film did raise concerns, particularly as Davis, played by Julian Firth, is presented within the narrative as a vulnerable child. There is no correspondence to suggest that the production company disputed the 'X' certificate, and the deliberate use of the category within the marketing of the film implies that the cultural clout of the 'X' was being capitalised upon.

The way the film was promoted also focuses attention on the involvement of Don Boyd. Boyd's success as an independent producer within the 1970s earned him the youthful sobriquet of 'the Boyd wonder,' and his contribution to the financing and production of films within the period was critically important.[16] Boyd's memories of working on *Scum* are interesting, as he recalls, 'I was the owner of the production company and had complete artistic and commercial control over every element of the film.'[17] Despite this high level of involvement in the production process, Boyd gave Clarke the space he needed in order to shoot the film. He remembers, 'I left Alan completely alone on the floor.

Deliberately. He knew what he was doing and only needed efficient production management.'[18]

This approach to filmmaking was pragmatic and sympathetic. Boyd passionately believed in *Scum* and his supportive letters to Clarke reveal not only how significant he considered the film to be, but how critical it was to British cinema:

> I am very proud that my company is making *Scum* for many reasons but the first and more important reason is that for a change, the British cinema is making a film which previously has just been aired on television. I know you are helping to make a brilliant film and I wish you the best of luck during its production.[19]

Boyd himself later came to believe that *Scum* and the debate surrounding the film hastened the abolition of the borstal system under the 1982 Criminal Justice Act.[20] One ex-borstal boy who was released in 1979 and interviewed about the film certainly considered that the film got it 'spot on' in its depiction of life within the borstal system and he uses the same language as the film does, talking of 'screws' and 'the daddy' to describe his own experiences.[21]

Boyd's achievements as producer and director were partly due to the skills of financier Roy Tucker, who ensured that Boyd's films made money by offsetting costs as tax losses and profits were ploughed back into new projects. However, Tucker was worried that the controversy around *Scum* would bring the company into ill repute. Executive producer Michael Relph wrote to Tucker in early 1979 to reassure him:

> I think that it is the most likely property that we have currently in production to achieve an important critical and artistic success. It is certain however, to be controversial and I shall be very surprised if we do not accrue prestige for having been daring enough to make it. I also think the film will do very well with the large of amount of publicity which I am sure it will receive.[22]

Tucker appears to have been persuaded and *Scum* was distributed throughout Britain by GTO films as part of a package of Boyd's Co films which included *Hussy* (1979) with Helen Mirren and Derek Jarman's *The Tempest* (1979). By November 1979, *Scum* was being referred to by the production company as the 'gem' in the line-up and considered as the film most likely to be profitable.[23] While impossible to fully discern the exact profit made by the film, a memo from the archives estimates that this collection of Boyd's Co films, when combined with monies received from the Eady Levy, would generate over £800,000 by November 1980.[24]

Without Boyd's support, it is unlikely that the film version of *Scum* would have been financed. As controller of the money, Boyd had a great deal of influence over the film's production and was heavily involved in specific aspects of production, notably in the final editing of two of the most significant and visceral scenes in the film, the suicide and the rape scenes. Boyd recalled;

> Alan asked me to see both versions – privately. We ran them and I was absolutely adamant that particularly in the case of the suicide (Parsons and Belling wanted the scene shortened and to end before the wrists cutting and the blood began to pouring blood). I was clear – to give justification to the riot and to heighten the appalling abuses of the system, the horror of the scene in its full version was essential. Alan agreed with me. The rape scene was equally important for similar reasons.[25]

Boyd's saw his role as supporting the vision of the director, but he was also able to support Roy Minton over changes made to the script and to overrule Parsons' desire to have music within the film.[26]

For all its thematic and visual similarity to the television version, *Scum* had a different cinematographer, camera operator and art director. Anthony Clarke was the production designer for the television drama and had previously worked on *Hallelujah Handshake* (1970), part of the *Play for Today* strand, which was directed by Alan Clarke. For the film version, Phil Mehaux was director of photography. Mehaux had also worked on a number of the *Play for Today* television productions, notably those directed by John Mackenzie. Mackenzie would later go on to direct *The Long Good Friday* (1980) and for this film, Mehaux, camera operator Mike Sweeney and editor Mike Bradsall would all work together again, reprising a working relationship first established on the feature film version of *Scum*.

Although *The Long Good Friday* is visually very different from *Scum*, both films were originally intended for television. As previously noted, *Scum* was refused a release by a nervous BBC, while the script for *The Long Good Friday* was shelved by an equally nervous Lew Grade and ATV. This project was finally picked up by Handmade Films and filmed as a feature film. Both films anticipated the following decade and the coming of Thatcherism and *Scum*'s affirmation of patriarchy and the power of discipline and control anticipated the re-emergence of the right in

British society and politics. The visual style of *Scum* is a result of the work of many of these practitioners, whose previous television experience and methods of working were well suited to the interior location shooting, confined spaces and realist settings. It is possible to see the television roots of the feature film, within in its script, visual style, camerawork, editing and use of locations and its similarity to Alan Clarke's earlier television work. It also could be usefully compared to powerful dramas such as Ken Loach and Tony Garnett's *Cathy Come Home* (1966), which combined television drama narrative with a social realist aesthetic, and also to the films of the British New Wave.

As part of the British New Wave, *The Loneliness of the Long Distance Runner* (1962) combines the social realist aesthetic of northern industrial landscapes with a political subject matter of a borstal boy attempting to beat the system. This film allows for debates about institutional systems, youth culture and the establishment with petty thief Colin Smith (Tom Courtenay) finally deciding that working with the system to achieve success and early release was no substitute for asserting his own independence, albeit in a self-destructive way. There is a similarity in early scenes from both films; close up shots playing on a range of youthful faces aboard the minibus before moving to focus on cuffed wrists. In deliberately referencing the earlier film in *Scum*, Clarke locates the film within the visual conventions of social realism which characterised the New Wave. The gritty graininess of the colour palette and the shaky camerawork again suggest social realism; the drab colours and anonymous mise-en-scène are entirely deliberate and create a look that fits in perfectly with the institutional setting. In *Scum*, the predominant colours are grey, navy and brown, again drawing comparisons to the black and white visuals of *The Loneliness of the Long Distance Runner*. In *Scum,* the only flashes of colour are the frequent gushes of blood. The visceral vividness of the blood which flows from Richards' smashed face, Banks' broken nose and Davis' slashed wrists is rendered more shocking against the drabness of the background and the uniformity of the setting.

The claustrophobia of institutional life is perfectly encapsulated by the long corridors and cramped spaces; the order which dominates the lives of the inmates is discernible in the meticulously arranged dining hall, symmetrical room layouts and precision of angle. Right angles dominate the frame; beds, windows, stairs, corridors and tables are all carefully aligned and these details reiterate the control and order which prevails within the institution. Such order is not the case in *The Loneliness of the Long Distance Runner*; while the institutional setting is comparable, there is a great deal less uniformity within the visual style, specifically in the way the camera is used. Within the earlier film, the camera roams freely, providing a variety of detailed visuals, while in *Scum*, the camera predominantly remains fixed, reiterating control and preventing any unusual insight into institutional life beyond that which exists in front of the firmly fixed gaze of the camera. While *Scum* is similar to some social realist filmmaking, there are important differences. The film does not allow the viewer any prior knowledge; there are no flashbacks or voiceovers to further character development and past events to provide contextual detail. *The Loneliness of the Long Distance Runner* utilises extensive flashback sequences which trace Colin's experiences leading up to his incarceration in the borstal. It is only by understanding his past – his dying father, his formidable mother, his petty criminal behaviour – that we understand his desire to beat the system in the conclusion of the film. This is not the case with *Scum*. In resisting attempts to open up the narrative by evoking sympathy or allowing character development, the script and mise-en-scène of *Scum* create total realism. In this way the film extends beyond social realism as its visual presentation allows for no explorations or explanations and is fiercely uncompromising.

This uncompromising vision is unusual in social realism and unusual for the period. Social realist texts *Pressure* (1975) and *Babylon* (1980) also addressed issues of youth culture and political and social injustice, yet avoid the entrenched positions held by *Scum*. *Scum* draws clear binary distinctions; black/white, empowered/disempowered, victim/oppressor, while *Pressure* and *Babylon* deliberately resist these easy distinctions. While *Pressure* and *Babylon* utilise the techniques of social and neo-realism, using non-professional actors and location filming, *Scum* does not. Unlike *Babylon*, which utilises local people and the crowded streets of Deptford for its filming, *Scum* does not rely upon location, time, space or place to render its presentation accurate and authentic. Where all three films converge is in their uncompromising presentation of authority figures. In refusing to compromise on this presentation, all three films can be seen to be attacking the institutional system and the society that creates and fosters such institutions.

The examination of British institutions within film dates back to Ealing comedies, early Boulting brothers and *Carry On* films. Films such as *Passport to Pimlico* (1949), *Lucky Jim* (1957), *Carry On Sergeant* (1958) and *Carry On Nurse* (1959) parody and critique the British institutions of the political bureaucracy, academia, national service and the hospital, but with affection. Within *A Clockwork Orange* (1971), the institution is again presented as a means of control, but it is peopled by buffoons in uniform, and the scathing humour and presentation of institutional life allows for the parody to continue. Another important institution-based visual text within the decade is *Porridge*. The television series ran from 1974 to 1977 and a feature film was released in 1979, the same year as *Scum*. Within *Porridge*, the institution is shown to be domestic, cosy and protective; the sympathetic and comical community which exists within its walls is a huge contrast to the brutality evident in *Scum*. *Porridge*'s depiction of institutional life fits in much more with the nostalgic and comedic presentations of the 1940s and 1950s, when such institutions were affectionately parodied.

The late 1960s and early 1970s was a period in which established institutions came to be actively questioned and challenged. From the indictment of the military establishment in Tony Richardson's *Charge of the Light Brigade* (1968) to Pete Walker's attack on the penal institution in *House of Whipcord* (1974) and the church in *The House of Mortal Sin* (1976), it is evident that established regimes and structures were under attack. Even the institution of the family was targeted with Ken Loach's *Family Life* (1971) presenting a polarised, dysfunctional family struggling to cope with mental illness and teenage pregnancy. It is significant that these attacks on a range of British institutions took place in the early years of the decade. By the time *Scum* was released in 1979, a backlash had taken place which coincided with a shift to the right within politics. Mark Garnett notes a series of crushing defeats suffered by the Left in the latter years of the decade and the rise of the political Right and the increasing prominence of the National Front.[27]

While Lindsay Anderson's *If . . .* (1968) advocated revolution and is indicative of a rebellious, youthful activism, the narrative of *Scum*, released a decade later, is deeply reactionary. Within *Scum*, the role and function of the institution is presented in a traditional and conventional way; deliberately reiterating the importance of the institution rather than parodying it. Order is established, briefly challenged and finally reasserted. The comfort from the text comes from the lack of ambiguity and the fixed and uncompromising notions of establishment and the institution which are articulated by the text. Unlike the prison in *A Clockwork Orange* or *Porridge*, the borstal in *Scum* is an example of Goffman's 'total institution'; nothing exists beyond its walls and the lives of the inmates do not extend into the outside world.[28] The inmates of *Scum* (unlike Colin Smith, Fletcher or Alex DeLarge), do not exist before they enter the institution. As Goffman illustrates in his work on asylums, the conditions created by total institutions actively and deliberately prevent individuality and advocate denial of the self.[29] Goffman considers, 'the barrier that total institutions place between the inmate and the wider world marks the first curtailment of self.'[30] And as Mary Douglas reminds us, the function of the institution is to establish certainty and to deliberately harness and create a sense of uniformity out of distinctly disparate elements. Douglas states:

> The institutional community blocks personal curiosity, organises public memory and heroically imposes certainty on uncertainty. In marking its own boundaries, it affects all lower-level thinking, so that persons realise their own identities and classify each other through community affiliation.[31]

If we apply this to the borstal within *Scum*, it is not simply the case that the boys have become institutionalised, but that they now see themselves in terms of the definitions accorded them by the system and they classify themselves and one another accordingly. The system establishes a power structure which allows and encourages a 'Daddy' figure, but also allows for other inmates to be categorised according to identity 'types,' which are then reiterated by the other inmates. The vulnerable Davis is referred to by the staff as 'a pathetic mardyarse,' whilst simultaneously being targeted by the other boys. The definition accorded to Davis is being reinforced by staff and by inmates and finally even by Davis himself. Even Archer, who prides himself on beating the system in his own way, comes to be classified as a troublemaker. He has been classified by the other inmates as strange, odd and difficult, in the same way that the staff have also sought to classify him. In conforming to these character stereotypes, the boys are not only establishing themselves within the institutional framework but are now defining themselves and each other in terms of these stereotypes.

Goffman acknowledges that the very conditions established within total institutions such as the denial of privileges, uniformity of dress, meals and strict timetables, while representing the restrictive conditions which are imposed, does allow for acts of individualism. He states: 'these conditions allow for different individualistic ways of meeting them, apart from any effort at collective subversive action.'[32] Within *Scum*, each boy has his own way of dealing with the conditions and the system itself: Archer seeks refuge in behaviour which causes as much inconvenience to the staff as possible; Carlin resorts to violence to ensure that he assumes a position of power and influence; Davis commits suicide, in his own way managing to beat the system. Despite these acts of individual resistance or rebellion, when the inmates unite behind a common cause and actively challenge the established rules and attempt 'collective, subversive action,' they fail. Following the deaths of Davis and Toyne, euphemistically described by the Warden as 'accidents,' the boys first refuse to eat and then riot. Neither the hunger strike nor the riot is successful; the final scenes, in which the Warden sternly informs the boys that they will work until the damages are paid for, is inter-cut with shots of the prone, bloody bodies of Carlin, Archer and Meakin being dragged unresisting into solitary confinement. Order has been restored and collective action has been effectively overturned by the system and by the strength of the institution. Within the film the institution seeks to reform but not rehabilitate. *Scum*'s overt rejection of any forms of group therapy and rehabilitation are evident when Matron attempts to encourage a small group of boys to discuss their feelings. Archer suggests the topic of 'trust' as an issue of importance, which Matron refuses to consider, while Meakin requests that Matron address them by their Christian names. This is also rejected for being against the rules. The focus is upon obedience and rules rather than learning or rehabilitation. The session ends with the boys in mutinous, self-imposed silence.

The way in which *Scum* reinforces the system of rules and unquestioning duty and responsibility actively rejects more progressive ideas about discipline and punishment which surfaced in the 1960s. The rejection of such idealism can also be read elsewhere in the text, for example, vegetarianism is shown to be merely a device for Archer to cause as much trouble to the borstal management as possible. He actively considers becoming a vegan and refuses to attend the church serves due to his self-professed atheism. All of these ideologies are shown to be utterly self-serving; he infuriates the prison warden by pondering a conversion to Islam. Archer is the only character within the film with the capacity to see himself outside the system and to comment upon the system itself. Through his acuity, intelligence and unorthodox methods of survival he emerges from the film as the bearer of its social and political message. The words of Roy Minton find resonance within the character and articulate the hopelessness of the current system, the lack of self-worth felt by the majority of the boys and the insolvable nature of the problem. Archer is a worthy successor to Mick Travis and Alex Delarge, yet unlike these characters, Archer is never permitted to beat the system.

While it is possible to read into the text the utter rejection of the notions of creative childrearing and education, vegetarianism and religion, nature and self-sufficiency which had emerged during the 1960s and early 1970s, the film also articulates a stronger message about authority and the re-emergence of the Right. The film's nihilism is particularly evident in its denouncement of patriarchy and it deliberately calls attention to the structures within the institution and how inmates and guards collude with established traditions.

It is easy to consider the establishment of patriarchy within *Scum* as an affirmation of masculinity under threat within an uncertain social period, yet this is too simplistic. Instead of a positive depiction of strength and resilience through community, shared experience and identity, masculinity is presented as reactive, violently aggressive and unequivocal. This reaffirmation of the strength of patriarchy can be tentatively linked back to the turbulent social period which was characterised by the collapse of the trade unions, widespread unemployment and the closure of traditionally masculine industries such as mining, but the film also articulates a response to the challenges of youth. As Archer reasons with one of the prison guards, 'I am only concerned about men being stripped of their dignity – cons and screws. We aren't much different in here you know.' The theme of out-of-control youth had already been seen in British cinema, notably in *If...*, yet again within this film, youth culture triumphs over existing institutions. In *Quadrophenia* (1979) Jimmy (Phil Daniels) celebrates his freedom in one final daring leap, effectively winning out against the system. *Scum* never suggests a triumph of youth over experience. Instead, Clarke and Minton highlight the ineffectual and limited protests which take place within the borstal, and how the system deals with such breaches of discipline. There is never any doubt as to the establishment of male power within the films; as Carlin affirms as he stands over Banks' bleeding body, 'I'm the Daddy now.' Carlin may be the self-proclaimed Daddy ruling over the other boys, but this status is only permitted with the collusion of the guards. When Carlin refuses to use his authority he is punished. The rules of patriarchy are clear and immovable and despite the similarities constantly drawn between the older boys and the prison guards, there is a clear hierarchy at work which is vigorously enforced when challenged.

Females are rarely referred to within the text and the only female character to feature is the formidable and unsympathetic Matron. Matron is presented as part of the system, is deliberately de-feminised in her dress and is devoid of feminine qualities. The absence of feminine characters suggests once again the importance of the patriarchal system, yet within the text, the younger more vulnerable male characters are deliberately feminised. The rape of Davis feminises the character and renders him sexually passive. Such sexual passivity and the violent and forced penetration of the child-like Davis within the domestic space of the greenhouse locates him as the female substitute. Davis's suffering firmly reinforces the dominance of both masculinity and patriarchy which render him both worthless and feminine. The illiterate and youthful Woods is also characterised as feminine and vulnerable, reliant upon Archer to help him decipher his letters from home. Woods represents the innocence, the youth and the optimism of childhood. He receives supportive and encouraging letters from his parents – although he is unable to read them – and his unaffected pleasure in the receipt of these letters offers some of the most poignant and comical moments in the film. Woods has retained his youthful exuberance even within the conditions of the borstal, yet he is treated with contempt by the housemaster who sees his academic limitations as failure. Both Davis and Woods are victims of the system and neither conforms to the dominant rules of patriarchy which the film so clearly establishes.

In addition to its important thematic and visual concerns, what makes *Scum* such a significant film is the way in which it was prepared for cinematic release and how test audiences' responses were used to help inform marketing and publicity decisions. Such deliberate marketing based on similar research may have been typical for films made in the period, yet few records survive. The audience response material for *Scum* found in the Don Boyd papers is useful and detailed, but is not without its limitations. The sample used was very small, with only 23 respondents, only seven females and only seven over 25.[33] The way the questions were structured illustrate that the production company was interested in gauging the audience's responses to specific aspects of the film. Firstly, how audiences described the film after viewing. Secondly, how they responded to individual scenes. Thirdly, what would constitute an appropriate audience for the film and if they would recommend it. Finally, they were asked how they rated the film. As can be seen from the data, the most popular term to describe the film was 'violent,' with 21 out of 23 respondents agreeing to this definition. 'Rough,' 'tense,' 'worthwhile' and 'frightening' also emerged as important terms amongst respondents, while none considered the film 'boring' or 'gentle' and only one considered it 'mainly fiction,' 'not believable' and 'relaxing.' Other terms used to describe the film, were 'true to life,' which garnered 12 responses, 'based on fact,' 'a documentary' and 'serious,' which all received 11. Only five respondents felt the film was 'exaggerated.' All this evidence suggests that the film could be and was viewed in a generally positive way and that the documentary and non-sensationalist style was identified as a visible strength. Paradoxically, the film would later be termed sensationalist by reviewers, whilst the 'true to life' and 'documentary' qualities identified by the test audiences were largely downplayed in the marketing of the film.

The selected scenes which elicited the most responses of 'extremely interested' were the riot scene and the scene in which Archer daubs 'I am happy' on the wall, each of which received 13 responses. Neither of these scenes is gratuitously violent, but instead show rebellion by the inmates. Such data suggest that some audience members considered such rebellion against the system to be more interesting than the violence. Other significant trends within the responses were the number of scenes involving the prison staff. Fourteen respondents were 'quite interested' in scenes where officers provoke Carlin into a fight, Carlin being punched by the Warden and Angel being beaten up by the Warden. This would again indicate that some of the well-received aspects of the film were presentations of institutional violence and racism. The only significant scene which was perceived to be 'of no interest' by a large number of respondents, was, predictably, the greenhouse scene where Davis is raped.

When the test audience were asked whom they thought the film would appeal to, the highest responses were, 'those aged 21–24,' which elicited 22 responses, 'those aged 18–20,' which received 21 and 'those aged 16–17,' which received 19. Clearly, the film was felt to be unsuitable for children under 16 with only three respondents deeming it suitable for a young audience and none considering it suitable for 'the whole family.' When considering the groups most likely to go and see the film, the highest figures were 'adults only,' with 17 responses and 'parents with teenage children,' which received 16 responses.

When it came to their own feelings about the film, the majority of the test audience rated the film either, 'good,' 'very good' or 'excellent' with 18 out of the 23 responses falling into these three categories. Whilst the largest group of male respondents (43%) placed the film within the 'very good' category, five out of the seven female respondents (71%) placed it within the 'good' category. The other two females considered the film to be 'excellent' and 'poor,' respectively. Although it is difficult to generalise on the female responses due to the size of the sample, it is important to note that not all the females consider the film to be 'poor' or 'fair' but that a clear majority felt that it was a 'good' film.

Another interesting indication from the data is that personal responses to the film do not directly correlate with the recorded responses about seeing the film. Despite only two respondents labelling the film as 'poor – one of the worst pictures I have ever seen,' over a quarter of the 23 respondents claimed that they 'would not see this film under any circumstances.' However, the largest single response to this question saw almost 40% of the respondents declare, 'I would definitely see this film,' a response which far exceeds the number of respondents who rated the film as 'excellent.' Perhaps the distinction needs to be made between the personal responses to the film, which were often not entirely positive, and the recognition of the *importance* of the film and its message. When asked if they would recommended the film, 48% agreed that they would 'recommend the film to *some* people I know,' while a further 34% stated, 'I would recommend it to *most* people I know.' Once these figures are combined, 82% of the test audience respondents felt that they would recommend the film to most or some of the people that they knew. This would suggest an overall positive response to the film and perhaps indicates that the importance of the narrative overcame some of the distasteful elements of the film, thus creating a film that *should* be seen and that was both significant and important, regardless of personal response to the material.

When it came to rating the film, no respondent considered that the film merited either a one or a two out of ten, and most respondents rated it either nine or ten. In total, 60% of all the respondents rated the film seven out of ten or above. Of the male respondents, 62% rated the film eight out of ten or higher, while the female respondents were more varied, rating the film between four and ten with a mean average of six.

Although interesting, these data must be viewed cautiously. However, some tentative conclusions can be drawn and perhaps corroborated by considering how these data were used to promote the film. Once the audience research was concluded and the results fed back to the production company, executive producer Michael Relph expressed concern about the way the film was being marketed:

> I should have thought that the audience perception figures indicate that there is little problem about appeal to the 16-24 male audience but a great danger that older audiences and females in particular will be put off. The female antipathy is particularly serious because male companions who would otherwise like to see the film will be dissuaded by their girlfriends.[34]

Publicist Laurence Myers responded:

> I would agree that we have been uncompromising in our efforts to get to this audience, the risk of possibly alienating the rest of the public... Nevertheless it is our intention to hit that young market

on the broadest possible level, which by definition is not the most sophisticated.[35]

Deliberately targeting a young, predominantly male audience, suggests that some of the important information indicated by the audience responses was ignored. While females did not respond as positively to the film as some of the male respondents, five out of the seven female respondents considered *Scum* to be 'about as good as most other pictures' and six out of seven agreed they would recommend it to 'some people.' These responses are not negative, and instead indicate that the female audience needed to be convinced by careful marketing. Instead, by focusing on the violent, exciting content and the 'X' certificate, the marketing campaign not only targeted the male audience, thus negating the opinions offered by the female respondents, it also failed to capitalise on the insights provided into the film's less obvious qualities. Indeed, it is possible to see in the use of the 'X' certificate a deliberate decision to embrace this category and its attendant controversy, rather than attempt to use the informative and educational aspects of the narrative, identified by the test audience to negotiate with the censor for a lower category.

Many of the respondents agreed that the film was 'worthwhile,' 'a documentary,' 'true to life' and 'based on fact.' These responses suggest that the film could have been presented in a more thoughtful way to capitalise on its realism and authenticity to appeal to a more thoughtful and discerning audience. Relph considered that this aspect of the film was being overlooked and suggested:

> The advertising should indicate that there are qualities in the film other than brutality and violence of an elementary kind.... I think the present poster to be crude and unsuitable in a most off putting way with the emphasis on the X harking back to the early days of X certificates in a most old-fashioned way. The lettering and colouring is crudely basic, the photographs do not register and the slogan is unconvincingly contrived.[36]

The slogan 'In Borstal survival rules' was eventually adapted for the film and fits in well with the sensationalist marketing campaign which, as the publicity company confirmed, was entirely deliberate:

> The design of the *Scum* poster was arrived at after an enormous amount of consideration. It certainly is crudely basic, purposely so,

in order to appeal to the under thirties who we believe on any basis will constitute 75-80% of the audience for this film.[37]

This selling of the film as sensational and exciting rather than thought-provoking and serious, can be seen as evidence of the Parsons strategy of selling the film based upon its 'exciting story' rather than any political message focus on social issues. Relph firmly believed that the film should try and market itself alongside 'quality' films by:

> Suggesting a touch of class by its advertising and emphasising the human elements of the film by identifying individual characters.... surely something like this would be suitable for *Scum* – pulling out the diverse characters and suggesting the emotional and humorous qualities of the film as well as the violent ones.[38]

This desire to sell *Scum* as a 'quality' British film was not be realised and although the marketing was crudely basic, it did ensure that the film received coverage once it was released. Despite a great deal of the critical response being negative and focusing on the violence, such reviews did ensure that the film garnered a great deal of attention. *Films and Filming* claimed; 'it states its case so vigorously that it can hardly help looking like sensationalism' and, 'the film would be an imposition on the eyes were it not so gruesomely enlivened at frequent intervals by vivid atrocities,' whilst the *Monthly Film Bulletin* considered it, 'prurient' and 'lacking a moral perspective.'[39]

An undoubtedly important film within British cinema, *Scum* offers an unrelenting critique of the borstal system, with its dependence on violence, patriarchal order and institutionalisation of young offenders. It is unfortunate that the audience research, which yielded such interesting results was ignored in favour of a more predictable campaign capitalising upon the film's violence, controversial appeal and its 'X' certification. The less than subtle approach moves the film further from the authenticity of the original research and the desire of Clarke and Minton to represent an accurate and realistic portrayal of life within a borstal. Minton's screenplay and Clarke's direction create a text which critiques the borstal while simultaneously drawing attention to a wider social system which allows such institutions to exist. The film's nihilism and narrative resolution reveal the extent to which it is a closed text and may account for its lack of popularity with audiences.

Scum offers the audience a single position from its straightforward and relentless narrative. In this way the film suffers from its television roots with the text and subject matter being much better suited to the medium of television. Subsequent showings of the film on television have garnered much critical attention and the film's success in this medium reinforces how unsuitable the film was for the cinema which privileges visual style over narrative. *Scum* offers very little in terms of visual pleasure. The film is not visually arresting either in its visual style, costumes or locations, yet this is entirely fitting with the institutional setting and draws on residual visual motifs within British cinema, such as those of the New Wave and social realist filmmaking. The film addresses important themes, yet it has consistently been regarded as yet another example of violent and excessive 1970s filmmaking, instead of a careful and thoughtful critique of contemporary social issues and mores.

13

The Tempest: A Brave New World of Creative Endeavour?

With its creative cinematography, innovative set designs and sublime costumes, Derek Jarman's *The Tempest* (1979) is one of the most distinctive and exciting 1970s visual texts. Filmed entirely on location at Stoneleigh Abbey in Warwickshire and Bamburgh Castle in Northumberland and financed by Don Boyd for £150,000, *The Tempest* was an innovative and evocative adaptation. Though lauded for its beauty and vision, some considered that Jarman's film lacked coherence as much of Shakespeare's dialogue and narrative were sacrificed. Jarman's decision to cast non-Shakespearian actors was also heavily criticised, one reviewer termed this decision 'audacious' and the performances of magician and poet Heathcote Williams as Prospero, punk rock singer and actress Toyah Willcox as Miranda and blind physical actor Jack Birkett as Caliban were heavily scrutinised.[1]

Jarman's carefully preserved diaries and notebooks demonstrate how his creative ideas were critical to the construction of the film, yet the visual style was achieved through the work of the talented team he gathered around him which included cinematographer Peter Middleton and designer Yolanda Sonnabend and the financial and creative support of Executive Producer Don Boyd. Although Boyd remains firm in his belief that *The Tempest* was Jarman's own 'unique brilliant creation,' he does acknowledge that he was 'heavily involved' in the creative elements of the film and that Jarman welcomed his input.[2]

While there is a strong tradition within British cinema of adaptation of Shakespeare's work, Jarman's adaptation of *The Tempest* is an entirely different visualisation from previous re-workings of Shakespeare's play, and it differs significantly from the source text. As George Bluestone argues, adaptations do more than simply convert one medium into another and in many cases the raw material of the original text is entirely refashioned.[3] This idea of remodelling the text fits in perfectly with Jarman's approach to *The Tempest* and within his wider working practices. The eclecticism of Jarman's influences as well as the restructuring of the text in order to make it more cinematic, firmly positions Jarman's *The Tempest* as a film which draws upon the narrative and characters of the original play, yet develops all these elements in a entirely new and original way. In an interview with the author, Don Boyd termed Jarman's adaptation 'a masterpiece,' which was 'an astonishingly brilliant cinema evocation of the Shakespeare play which the Bard would have loved too.'[4] As Boyd recognises, the film is an evocation or translation, rather than an adaptation and should not be considered as such nor criticised for its lack of fidelity to the source text. Jarman's interpretation presages Peter Greenaway's *Prospero's Books* (1991), which also utilised Shakespeare's play in a way which rejected much of the narrative and many of the characters, yet still owes much to the original material.

Jarman himself considered *The Tempest*: 'the most extraordinary of Shakespeare's plays [...] the one which is most misunderstood.'[5] He believed that the play was 'Shakespeare's most personal and internalised comment on his conditions' which effectively captured 'the loneliness of the old poet at odds with the society in which he lives.'[6] Jarman was convinced that *The Tempest* reflected Shakespeare's dissatisfaction with Jacobean England following the vibrant and progressive Elizabethan age. In a commentary which accompanies the film on DVD, Toyah Willcox suggests that the isolation of both Prospero and of Shakespeare remained an enduring fascination for Jarman, noting, 'Derek had an understanding of what it was like to be dispossessed and to be judged.'[7] Jarman was keenly aware that he could take liberties with Shakespeare's text and offer a new interpretation of the play which utilised his own creative ideas in a style which Gomez considers as part of the 'British non-realist tradition of visual excess.'[8] Certainly visual excess is evident throughout the film, culminating in the flamboyant masque sequence which is a riotous pageant of 'camp sensibility' replete with gay sailors, gold leaf and Elisabeth Welch as 'The Goddess.'[9] When discussing the inclusion of the song 'Stormy Weather' in the film, Willcox speculated that its inclusion was linked to the storm at the start of the play, whereas cinematographer Peter Middleton believed that it was simply a whim of Jarman's and that 'he didn't need a reason,' offering an intriguing insight into Jarman's creative working practices.'[10]

Jarman's own interests are discernible within the film, particularly his preoccupations with magic and the occult as well as his fervent interest in the Renaissance. His fascination with this historical period was first realised in *Jubilee* (1977) and was a period to which he would return in *Caravaggio* (1986) and his adaptation of Marlowe's *Edward II* (1991). However, within *The Tempest* it is possible to discern influences from a multiplicity of historical periods with evidence of the Gothic in the costumes, lighting and visual style. Jarman's background as an artist and his attention to historical detail are perhaps two of the most important contributions to his adaptation of *The Tempest*. His creative and entirely deliberate sampling from different historical periods creates an unsettling and often confusing text. Such sampling allows the viewer to interpret the meaning of the film and to take whatever references they chose. Although history is being utilised within Jarman's film, it is being used in a very deliberate way. The past is not simply being celebrated but rather being made useful as it is re-fashioned for the present.

The film recreates images from classical art and sculpture, notably in the scenes with Ferdinand and Miranda. Within the wedding masque sequence, Miranda appears without her childish plaits, with her white-blond hair held underneath an enormous hat festooned with lace veil, feathers and sheaves of corn. In her pose and in her dress with its intricate ruffles and garlands, she closely resembles the famous Vigee-Lebrun portraits of Marie Antoinette or the Gainsborough portrait of Georgiana, Duchess of Devonshire. This level of intricate detail specifically references a distinct historical era while simultaneously allowing conflicting historical influences; the sheaves of corn in the hair of Elisabeth Welch, the white-gloved Ariel, the hornpipe-dancing sailors. All these elements conflict with the classically posed and dressed Miranda, yet ultimately combine in a scene which refuses to commit itself to a single visual influence or a defined historical period. Jarman's historical preoccupations are not limited to classical moments from British history but rather represent an eclectic bricolage of European historical influences in a manner reminiscent of Shakespeare's own use of classical and historical references. Jarman felt that the film should not be confined to any specific era, period or location, believing instead that the right setting would allow the film to be 'timeless – a twilight never-never land.'[11]

Correspondence from designer and artist Christopher Hobbs who had worked on *Jubilee* further reveals the ideas of timelessness which are utilised in *The Tempest*. Hobbs wrote to Jarman in 1976, suggesting:

> In the house, not only should one see strange people doing strange things, but strange objects of all times i.e. a table with geometric forms white as eggs, a computer element (or something equally

space-age) on rich rotting velvet covered in dust under a glass dome (which obviously might link with Ariel's digital watch).[12]

Hobbs' ideas were accompanied by a detailed illustration of the table he so vividly describes, as well as a sketch of a mythical set complete with pyramids, stone lions and obelisks.[13] Although much of this did not feature in the final film, the rotting velvet and mysterious geometrical forms are part of Prospero's magical paraphernalia and the chalk cabalistic drawings on the floors feature mythical symbols which include Egyptian hieroglyphics. Here again is the creative and artistic sampling which dramatically invokes the Gothic style with its heavy fabrics, chirascuro lighting, symbols and columns.

In the press book for the film, Jarman elaborates on his historical placement of *The Tempest*: 'the film is not set in the Elizabethan period of Shakespeare, nor is it modern. Rather it is an indistinct past, a conglomerate of many styles emphasising the timelessness of the play.'[14] David Hawkes considers that 'Jarman's treatment of Marlowe's *Edward II* and Shakespeare's *The Tempest* call attention to these play's mediations on identity, sexuality and history,' yet Jarman does not focus on these issues to the exclusion of all else and instead utilises time and location in a playful, often contradictory non-narrative way to address these issues.[15] As Harris and Jackson note, 'Jarman jettisons the bulk of the dialogue and reorders much of what he keeps [...] [he] breaks Shakespeare's scenes into smaller units which he interweaves.'[16] Jarman moves around a great deal of the dialogue in order to focus the narrative upon the themes and events which he deems important. One of the more significant changes he makes is reducing the role and function of the courtiers. In eliminating the minor characters of Francisco and Adrian and reducing the lengthy plotting between Sebastian and Antonio, Jarman refocuses the text around the respective plots of Prospero, Caliban and Ariel and the courtship of Ferdinand and Miranda. The reduction of the courtier scenes serves to make the play much more suitable for the cinema; key plot elements are retained but are predominantly established through atmosphere rather than extensive dialogue. Perhaps most important is the omission of the politics which have such an important part in the original play. References to the political machinations of Alonso, Sebastian and Prospero are all removed, suggesting that Jarman's preoccupations were elsewhere.

Jarman stated in an interview that he only ever made the films that he wanted to make and that *The Tempest* was no exception.[17] While Jarman's authorship of the project is not in question, his vision was brought to the screen with the help of the technically innovative and gifted creative team he gathered around him. Although the film utilised many of the same technical crew who had worked with Jarman on *The Devils* (1971), the director himself acknowledged that on *The Tempest* 'there was a co-operation and pooling of ideas that went beyond anything in my previous projects. My real role was as a kind of ringmaster.'[18] While Jarman's interest in *The Tempest* dated back to his school days and his notebooks document his personal and passionate attachment to the project, his directorial style permitted individual creative autonomy to flourish. In a *Time Out* interview in 1980, Jarman explained his approach to filming *The Tempest*, 'I had a very strong view about interpretation which I buried when we got to making the film. When it came to reality faced with real people, I didn't want to impose an intellectual conception of the play.'[19] Although the film was a labour of love for Jarman, he was willing to allow other people's skills to contribute to his vision and this is a testament to his directorial style. In an interview shortly after the film's release, Toyah Willcox commented on Jarman's approach to filmmaking:

> The good thing about a Jarman movie is that you can say to the lighting men, 'Why don't you put some light over there?' and they won't go 'Fuck off, you're not in the union.' It's a joint thing, Derek creates that kind of magic. I've never met anyone that creates the atmosphere he can create.[20]

Jarman's thoughtful directorial approach allowed his technical crew and actors some creative autonomy. It is possible that Jarman was permitting collaboration, yet remained firmly wedded to his vision and the only ideas that were incorporated into the film were the ones which he personally selected.

In a recent interview with the author, executive producer Don Boyd revealed that he was actively involved in all aspects of production on *The Tempest* from 'conception, casting, rushes, editing and mix.'[21] Such involvement suggests that Boyd's role on the film was not that of a typical producer. Boyd remembers that Jarman used him as 'an important, consistent and trustworthy creative partner,' a description which supports the idea of a producer involved in a film both artistically and financially.[22] Boyd's occupation of this creative-producer role is similar to that of the position often assumed by David Puttnam in the decade and indicates a break from previous production practices within British cinema. Boyd's contribution to *The Tempest* was not solely financial, though his commitment to the project did enable Jarman to realise a much-desired project. Perhaps most importantly he trusted Jarman and gave him the space in which to make his film, allowing for an easy and productive working relationship.

Jarman also considered his technical crew for *The Tempest* to have been 'a very good gang,' with important members including cinematographer Peter Middleton who had worked on *Sebastiane* (1976) and *Jubilee*, experienced art director Ian Whittaker, and newcomer Yolanda Sonnabend who designed the set and the costumes.[23] Cinematographer Peter Middleton remembers that during filming of *The Tempest* the day-to-day filming decisions were left up to him. In an interview to accompany the release of the film on DVD, Middleton recalled, 'Derek Jarman wasn't a technical director, we just did it and he just tagged along [...] [I was] very much left to my own devices.'[24] He remembers that shooting began in early 1979 but after a few days of reviewing the rushes, he and Jarman were both unimpressed by the progress made, so began shooting everything again! This suggests not only a collaborative process, but also the clarity of Jarman's vision and the way he imagined the finished film. Middleton also recalls that Jarman was satisfied with a small number of takes and was, 'a bit economical' with his retakes, usually preferring the first take of most of the scenes.[25]

Middleton's cinematography helped create the world Jarman desired, 'a mesmeric, alienated world of deserted rooms, ghosts, ESP and hypnotism.'[26] The scenes within the decaying rooms of Stoneleigh Abbey are all shot in partial darkness. The candlelight, which appears to light the interior scenes was achieved through huge table lamps placed off camera and the shadows cast by this technique created a claustrophobic atmosphere. The actors slip in and out of the shadows, with specific characters utilising the darkness and light in particular ways. Ariel and Prospero both lurk in shadows, many times standing motionless and unlit within a scene before moving into the line of the camera and into the pools of light. This visual effect also allows for character and narrative devices to be achieved; the spirit-like, all-seeing quality which both characters possess within the film is linked to their movements and is enhanced by the lighting. Such deliberate movements are suggestive of a gothic nightmare and evoke the visual world of German Expressionism, which Jarman cited as one of his influences for the film. In his diary for autumn 1974, Jarman noted that his planned film would 'take great freedom... The main body of the film will be in black and white, shot like a German expressionist horror

(*Nosferatu*) with deep shadows and highlights and atmospheric rather than natural lighting.'[27] The visual inspiration for the film that Jarman describes here can clearly be seen in the finished text, yet it was also the setting of Stoneleigh Abbey which contributed so significantly to the film's crafted atmosphere.[28] The Abbey's function as a former aristocratic home, now partially derelict, also implies the decline of the old social order which is highlighted more explicitly in *The Go-Between*. Peter Middleton suggested that the desolate, fire-ravaged and partially furnished Abbey was the perfect location for the film and that there was 'very little set dressing at all... mainly wheelbarrows and logs.' Material from an undated scenario for the film articulates Jarman's thoughts on his interior location:

> The gothic manner of the film is enforced by situating the film in the empty rooms of Stoneleigh Abbey which reveal strange perspectives and corridors, off which rooms full of surprises are opened like Chinese boxes. With the ghostly elegance of the rooms, one is always at a degree of disorientation inside this vast location [...] Many rooms are empty, others reveal Magritte like images.[29]

Jarman also felt that the bleakness of the interior locations fitted in well with what he wanted for the exterior location shooting. Bamburgh Castle in Northumberland served as a location for the exterior shots, while the nearby windswept and snow-covered beaches were used for the few island scenes. These scenes are bathed in a clinical light using blue filters which drain most of the colour from these sequences. Instead of creating Prospero's world of magic and illusion with sinister light, harsh and artificial lighting is used for the exterior shots. The cluttered and confusing world within the castle walls, although heavily stylised, is presented more realistically than the deliberately artificial outside world with its unforgiving light, painted backdrops and barren emptiness. The isolation of the locations and the frequent shifts in camera angle and perspective create a disorientating effect in keeping with Prospero's machinations and Jarman's own desires to present his narrative as a dreamlike thread, reliant more upon atmosphere than narrative. The camerawork, the lighting and the way in which the locations are used all combine to create a distinctive and unusual visual style for the film which owes a great deal to experienced art director Ian Whittaker.

Whittaker had worked on a range of important 1970s films including *The Music Lovers* (1970), *The Devils*, *The Boyfriend* (1971), *Savage Messiah* (1972), *Tommy* (1975) and *Lisztomania* (1975) for Ken Russell, as well as *Swallows and Amazons* (1974), *The Rocky Horror Picture Show* (1975) and *Joseph Andrews* (1977). Whittaker would later contribute to the success of productions as diverse as *Alien* (1979) and *Sense and Sensibility* (1995) and win an Oscar for his work on *Howards End* (1992). Although Whittaker had worked with Jarman on both *The Devils* and *Savage Messiah*, *The Tempest* was his first involvement in a Jarman-directed production. Working with Whittaker was film design novice Yolanda Sonnabend. Sonnabend had predominantly worked in the theatre, creating set designs for the English National Ballet and the Royal Shakespeare Company for productions of *Cinderella*, *Swan Lake*, *The Nutcracker* and *Anthony and Cleopatra*.[30] Her stunning production design for *The Tempest* creates a textured and detailed history and narrative as well as suggesting important character depth. It is significant that Sonnabend was given a huge responsibility on Jarman's film. Much as Ken Russell had offered him an early opportunity, Jarman himself offered Sonnabend her first and only opportunity to design a feature film. Although her film experience was limited, her years at the Slade School of Fine Art – where Jarman also studied – coupled with her theatrical experience, provided Sonnabend with the skills to create a sensitive and memorable design for the production.

The exterior locations are enhanced by painted backdrops reminiscent of stage scenery, which create an oppressive and constricted space and limit the boundaries of the island. The parameters of the island are clearly within the rooms of the abbey and on the beach; the island is not a limitless expanse and everyone outside the abbey eventually finds their way within its walls. The interior rooms of the abbey are a maze of dark corridors and contradictory furnishings; elaborate chandeliers hang from the ceilings, antique mouldings and period furniture grace rooms full of straw and dead leaves. Rich, decayed velvet hangings recall the sumptuousness and opulence of an earlier age. The wealth of textual detail adds to a sense of decaying hopelessness; the stuccoed walls, marble mantelpieces and the striped wallpaper are concealed by cobwebs and charred curtains. One review would later consider the film a 'bric-à-brac brainstorm' and this perfectly encapsulates the creative, innovative and exciting design.[31]

There are also visual touches throughout which draw attention to both Jarman and Sonnabend's background in painting. In the first scene where Miranda and Ferdinand are alone together, they sit side by side on a brocaded and gilded *chaise-lounge*. The camera pulls back to frame the couple: Miranda seated demurely with her hands folded in her lap with her back straight and Ferdinand turned slightly towards her with outstretched hands. This heavily stylised yet perfectly recreated tableaux of an aristocratic couple, is reminiscent of a classical 18th Century painting. It is only as this scene develops that this perfect tableau is shown to be false. There is straw, not carpet or polished wood on the floor of the chamber, while the wheelbarrow full of logs and the tools of the manual worker, through which Ferdinand must win his freedom, all subvert the aristocratic image. Such touches within the staging and set design make the film much more than a beautiful visual feast and the clever design drew great acclaim from the critics. Philip French considered it 'a gothic extravaganza [...] a darkly comic box of theatrical tricks,' while *Screen International* felt it was 'a feast of visual delights most ingeniously achieved without a lavish budget.'[32]

Sonnabend's contribution to the film was not limited to the set design, she also designed the costumes which are such an integral part of the film's visual style. Back in 1975 Jarman considered that the costumes for his production would be 'renaissance and very accurate and simple.'[33] Yet this early decision was unrealised in the finished film, and costume became an important aspect of the text where historical authenticity was avoided in favour of deliberate anachronism. The sequinned golden gown worn by Elisabeth Welch, combined with gold leaf cap and yellow feathers and corn-sheaves is fantastic rather than historically situated, while Ariel's white boiler suit and string vest are deliberately modern and possibly reference Jarman himself. Wymer considers that these anachronisms 'opened up the possibility of a living relationship between past, present and future,' yet Jarman does not utilise history and historical objects to draw out differences between past and present.[34] Instead, he creates a smorgasbord of visual codes and references in which the past and the present are offered to the viewer seemingly without distinction or discrimination, enabling them to select and sample as they choose.

Prospero's ruffled shirt, unkempt hair, lace cuffs and velvet waistcoat invoke a dissolute nobleman fallen on hard times, whilst also referencing the gothic flamboyance of the Elizabethan, Georgian or Regency periods. Such a design suggests Sonnabend's influence, for in his notebooks Jarman believed that Prospero should wear a 'black shiny costume like Robespierre.'[35] While the reference to Robespierre continues to locate the film at the end of the 18th Century, the sumptuous fabrics and textures which form such a vital part of Prospero's costumes reflect the theatrical background of the designer. The wisps of net and lace which adorn Miranda's dresses and the feathers, beads and pearls in her hair are straight out of *Giselle* or *Swan Lake* and deliberately soften the character.

Willcox remembers Sonnabend's contribution to Miranda's costumes, 'she was so creative, so wonderful [...] dressing a virgin child in a skeleton structure which represented femininity but also represented abandonment as well [...] everything lent itself to character.'[36]

Willcox recalls how she herself had firm ideas about the character and how Sonnabend incorporated such suggestions into her designs, particularly for the costumes. Willcox stated, 'I tried to do her femininity by her being creative; wearing masks, a fan, or putting shells on the dress. I wanted the hair in plaits because she wouldn't know how to style her hair.'[37] The embellished dress which Miranda wears for the majority of the film is closely fitted, yet allows for childish scampering, indicating both the child-like dressing up which such a costume suggests and the burgeoning sexuality of the low-cut and heavily boned corset. The pearls in her hair imply virgin purity but the dreadlock plaits which hold them in place suggest the child far removed from the outward sophistication of a dress of lace, feathers, satin and tulle. The heavy skirts and shape of the dress is again suggestive of the courtly wear of the 1800s, whilst her use of the skeletal fan she plays with when she first glimpses Ferdinand mimics the skilful coquette. As she approaches the sleeping Ferdinand, Miranda flutters her fan, aping the tricks of flirtation, yet the gaps within the sticks allow her to peep through like a child with enthusiasm and candour.

Wymer considers that, for Jarman, *The Tempest* was partially concerned with 'the loss of childhood' and certainly childhood and maturity is a key theme which runs through the set designs and costumes of the child-woman Miranda.[38] Her sexual awareness is implied by the 'riding' of the rocking horse during which she chants the marriage ritual as she has seen Ariel do, she mimics his behaviour and in doing so acquires sexual knowledge, yet the singsong cadence of her voice carries with it suggestions of the nursery rhyme to accompany child-like play on a favourite toy. Yet again, she is both child and woman carefully positioned on the cusp of adolescence; sometimes the leggy and graceless tomboy, at other times a sexually predatory female. For Willcox, this paradox was a central part of her performance. She considered that Miranda was motivated by her 'uncontrolled sexual desire when her sexuality is awakened but [she is] also a wild survival child.'[39] This combination of child and adult is rendered yet more important when considering that the original Miranda would have been more likely to have been in her early rather than late teens. The play was conceived many years before Victorian ideals of childhood were first considered and the young upper-class girls of the Elizabethan and Jacobean age were often married at 14 or 15. As Shakespeare observed about 15-year-old Juliet, 'younger than she are happy mothers made.' The childlike behaviour of Miranda throughout the film acts as a bridge to link in ideas of precocious sexuality, behaviour and knowledge with more modern conception of childhood and adolescence.

Caliban's clothes are a parody of a butler's uniform, and his shapeless shuffling is perfectly contained within his over-large coat and cumbersome shoes. Both Trinculo and Stephano are dressed according to their characters as sailor and cook but Trinculo casts off his clothes to romp in Miranda's wardrobe with wild abandon. He emerges with fan, feathers and mask, deliberately feminising an already feminine persona. In the final scenes he is elaborately costumed and grotesquely made up with rouge and false eyelashes as a parody of femininity. Trinculo, Stephano and Miranda all play with gendered characteristics, deliberately subverting sexual stereotypes and demonstrating that previously defined gendered positions and characteristics are similar to costumes which can be assumed at will. In his notebooks, Jarman noted that Antonio and Sebastian were to be dressed as Guards officers, while in the film Antonio is dressed like a Cossack soldier with a black military greatcoat with epaulettes and Sebastian is a bespectacled cardinal.[40] Some of the military associations Jarman intended remain, yet Sonnabend's costumes become more nuanced, with the exact implications of Sebastian's rosary beads and Antonio's jackboots being open to interpretation. Again, this allows for a range of inferences to be drawn from the costumes, while still maintaining their simple narrative function. In allowing Sonnabend to moderate his vision, Jarman's authorial intentions become slightly obscured, which fits in perfectly with the multiplicity of historical and textual meanings deployed elsewhere throughout the film.

Drawing on the stunning sets, costumes and locations and aided by atmospheric lighting and cinematography, the cast began translating Jarman's vision to the final film. Jarman had always considered that in his adaptation, 'the actors with the exception of the Prospero will not be the sort of actors normally associated with a conventional Shakespeare production.'[41]

While this is true, many of Jarman's ideas about character were transformed as the project evolved. Jarman initially envisaged Caliban as 'the natural islander, black and very beautiful,' while prior to Elizabeth Welch's involvement, the trio of Caliban, Stephano and Trinculo were to have played Ceres, Juno and Isis in the concluding masque sequence, all garbed as goddesses in drag![42] As Jarman himself recognised, it was impossible to retain his intellectual vision of the play when confronted with actors who brought such individuality to the project. The characters and resulting performances are perhaps best considered as a fusion of Jarman's initial ideas and creative inspirations coupled with contributions from the individual actors. For example, Williams' Prospero incorporates many of Jarman's early ideas, while also bringing elements of his own persona to the multifaceted character. Unlike Willcox, he does not appear to struggle with the iambic pentameter, yet manages to present a menacingly patriarchal figure tempered with wry humour and mockery. One of the keys to this powerful performance is the way in which Williams uses his voice. Instead of loudly declaiming, he softly ponders and muses. Willcox remembers this as a 'wonderful quality' of Williams and such a deliberately controlled performance helps to humanise his Prospero, as does Jarman's decision to cut out many of the lengthy soliloquies.[43] Although at times frightening, sadistic and benevolent, Williams truly represents the poet and sage that Jarman envisaged Prospero to be; peering over his half-moon glasses, crouched on the floor examining his chalk markings and muttering to himself by candlelight, he evokes the absent-minded professor. Jarman always envisaged Prospero as a possessor of knowledge rather than an exiled nobleman. In 1975, he felt that his Prospero was 'given over to cabbalistic pursuits and [was] the possessor of esoteric knowledge [...] [he] loses contact with the reality necessary to cope with the daily affairs of a renaissance prince.'[44] Visually, Jarman considered Prospero to be 'haggard and withdrawn but [he] has obviously possessed great and charismatic beauty which he has sacrificed in his pursuit of knowledge.'[45]

In early 1975, Jarman was considering utilising the character of Prospero as a combination of Caliban, Ariel, Miranda and Ferdinand. He felt that these different characters were all warring parts of the Prospero's own personality. Jarman noted:

Within his personality, Prospero contains the spirit of Ariel – fire and ice - and also its obverse – Caliban, earth and water. Continually at war – Miranda his female animal and Ferdinand a vision backwards in time of his youth – both are possessed of great beauty. It would be necessary for the actor who plays Prospero to convince us that these four characters are divergent parts of his persona.[46]

Within the film it is initially unclear if Ariel is a visual presence or simply a voice within Prospero's mind. The themes of madness and insanity run throughout the course of the play, and Williams' performance as the single-minded cabbalistic sorcerer is presented as scholarly madness, whose frightening and obsessive preoccupations add a sinister layer to the character. In an interview following the production of the film, Williams claimed that Prospero was 'a psychopath in a sensory deprived chamber' and within his performance, much of the narrative action is focused around the character's whims, ideas, pleasures and tantrums.[47] While David Hawkes considers that Prospero is 'an overtly sadistic tyrant,' it is insufficient to simply see him as a vengeful sorcerer.[48] Indeed, the interpretation offered by Williams conforms more closely to Jarman's own ideas about the 'divergent parts of his persona' and this can be seen most closely in his relationship with Ariel. The relationship between the two characters is complex; at times they are mischievous collaborators or rivals, yet always remain as master and servant. At key points within scenes the camera shifts from one to the other, with Ariel appearing where Prospero was standing and cutting quickly between the two characters as if to suggest their similarities. Within the frame they are often located opposite one another as if to suggest two halves of a whole.

While the idea of Ariel as part of Prospero's own personality can be seen in aspects of Williams' performance as Prospero, Karl Johnson's presentation of Ariel resists such categorisation. Ariel is bonded to Prospero through servitude, yet at the same time is entirely separate and 'othered' by his modernity of dress and manner. Clad in a white boiler suit, string vest and boots with a pearl stud in one ear and white gloves, Ariel is modern and anachronistic, while the boiler suit links him irrevocably to Jarman himself. Johnson's Ariel is forever on the sidelines, out of place and out of time; an observer rather than an active protagonist and visual example of Jarman's contention that the play should be timeless. He acts as a voyeur throughout the play, appearing through closed doors, from behind furniture, and within mirrors. The character interacts with no-one but Prospero, which allows for continued questions to be raised about Prospero's sanity as he converses with a spirit no-one else can see. The positioning of Ariel slightly outside the main narrative could also be seen as indicative of where Jarman placed himself. He referred to his role within the production as a 'ringmaster' and this description could also be used to characterise Ariel; while outside the narrative action, Ariel is the character with all the supernatural power and who acts as master of ceremonies, not just in the final sequence, but throughout the film.

Johnson's Ariel reflects the melancholy aspects of the spirit and even comical moments where he toys with the courtiers and barking like a dog to confound Trinculo, Caliban and Stephano are accompanied with a wistful, mocking smile and a flat, fixed expression. It is not possible to see in Jarman's Ariel the playful spirit which Shakespeare created, yet the loneliness, isolation and claustrophobia which form such critical themes within the play are all discernable within Johnson's performance. His dance with the sailors in the final masque sequence is nostalgic, mournful and stilted, with none of the pantomime elements of performance affected by Trinculo, Caliban or Stephano. The performances of Trinculo and Stephano justify many of the descriptions of Jarman's *The Tempest* as a 'camp' film, as both of these characters affect a camp style of performance which is highly excessive; flamboyant verbal delivery, wild gesticulating movements and visual performance which draws heavily on pantomime. There is very little dialogue given to either character and they exist as camp characters and are the most obvious representation within the production of a gay relationship. Jarman had no doubts about the relationship between them, his annotated script reads, 'Stephano, Alonso's butler is fat, jolly and gay. Trinculo is his tough, rather stupid sailor lover.'[49]

Toyah Willcox's performance has no elements of camp, yet is at times suggestive, comical, childish and awkward. Miranda's lines have been drastically reduced and Willcox utilises a range of performance ideas in order to develop the limited character of the original play. Willcox experimented with mime, gesture, dance and voice to demonstrate character using a range of Brechtian techniques to communicate meaning beyond her limited dialogue and narrative role. When interviewed, Willcox explained that she utilised such techniques to move beyond her discomfort with the dialogue, 'I put everything into mime, it was the only way I could put the part over.'[50] When planning his production, Jarman felt, 'Miranda has no history. She never knows where she came from. She is ignorant of the normal rules of society. She appears to Ferdinand as a nymphomaniac, wild, untamed. Her character is less structured than Caliban's,' while Willcox believed, 'I don't think she's innocent because she doesn't know what innocence was or virginity [...] she was a tribal animal rather than a human being.'[51] Willcox's movements reflect this animalistic quality. She moves fluently but is bouncy and uncoordinated rather than graceful, bending from the waist rather than the knees and scrabbling, squatting and crawling. Her attempts to trip gracefully down the stairs are unsuccessful and she attempts to repeat this performance before quickly tiring of her lack of coordination and grace.

While Caliban uses pantomime gestures and excessive theatricality in a similar way to Trinculo and Stephano, the animalistic qualities attributed to the character by Shakespeare are not realised within the performance of Jack Birkett. Caliban moves with rare grace, which reveals Birkett's extensive experience within physical and experimental theatre. He turns cartwheels on the beach, flops motionless on the sand and trips gracefully down poorly lit stairs with careful dance-like steps, which deliberately contrast with the more clumsy movements of Miranda. There is dance-like fluidity to his movements and despite his physical appearance he is not the sinister and unattractive character who features in Shakespeare's play. Indeed, Jarman wanted to make Caliban sympathetic, with his planned overthrow of Prospero viewed as a legitimate attempt at freedom from an oppressive tyrant.[52] With his thick regional accent, lascivious leer and high-pitched cackle, Birkett's Caliban is a pantomime villain, yet he lacks the menace which is hinted at in the original play. His few interactions with Miranda consist of childish face-pulling and noise-making; when he spies on her as she washes herself, he retreats when she throws her sponge at him and slams the door. Certainly the pain on his face when Prospero stamps upon his fingers and the way he cowers when berated for clumsiness places him as a sympathetic character within the play who is, like Ariel, a victim of Prospero's machinations. While some critical reviewers of the film focused negatively on the performances of the non-Shakespearian actors, much of the critical response to the film was positive.

The film's success within art house theatres was the result of careful marketing and distribution. As part of the Boyd's Co programme of films, *The Tempest* enjoyed success throughout the UK, opening in a selection of art house cinemas in cities including Bristol, Brighton, Oxford and Salisbury.[53] Following a six-week run at the Screen on the Hill in London, the film had cleared over £63,000, an impressive total for an 'art house' film.[54]

When interviewed by the author about the financial prospects of the film, executive producer Don Boyd stated that he always considered 'Derek's audience would cover its [the film's] costs.'[55] The production company was fully aware that the film would never be a straightforward commercial success, but would instead appeal to an art house or avant-garde audience; an audience who had previously enjoyed Jarman's films. Despite his background in experimental film, Jarman disliked being characterised as an avant-garde or artistic filmmaker and simply saw himself as a filmmaker. In an interview following the film's release, Jarman himself questioned the reaction to the film:

> The reaction has been extraordinarily positive; it's the first of my films that people all seem to like. And that worries me slightly, because in a sense, I think it better to be disliked, to be slightly more dangerous as an artist than *The Tempest* allows. I adore *The Tempest* as a play, so obviously, the right reaction is that it shouldn't be controversial and I'm pleased that people like it.[56]

The Tempest was the first of Jarman's films that generated such positive publicity with critics hailing it as, 'bold,' 'imaginative' and 'beguiling.'[57] It also attracted attention from unexpected quarters with the British Council requesting a print of the film in 1982 to screen as part of a programme for 'promotion of British cultural, educational and technological achievements' across the world, and schools began to screen it to accompany the school syllabus.[58]

Despite the positive responses in Britain, much to Jarman's disappointment the film was notably unsuccessful in America. The *New York Times* review was ferocious and likened the production to 'a fingernail scratched along a blackboard, sand in spinach, a 33 rpm record recording of *Don Giovanni* played at 78 rpm.'[59] Such a scathing critique from this powerful newspaper effectively ended any chance the film had of success in America. When interviewed shortly before his death, Jarman revealed that it was not just that the film was reviewed poorly in America that was so upsetting, but also that its financial failure within the US meant his future projects could not be funded using American profits.[60] Such an awareness of the way in which the film industry operated demonstrates that although Jarman located himself firmly outside mainstream commercial cinema, he was by no means impervious to the financial benefit and future opportunities that commercial success could provide.

While Shakespeare's major thematic concerns of loss, childhood, isolation and disillusion are preserved within the film, to these are added Jarman's own preoccupations with sexuality, gender, madness and the occult. The costumes and set design are key to the film's exploration of these themes while character development is also heavily dependent upon the stylised set and atmospheric lighting and visuals. The creative autonomy given to Yolanda Sonnabend in designing the space for *The Tempest* as well as creative ideas offered by Ian Whittaker, Peter

Middleton and Christopher Hobbs fuse with Jarman's own artistic ideas to formulate an arresting visual style.

In allowing his actors to utilise their own backgrounds and offer ideas about character to inform their performances, the range of performance styles and techniques at work within the text, again represent a fusion of creative ideas and influences. In allowing things to happen 'by accident,' Jarman permitted his own ideas to be enhanced, challenged and developed by his cast, ensuring a high degree of creative autonomy.[61] The range of creative ideas which are at work within the film and which contributed to its visual style reveal a complex process of creative endeavour and highlight important issue of film authorship.

In creating a postmodern text which refuses to remain firmly rooted in place, space or time, Jarman succeeds in creating a world which is accessible yet fantastical. Jarman's reliance on historical and textual borrowing creates a postmodern bricolage, incorporating important cultural references whilst allowing the film to occupy a transitional space unfettered by historical period. As one reviewer noted, 'Jarman's major achievement is to displace Bardolatory with humour and literature with visual pleasure evoking all the giddy enchantment of the play with a golden-hued rendering of the wedding masque.'[62] Herein lies the success of the film; the beauty and innovation of a text achieved through independent creativity offers a distinctive 1970s film which captures the humour and darkness of Shakespeare's play, while incorporating the fantastical flamboyance of the period. The film also succeeds because of its ambiguity and openness. It offers itself to the viewer and allows for independent conclusions to be drawn, while at the same time also allowing for the visual splendour of the film to be enjoyed without constraint.

Drawing on avant-garde and artistic influences and through collaboration with those outside the film world and backed by a creative producer like Boyd, Jarman moved beyond the constraints of British film production. *The Tempest* showcased the creative skill of technicians and artists and demonstrated that here at last, at the end of a chaotic decade, was a 'brave new world' of filmmaking which opened upon the possibilities of technical collaboration and innovation as well as artistic crossover into the commercial world of the mainstream.

Conclusion

The 1970s is not the cultural wasteland which previous studies have suggested. The fragility of an industry which created an uncertain and unstable film culture was brought about by industrial changes and allowed for exciting innovation. Fostered by the entrepreneurial culture of the 1960s, the 1970s film industry permitted relatively inexperienced producers to flourish. The working practices adopted by entrepreneurial producers and financiers passed benefits on to filmmakers who may not have otherwise secured funding. I have highlighted Don Boyd's work with Alan Clarke and Derek Jarman, but other important partnerships were forged in the period, which directly contributed to this eclectic film culture. David Puttnam and Sandy Lieberson collaborated with Ken Russell on *Mahler* (1974) and *Lizstomania* (1975), and also offered feature film opportunities to Alan Parker, Ridley Scott and Terry Gilliam. The activities of Michael Klinger throughout the 1970s also demonstrate how crucial it was to secure alternative methods of funding. Similarly to Klinger's work with independent financiers to fund the *Confessions* series, the Monty Python team also drew the funding for their first feature film from investments made by bands Pink Floyd and Led Zeppelin. Such innovative production methods were the direct result of the failure of existing forms of financial support from the American studios, Rank, EMI and the NFFC. This entrepreneurial culture has often been associated with the 1960s, and while its roots were embedded within the earlier decade, it truly came to fruition in the 1970s.

The innovative and adventurous film culture provided a range of opportunities fostered by ad hoc methods of production and finance, yet also had huge weaknesses. Reckless and immoderate behaviour in some areas of film production and finance and the retirement of some of the more conservative elder statesmen of the industry, led to massive losses, high-profile flops and a weakened and fragmented industrial structure. This was a new era in British film production which saw the death rattle of the British studio system, along with the rise of independent and innovative producers and directors who operated outside existing structures of production. The weaknesses of the industry were compounded by the inconsistency of the government's approach to the film industry. Government bodies such as the NFFC and the CFC had a marked influence upon the film industry and film culture in the 1970s. All of these institutions and organisations were struggling to keep pace with social change and popular taste, within a changing culture of permission, with varying degrees of success.

The attitude of successive governments also directly contributed to the uncertain culture of production and failed to secure the future of the industry or protect it from wider economic problems. Yet, despite this uncertainty (or perhaps because of it), a number of thematic trends are evident within some of the films I have examined.

For example, the central protagonist of *Stardust* is the Picaro: a rootless, classless masculine figure who epitomises anxieties surrounding gender and class in the decade. These picaresque figures are evident in *Sunday Bloody Sunday, Confessions of a Window Cleaner* and *The Tempest* as well as *Performance* (1970), *O Lucky Man!* (1973), *Joseph Andrews* (1977) and many others. While it would be easy to characterise the 1970s as a decade in which predominantly masculine anxieties emerged on and through film, this is too simplistic. Anxiety about masculinity does feature in a large number of films throughout the decade, but is manifested in a variety of forms and performs different cultural tasks. As well as the easily identifiable figures that embody masculine anxiety, such as the sexually inadequate window cleaner or the vacuous pop star, the anxieties surrounding masculinity are frequently posited in relation to the changing role of women. For example, the predatory Marian in *The Go-Between* destroys the lives of the male characters around her through her overt and selfish sexuality, while the dissatisfied wife of *The Romantic Englishwoman* (1975), is shown to destroy home, family and marriage through her wilful pursuit of sexual pleasure and fulfilment.

These anxieties about femininity not only represent the threats and challenges posed to male identity but also to the uncertainties surrounding shifting and emerging feminine roles. Anxieties about feminine roles are evident throughout films of the period, from the unease which is associated with sexually carefree women in *Confessions of a Window Cleaner*, to the anxieties and uncertainties of Glenda Jackson's character in *Sunday Bloody Sunday*. Within this film, the confusion and unhappiness of Alex as she struggles to cope with the changes which have taken place within marriage, sexual relationships and family, are echoed by Julie Christie's Marian in *The Go-Between*. Alex is reluctantly embracing a sexually liberated relationship amid anxieties about the future, while Marian's modernity of manner contrasts awkwardly with the period setting, costumes and narrative which confine her. Both of these characters are modern, liberated and aware, yet are trapped by their circumstances. Christie's Marian is trapped by the restrictions imposed upon her by society and family, while Jackson's Alex is constrained by her unhappy open relationship and she privately yearns for a more stable, settled time.

As shown in previous chapters, both of these characters exhibit a knowingness, indicating a new female assuredness, while at the same time remaining firmly restricted in older, more conventional feminine roles. Film culture is responding in a mixed way to show both the positives and the negatives of the new sexual roles and mores. And it also illustrated that while questions had been raised about female sexuality and identity it was also apparent that there were no easy answers. The frequent references to older models of femininity are easily discernible in films including *The Beast in the Cellar* (1970), *The Triple Echo* (1972) and *The Four Feathers* (1978), yet films of the decade also contain female characters who exhibit an awareness and candour and are unrestricted by older models of feminine identity. This female knowingness is evident in *The Tempest*, as Toyah Willcox's youthful Miranda recognises her burgeoning sexuality and the power that comes with it. This characterisation emerges at the end of the decade and has shaken loose some of the more cloying restrictions which prevailed at the start of the decade. This emergence of a new, highly-contested feminine identity can be identified as one of the most important shifts within British cinema of the period.

Although *The Go-Between* is concerned with sexuality and the loss of innocence in much the same way as *The Tempest*, it also foregrounds important issues of class. The decline of the class system and the uncertainties which emerge following the social changes of the 1960s can be discerned within a number of 1970s cultural texts. As well as being one of the main preoccupations of *The Go-Between*, the decline of the aristocracy features obliquely in *Stardust*, where the fledging rock stars showcase their skills at a country house and Jim retreats to his Spanish castle, purchased with his rock-star earnings. In *The Tempest*, Prospero's cell is visualised within the decaying rooms and corridors of a stately home destroyed by fire and neglect. In this decade, the aristocracy as a symbol is not fixed or certain as it has been in other periods. It is no longer the potent symbol it had been in earlier film cultures.

The Tempest also uses history more generally as a means of evoking details about character and setting. However, the eclecticism of the historical references do not seek to locate the film within an ordered, historical past. Rather, Jarman's film includes a range of historical details which often contradict and challenge each other, as modern, medieval and renaissance images are muddled together. Such textual borrowing also operates in *Stardust,* where images of rock stars past and present are deliberately evoked through hairstyles and costumes, to place the central character within an easily recognisable setting and timeframe. The plundering of history which occurs in both *Stardust* and *The Tempest* also characterises *Monty Python and the Holy Grail* (1975), where historical references create a smorgasbord of textual and visual detail. The postmodern tendencies observed in films of the period allow for the viewer to interpret what he or she will from the film, in the manner of the historian selecting 'facts.' Such historical and textual borrowing also places these films outside easily recognisable historical or temporal settings.

As well as using the past and history in a distinctive way, many 1970s films look forward to the next decade. *Sunday Bloody Sunday's* visual style emphasises an uncomfortable modernity, and Bob's technological inventions prove pivotal to the resolution of the narrative. Similar thematic preoccupations of technological innovation and scientific progress are also present in *Doomwatch* (1972), *The Beast Must Die* (1974) and *Warlords of Atlantis* (1978). *The Tempest* is also preoccupied with the future, and the film's anachronistic touches present the modern alongside the historical, suggesting temporal links between the cultural capital of the past and the technological promise of the future. Even *Scum* appears to point towards the next decade. Its firm narrative resolution and the triumph of the systems of institution and patriarchy indicate the shift to the Right which had occurred within British society and politics. It presciently anticipates Thatcherism much as other films did, such as *The Long Good Friday* (1980).

The concept of time which is so important to the narrative of *The Tempest* is also pivotal to *The Go-Between.* The clever use of flashbacks and the innovative narrative structure allow for a text which moves fluently between past, present and future. *The Go-Between* looks back to the past, but in doing so, critiques it and suggests how nostalgic images are worthless and harmful, rather than pleasurable. The nostalgia about the past which is absent in *The Go-Between* is an important feature in a number of films of the decade, and can be seen in *Stardust*, *Confessions of a Window Cleaner* and *Sunday Bloody Sunday*, albeit in very different forms. *Confessions of a Window Cleaner* uses nostalgia in a straightforward way and the past is revered as a more ordered place, undisturbed by sexually demanding females. Such nostalgia is also evident in other films which have their roots in earlier periods, for example *On the Buses* (1971) and *The Likely Lads* (1976). Nostalgia permeates much of 1970s culture and is manifest in the high number of literary adaptations and children's films including *Swallows and Amazons* (1974), *Murder on the Orient Express* (1974) and *The Slipper and the Rose* (1976). Yet, not all films of the 1970s use nostalgia in such an uninflected way. *Sunday Bloody Sunday* is particularly preoccupied with the faded promise of the 1960s, as is *Stardust*. While both films reflect upon the lost dreams of the earlier decade, *Stardust* allowed the viewer to revel in the hedonism of the 1960s whilst critiquing it, whereas *Sunday Bloody Sunday* offers more bitter and sombre reflections. *Stardust* permitted nostalgia, but *Sunday Bloody Sunday*, like *The Go-Between* showed the past and all that it promised to be empty and false. *Scum* is not nostalgic for an earlier period, but rather looks back approvingly to a more ordered time. While the film's screenplay and characters articulate the inhumanity of the borstal system, the uncompromising narrative and visual style affirms the need for order, structure and method. *Scum* is only one of the films of the period which critiques the role of the institution and challenges its purpose and efficacy. Films from a variety of genres critique a range of social institutions, and these texts include *Family Life* (1971), *Frightmare* (1974), *The House of Whipcord* (1974) and *Royal Flash* (1975).

While *Scum*'s narrative may have been unambiguous, its marketing and publicity were less straightforward. The film was deliberately marketed as sensationalist and dramatic, while its director and writer were keen to adopt a social realist approach, which drew heavily on their own research, to make a film about a social problem. This suggests both a dependence on the residual quality of British social realist cinema and television, as well as an awareness of the potency of the X certificate.

The power of the X certificate was a major factor within film production in the decade and just as the film industry saw new collaborations in the 1970s it was also working closely with existing institutions such as the BBFC and adapting to its changing relationship with television. Some feature films, including *Scum*, had television roots and influences and the interrelationship between the film and television industries played an important role in the period and significantly affected film production, as evidenced by the high number of films of TV sitcoms made, which were phenomenally successful in the early years of the decade.

While there are some similar themes and issues within the films I have studied, the film texts I have selected do not define or typify the film culture of the period and, as I have also shown, can only be adequately understood when placed within their production context. One of the key production trends which can be identified for films of the 1970s is the notion of increased creative and practical collaboration. As well as established collaborations between literature and the film industry, practitioners from the theatre as well as from the music, television and advertising industries were called in to facilitate and finance film production. The talents of theatre designer Yolanda Sonnabend, playwright Harold Pinter, musicians Alan Price, Dave Edmunds and Pete Townshend, television practitioners including Alan Clarke, Frank Roddam and Claude Whattham and David Puttnam, Ridley Scott and Alan Parker from the world of advertising all became involved in the film industry in the 1970s. As I have shown, the involvement of individuals from across different industries demonstrates the new types of collaboration within British cinema.

Film production was influenced by finance and government investment, as the funding offered by the NFFC actively determined what films were made and established a precedent for future funding. Attempts made throughout the decade by members of the film industry, such as the FPA or the trade unions to circumnavigate or confront a series of controls are indicative of other socio-political struggles. In this way, the struggles of film entrepreneurs and industry representatives against industrial constraints mirrors the paradigm of the individual verses the institution which can be seen throughout the 1970s period.

The 1970s is a crucially important decade which sits uneasily between the 1960s and 1980s. The decade is one of the last periods in which an independent and indigenous, albeit only moderately successful, British film culture existed. In the decade that followed, the American blockbuster reigned supreme at the box office and within the newly created multiplexes, while the influence and popularity of television steadily increased with the launch of Channel 4 in 1982. Video technology also irrevocably altered patterns of film-watching and the rise of MTV indicated the possibilities for this emergent technology. Such technological changes fundamentally altered the practices of cinema-going, as film consumption shifted from the public space of the cinema to the private space of the home. These changes had a massive impact upon the

British film industry, which became in the 1980s even more fragmented and pluralised than it had been in the later years of the 1970s.

As well as exploring cultures of production and shining new light on British films and filmmaking, this study has also utilised a historical and cultural approach for the study of film. It has challenged previous assumptions about the decade, both in terms of a period not worthy of study and also as a period devoid of sources. Using archival material alongside close textual analysis and economic and institutional frameworks has revealed a very different industry to the one frequently identified as one of the low points of British cultural production. Such an approach can be usefully applied to any decade in British film history and could be used to re-examine periods which have hitherto been seen in straightforward terms. The 1970s was a complex and uncertain time for British filmmaking, yet the financial constraints and high level of innovation and collaboration required prompted new cultures of production and the creation of high-quality, popular and exciting British films. Although a great deal remains to be done, this study seeks to contribute to the reappraisal of this important decade and to suggest that the 1970s British film industry should be viewed as collaborative, innovative and energetic, rather than simply as an industry in decline, beset by crisis and preoccupied only with lowbrow culture.

Notes

1 Film and Cultural History

1. S. Harper and V. Porter, *British Cinema of the 1950s: The Decline of Deference* (Oxford: Oxford University Press, 2003), p. 3.
2. *Ibid.*, p. 5.
3. R. Durgnat, *A Mirror for England: British Movies from Austerity to Affluence* (London: Faber and Faber, 1970).
4. J. Richards, 'Film and TV: The Moving Image,' in S. Barber and C.M Penniston-Bird (eds), *History Beyond the Text: A Student's Guide to Approaching Alternative Sources* (Abingdon: Routledge, 2009), p. 74.
5. R. Williams, *Problems in Materialism and Culture* (London: Verso Editions and NLB, 1980).
6. R. Allen and D. Gomery, *Film History: Theory and Practice* (New York: McGraw-Hill, 1985), p. 37.
7. J. Chapman, *Past and Present: National Identity and the British Historical Film* (London: I.B. Tauris, 2005), p. 11.
8. R. Allen and D. Gomery, *Film History, op. cit.*, p. 13.
9. J. Richards, 'Rethinking British Cinema,' in J. Ashby and A. Higson (eds), *British Cinema, Past and Present* (London: Routledge, 2000), pp. 21–34.
10. J. Chapman, M. Glancy and S. Harper (eds), *The New Film History* (Basingstoke: Palgrave Macmillan, 2007), p. 5.
11. A. Spicer, 'Film Studies and the Turn to History,' *Journal of Contemporary History*, Volume 39, Number 2 (2004), pp. 147–155.
12. J. Richards, *The Age of the Dream Palace: Cinema and Society 1930–1939* (London: Routledge and Kegan Paul, 1984) and S. Harper and V. Porter, *British Cinema of the 1950s: The Decline of Deference* (Oxford: Oxford University Press, 2003).
13. R. Murphy, *Sixties British Cinema* (London: BFI Publishing, 1992) and J. Hill, *British Cinema in the 1980s* (Oxford: Clarendon Press, 1999).
14. S. Harper and V. Porter, 'Beyond Media History: The Challenge of Visual Style,' *Journal of British Cinema and Television*, Volume 2, Number 1 (2005), pp. 1–17.
15. S. Street, 'Designing for Motion Pictures.' Paper given at Archives and Auteurs Conference, University of Stirling, 4 September 2009.
16. S. Street, *British Cinema in Documents* (London: Routledge, 2000), p. 2.
17. A. Spicer 'Understanding the Independent Film Producer: Michael Klinger and New Film History.' Paper given at Researching Film History: Perspectives and Practices in Film Historiography Conference, 7 July 2009.
18. L. Jordanova, *History in Practice* (London: Hodder Headline, 2000), p. 101.
19. J. Tosh, *The Pursuit of History*, 4th Edition (Harlow: Pearson Education, 2006), p. 60.

20. R. Samuel, *Theatres of Memory: Volume 1, Past and Present in Contemporary Culture* (London: Verso, 1994), p. 8.
21. Material from the Losey papers within the BFI Special Collections, pertaining to *The Romantic Englishwoman*.
22. S. Barber, *Censoring the 1970s: The BBFC and the Decade That Taste Forgot*, (Newcastle: Cambridge Scholars Press, 2011).
23. R. James, 'Kinematograph Weekly in the 1930s: Trade Attitudes Towards Audience Taste,' *Journal of British Cinema and Television*, Volume 3, Number 2 (2006), pp. 229–243. M. Glancy, *When Hollywood Loved Britain: The Hollywood 'British' Film, 1939–45* (Manchester: Manchester University Press, 1999). S. Harper, 'A Lower-Middle-Class Taste Community in the 1930s: Admission Figures at the Regent, Portsmouth,' *The Historical Journal of Film, Radio and Television*, Volume 24, Number 4 (2004), pp. 565–588. S. Harper, 'Fragmentation and Crisis: 1940s Admissions Figures at the Regent Cinema, Portsmouth, UK,' *The Historical Journal of Film, Radio and Television*, Volume 26, Number 3 (2006), pp. 361–394.
24. S. Barber, 'Beyond Sex, Bond and Star Wars: Exhibition Data from the Southampton Odeon 1972–1980,' *POST SCRIPT: Essays in Film and the Humanities*, Volume 30, Number 3 (2011), pp. 77–90.
25. R. Perks and A. Thomson (eds), *The Oral History Reader* (London: Routledge, 1998), p. ix.
26. A. Spicer, 'Film Studies and the Turn to History,' *Journal of Contemporary History*, Volume 39, Number 2 (2004), pp. 147–155, p. 152.

2 Understanding the 1970s

1. A. Sutcliffe, *An Economic and Social History of Western Europe Since 1945* (Harlow: Longman, 1996), p. 204.
2. D. Sandbrook, *State of Emergency. The Way We Were: Britain 1970–1974* (Penguin Books; London 2011).
3. *Ibid.*, p. 30.
4. *Ibid.*, p. 41.
5. N. Shrapnel, *The 70's: Britain's Inward March* (London: Constable, 1980), p. 13. C. Booker, *The 70s: Portrait of a Decade* (London: Penguin Books, 1980). A. Walker, *National Heroes: British Cinema in the 70s and 80s* (London: Harrap, 1985).
6. M. Bloch, *The Historian's Craft*, 7th Edition (Manchester: Manchester University Press, 1992), p. 48.
7. R. Weight, *Patriots: National Identity in Britain 1940–2000* (London: Macmillan Press, 2002). A. Marr, *A History of Modern Britain* (London: Macmillan Press, 2007).
8. A. Marwick, 'Locating Key Texts Amid the Distinctive Landscape of the Sixties,' in A. Aldgate, J. Chapman and A. Marwick (eds), *Windows on the Sixties: Exploring key texts of Media and Culture* (London: I.B. Tauris, 2000), p. xii.
9. N. Shrapnel, *The 70's*, *op. cit.*, p. 13. A.W. Turner, *Crisis? What Crisis? Britain in the 1970s* (London: Aurum Press, 2008).
10. E. Hobsbawm, *Age of Extremes: The Short 20th Century 1914–1991* (London: Michael Joseph, 1984), p. 404.

11. M. Garnett, *From Apathy to Anger: The Story of Politics, Society and Popular Culture in Britain since 1975* (London: Vintage Books, 2008).
12. A. Beckett, *When the Lights Went Out: Britain in the 1970s* (London: Faber and Faber, 2009), p. 5.
13. A. Marwick, *Culture in Britain Since 1945* (Oxford: Basil Blackwell, 1991), p. 97 and A. Marr, *A History of Modern Britain, op. cit.*, p. 359.
14. R. Weight, *Patriots, op. cit.*, p. 18.
15. H. Sounes, *Seventies: The Sights, Sounds and Ideas of a Brilliant Decade* (London: Simon & Schuster, 2006).
16. A.W. Turner, *Crisis? What Crisis? op. cit.*, p. ix.
17. B. Moore-Gilbert (ed), *The Arts in the 1970s: Cultural Closure?* (London: Routledge, 1994).
18. R. Hewison, *Too Much: Art and Society in the Sixties 1960–75* (London: Methuen, 1986).
19. J.A. Walker, *Left Shift: Radical Art in 1970s Britain* (London: I.B Tauris, 2002).
20. R. Williams, *Problems in Materialism and Culture* (London: Verso Editions and NLB, 1980), p. 38.
21. *Ibid.*, p. 40.
22. *Ibid.*, p. 41.
23. A. Walker, *National Heroes, op. cit.*
24. J. Walker, *The Once and Future Film: British Cinema in the Seventies and Eighties* (London: Methuen, 1985).
25. E. Betts, *The Film Business* (London: George Allen and Unwin, 1973). M. Dickinson and S. Street, *Cinema and State: The Film Industry and the British Government 1927–1984* (London: BFI Publishing, 1985). B. Baillieu and J. Goodchild, *The British Film Business* (Chichester: John Wiley and Sons, 2002).
26. S. Street, *British National Cinema* (London: Routledge: 1997). J. Leach, *British Film* (Cambridge: Cambridge University Press, 2004). A. Sargeant, *British Cinema: A Critical History* (London: BFI Publishing, 2005).
27. L. Hunt, *British Low Culture: From Safari Suits to Sexploitation* (London: Routledge. 1998).
28. A. Higson, 'A Diversity of Film Practices: Renewing British Cinema in the 1970s,' in Bart Moore-Gilbert (ed), *The Arts in the 1970s: Cultural Closure?* (London: Routledge, 1994), pp. 218–237, p. 227.
29. S. Chibnall and J. Petley (eds), *British Horror Cinema* (London: Routledge, 2002). A. Medhurst, 'Music Hall and British Cinema,' in C. Barr (ed), *All Our Yesterdays: Ninety Years of British Cinema* (London: BFI Publishing, 1986), pp. 168–188 and 'Carry On Camp,' *Sight and Sound*, Volume 2, Number 4 (1992), pp. 16–19. P. Hutchings, 'The Problem of British Horror,' in M. Jancovich (ed), *Horror: The Film Reader* (London: Routledge, 2002), pp. 117–124 and *Hammer and Beyond: The British Horror Film* (Manchester: Manchester University Press, 1993).
30. G.A. Smith, *Uneasy Dreams: The Golden Age of British Horror Films 1956–1976* (London: McFarland and Company, 2000). S. Chibnall, 'A Heritage of Evil: Pete Walker and the Politics of Gothic Revisionism,' in S. Chibnall and J. Petley (eds), *British Horror Cinema* (London: Routledge, 2002), pp. 156–171.
31. Publications which cover *Carry On* and the sexploitation film include D. McGillivray, *Doing Rude Things: The History of the British Sex Film*

1957–1981 (London: Sun Tavern Fields, 1992). S. Sheridan, *Keeping the British End Up: Four Decades of Saucy Cinema* (Richmond: Reynolds and Hearn, 2005). M. Bright and R. Ross, *Carry On Uncensored* (London: Boxtree 1999). I. Conrich, 'Forgotten Cinema: The British Style of Sexploitation,' *Journal of Popular British Cinema*, Volume 1, Number 1 (1998) pp. 87–100. M. Anderson 'Stop Messing About: The Gay Fool in *Carry On* Films,' *Journal of Popular British Cinema*, Volume 1, Number 1 (1998), pp. 37–47.

32. C. McCabe, *Performance*, BFI Film Classics (London: BFI Publishing, 1998), S. Chibnall, *Get Carter* British Film Guides series (London: I.B. Tauris, 2003) and M. Sanderson, *Don't Look Now*, BFI Film Classics (London: BFI Publishing, 1996).

33. J. Chapman, 'From Amicus to Atlantis: The Lost Worlds of 1970s British Cinema,' in R. Shail (ed), *Seventies British Cinema* (London: BFI/Palgrave Macmillan, 2008), pp. 56–64. J. Chapman, *Past and Present, op. cit.*

34. Biographies of key 1970s filmmakers include; J. Baxter, *An Appalling Talent: Ken Russell* (London: Joseph, 1973). J. Lanza, *Phallic Frenzy: Ken Russell and His Films* (London: Aurum Press, 2008). R. Wymer, *Derek Jarman* (Manchester: Manchester University Press, 2005). N. Sinyard, *The Films of Nicolas Roeg* (London: Letts, 1991). J. Palmer, *The Films of Joseph Losey* (Cambridge: Cambridge University Press). A. Yule, *Enigma: David Puttnam, The Story So Far* (Edinburgh: Mainstream, 1988). M. Deeley and M. Field, *Blade Runners, Deer Hunters and Blowing the Bloody Doors Off: My Life in Cult Movies* (London: Faber and Faber, 2008).

35. Work on production companies includes R. Murphy, 'Three Companies: Boyd's Co, Handmade and Goldcrest,' in M. Auty and N. Roddick (eds), *British Cinema Now* (London: BFI Publishing, 1985), pp. 43–56. R. Sellers, *Always Look on the Bright Side of Life: The Inside Story of Handmade Films* (London, Metro Books, 2003). J. Eberts and T. Ilot, *My Indecision Is Final: The Rise and Fall of Goldcrest Films* (London: Faber and Faber, 1990).

36. R. Shail (ed), *Seventies British Cinema* (London: BFI/Palgrave Macmillan, 2008).

37. P. Newland (ed), *Don't Look Now: British Cinema in the 1970s* (Bristol: Intellect Books, 2010).

38. L. Forster and S. Harper (eds), *British Culture and Society in the 1970s: The Lost Decade* (Newcastle: Cambridge Scholars, 2010).

39. S. Harper and J. Smith (eds), *British Film Culture in the 1970s: The Boundaries of Pleasure* (Edinburgh; EUP, 2011).

3 Film and Government

1. L. Napper, 'A Despicable Tradition?, Quota Quickies in the 1930s,' in R. Murphy (ed), *The British Cinema Book*, 2nd Edition (London: BFI Publishing, 2001), p. 47.

2. L. Napper, 'A Despicable Tradition?' *op. cit.* and S. Chibnall, *Quota Quickies: The Birth of the British 'B' Film* (London: BFI Publishing, 2007).

3. For a fuller discussion of the creation of the NFFC and the British Lion debacle see S. Harper and V. Porter, *British Cinema of the 1950s, op. cit.* and M. Dickinson and S. Street, *Cinema and State, op. cit.*

4. V. Porter, 'Film Policy for the 80s: Industry or Culture?,' *Sight and Sound*, Volume 48, Number 4 (1979), pp. 221–223, p. 226.
5. Figures taken from M. Dickinson and S. Street, *Cinema and State, op. cit.*, p. 231.
6. For further details on the loan-making capabilities of the NFFC see S. Harper and V. Porter, *British Cinema of the 1950s, op. cit.*, pp. 8–11.
7. L. Wood, *British Films 1971–1981* (London: BFI Library Services, 1983), p. 144.
8. All files from The National Archives will hereafter be abbreviated to TNA. TNA BT 383/14 – BT 383/23 Figures from British Film Fund Agency Committee: Minutes (1970–1980).
9. *Ibid.*
10. A. Lovell, *The British Film Institute Production Board* (London: BFI Publishing, 1976), p. 5.
11. *Ibid*, p. 1.
12. D. Todd, 'Freedom for the Flicks,' *Kinematograph Weekly*, 19 December 1970, pp. 3–4.
13. Letter to Editor from Lindsay Anderson et al., 'Financial Support for Film-Makers,' *The Times*, 5 August 1971, p. 13.
14. Gwyneth Dunwoody quoted in 'The £1 Million Offer: To Phase Out NFFC Aid,' *Kinematograph Weekly*, 3 July 1971, p. 3.
15. Parliamentary debates (Hansard) House of Commons official report. Volume 821, 15 July 1971, p. 876.
16. John Terry quoted in 'NFFC end of year hopes for Consortium,' *Kinematograph Weekly*, 4 September 1971, p. 13.
17. M. Dickinson and S. Street *op. cit.*, p. 241.
18. *NFFC Annual Report*, 1972, p. 1.
19. K. Courte, 'No Longer the Kindly Money Lenders,' *Today's Cinema*, 3 September 1971, p. 10.
20. P. Swern and M. Childs, *The Guinness Book of Box Office Hits* (Enfield: Guinness, 1995), p. 187.
21. Figures taken from National Film Finance Corporation Annual Reports 1969–1980.
22. *Ibid.*
23. *NFFC Annual Report* 1971, p. 3.
24. P. Swern and M. Childs, *The Guinness Book of Box Office Hits, op. cit.*, p. 192.
25. *NFFC Annual Report* 1974, p. 4.
26. *Ibid.*
27. P. Swern and M. Childs, *The Guinness Book of Box Office Hits, op. cit.*, p. 202 and p. 211.
28. *NFFC Annual Report* 1978, p. 7.
29. Parliamentary debates (Hansard) House of Commons official report. Volume 892, 17 June 1975, p. 395.
30. *NFFC Annual Report* 1976, p. 7.
31. *Great Britain: Future of the British Film Industry: Report of the Prime Minister's Working Party*, Cmnd 6372.
32. *Ibid.*
33. *Ibid.*
34. TNA FV 81/95, Ministers special meeting of the Cinematograph Films Council to discuss the Terry Report, 26 January 1976.

35. Films granted loans in this period which made no impact at the box office included *Captain Kronos-Vampire Hunter* (1974), *Ooh... You Are Awful* (1972), *Black Joy* (1977).
36. TNA FV 81/95, Ministers special meeting of the Cinematograph Films Council to discuss the Terry Report, 26 January 1976.
37. TNA FV 81/93, Personal Minute to the Secretary of State for Trade from Harold Wilson, Prime Minister dated 6 January 1976.
38. Parliamentary debates (Hansard) House of Commons official report. Volume 959, 27 November 1978, p. 4.
39. Parliamentary debates (Hansard) House of Commons official report. Volume 969, 2 July 1979, p. 884.
40. Parliamentary debates (Hansard) House of Commons official report. Volume 983, 25 April 1980, p. 859.
41. *Ibid.*, pp. 859–860.
42. *Ibid.*, p. 867.
43. *Ibid.*, p. 868.
44. Figures compiled from TNA BT 383/14 – BT 383/23 British Film Fund Agency Committee Minutes.
45. *Film Producers Association Annual Report* 1979/1980, p. 12. and figures compiled from TNA BT 383/14 – BT 383/23 British Film Fund Agency Committee Minutes.
46. Further details of the Eady Fund's fluctuations can be found in Appendix 2.

4 Funding Innovation

1. M. Dickinson and S. Street, *Cinema and State: The Film Industry and the British Government 1927–1984* (London: BFI Publishing, 1985), p. 237. and M. Dickinson, 'The State and the Consolidation of Monopoly,' in J. Curran and V. Porter (eds), *British Cinema History* (London: Weidenfeld and Nicholson, 1983), p. 92.
2. S. Street, *Transatlantic Crossings: British Feature Films in the Unites States* (London: Continuum International Publishing, 2002), p. 187.
3. Figures taken from A. Walker, *Hollywood England: The British Film Industry in the 1960s, op. cit.*, p. 442.
4. *EMI Annual Report* 1975, p. 5.
5. L. Wood, *British Films 1971–1981* (London: BFI Library Services, 1983), pp. 97–138.
6. Stephen Weeks in D. Pirie, 'New Blood,' *Sight and Sound*, Volume 40, Number 2 (1971), pp. 73–75.
7. In his ghost-written autobiography, Michael Deeley repeats the rumour that James Carreras began his horror films with a title and a poster design and then worked back to the script. M. Deeley and M. Field, *Blade Runners, Deer Hunters and Blowing the Bloody Doors Off: My Life in Cult Movies* (London: Faber and Faber, 2008), p. 110.
8. A. Barnes and M. Hearn, *The Hammer Story* (London: Titan Books, 1997), p. 133.
9. *Film Co-production Agreement between the Government of the United Kingdom of Great Britain Northern Ireland and the Government of the French Republic.* 21 September 1965, Cmnd 2781, p. 2.

10. *Ibid.*
11. *Co-production Guide to the Anglo-French and the Anglo-Italian Co-production Treaties* (London: Film Production Association of Great Britain, 1971), pp. 1–13.
12. *Ibid.*
13. *Ibid.*
14. *Ibid.*
15. F. Morris Dyson, 'A survey of the various legislative and fiscal devices adopted by members of the European community to promote and support their film industries together with the subsequent directives of film production by the EEC council' from written report of proceedings at Polytechnic of Central London conference 3–4 March 1972.
16. S. Caulkin, 'Movie Moguls look to Brussels for Fresh Aid,' *The Times*, 19 April 1972, p. 23.
17. Only these four of the 29 European co-productions made in this decade make it into the top twenty at the British box office. Figures from P. Swern and M. Childs, *The Guinness Book of Box Office Hits* (Enfield: Guinness, 1995).
18. *Ibid.*
19. Material from the Joseph Losey papers in the BFI special collections, pertaining to *The Romantic Englishwoman*.
20. S. Shaw, 'Picking up the Tab for the Whole Black Community?: Industrial, Social and Institutional Challenges as Exemplified in Babylon,' in S. Harper and J. Smith (ed), *British Film Culture in the 1970s: The Boundaries of Pleasure* (Edinburgh: EUP, 2011), p. 81.
21. Film projects including *Stardust* (1974), *The Europeans* (1979) and *Bugsy Malone* (1976) all did well at the UK box office and are examples of the NFFC making wise investment decisions.

5 Movers and Shakers

1. *EMI Annual Report* 1969, p. 4.
2. *Ibid.*, p. 9.
3. *EMI Annual Report* 1970, p. 4.
4. Details taken from A. Walker, *National Heroes* (London: Harrap, 1985), p. 129.
5. *EMI Annual Report* 1973, p. 4.
6. Electronics, Radio and equipment accounted for 13% of total profits at EMI at the end of 1970. Figure taken from 'City Comment,' *The Guardian*, 8 March 1971, p. 12.
7. Material taken from the Joseph Losey papers held at the BFI Special Collections and will hereafter be abbreviated to LPGB for *The Go-Between* and LPRE for *The Romantic Englishwoman*. LPGB, Joseph Losey to Bernard Delfont, telegram dated Friday 5 November 1971.
8. LPGB, James T Aubrey from EMI to Bernard Delfont, cable dated 10 March 1971.
9. *Ibid.*
10. T. Murari, 'Nat King Cohen,' *The Guardian*, 17 November 1973, p. 9.
11. *Ibid.*, p. 9.

12. *EMI Annual Report* 1975, p. 36.
13. For more information on the distribution deal in America, see A. Walker, *National Heroes, op. cit.*, p. 206.
14. *Ibid.*, p. 206.
15. Material taken from the Peter Rogers papers held at the BFI Special Collections and will hereafter be abbreviated to PR. PR file for *Carry On England*, John Terry of the NFFC to Gerard Thomas declining funding, letter dated 4 March 1976.
16. PR file for *Carry On England*, Richard Du Vivier at EMI to Peter Rogers suggesting some suitable names for the film, letter dated March 1976.
17. PR file for *Carry On Matron*, Peter Rogers to Graham Dawson of Rank, letter dated 6 September 1971.
18. Comments taken from unpublished interview with David Puttnam conducted by the author via telephone on 17 August 2009.
19. S. Clarke, 'Apple branches into Features,' *Kinematograph Weekly*, 25 November 1972, p. 9.
20. *Ibid.*
21. Comments taken from interview with Sandy Lieberson conducted by Sue Harper and Justin Smith on 6 March 2008.
22. Comments taken from unpublished interview with David Puttnam conducted by the author via telephone on 17 August 2009.
23. *Ibid.*
24. Comments taken from unpublished interview conducted with Don Boyd via email on 30 June 2009.
25. Boyd comments from A. Walker, *National Heroes, op. cit.*, p. 166. David Puttnam comments from unpublished interview with the author conducted by telephone on 17 August 2009.
26. R. Murphy, 'Three companies: Boyd's Co, HandMade and Goldcrest,' in M. Auty and N. Roddick (eds), *British Cinema Now* (London: BFI Publishing, 1985), p. 51.
27. For more detail on Don Boyd and his role during the 1970s see 'The Boyd Wonder' in A. Walker, *National Heroes, op. cit.*, pp. 144–166.
28. In an interview with the author Boyd recalled that he had originally been signed on as the director of *Honky Tonk Freeway* but pulled out after EMI pushed the budget to $15 million. He remained closely involved with the project bringing in John Schlesinger to direct and continued to work with Barry Spikings and Bernard Delfont. Boyd maintains that he was always keen to stay involved with the project but became uncomfortable when the proposed low-budget road movie evolved into a much larger film.
29. Comments from unpublished interview with Don Boyd conducted by the author via email on 11 June 2012 and an unpublished interview with David Puttnam conducted by the author via telephone on 17 August 2009.
30. *Ibid.*
31. S. Harper and J. Smith, *British Film Culture in the 1970s: The Boundaries of Pleasure* (Edinburgh: EUP, 2011), p. 132.
32. Broadcasting, Entertainment Cinematograph and Theatre Union (BECTU) interview with Lord Lew Grade. Interview number 290 with Lord Lew Grade conducted by Alan Sapper on 10 August 1993. Accessed

from: http://csedmac01.prs.uea.ac.uk:8080/Plone/bchrp-bectu-oral-history-project/document_view.

33. For more details on Lew Grade, ATV and ACC, see A. Walker, *National Heroes, op. cit.*, pp. 201–211.

6 Institutions and Organisations

1. 'Nationalising the film industry,' *ACTT Report*, August 1973, pp. 5–35.
2. *Ibid.*, p. 35.
3. TNA ED 245/54 Reports from the Cinematograph Films Council regarding financing the film industry, 1974–1976 and *Film Producers Association Annual Report*, 1974–1975, p. 10.
4. *Film Producers Association Annual Report*, 1974–1975, p. 19.
5. Q. Falk, 'Just how far should the Government be involved in the films industry?,' *CinemaTV Today*, 23 March 1974, p. 6.
6. *Ibid.*
7. *Film Producers Association Annual Report*, 1974–1975, p. 3.
8. Comments from Don Boyd at 1970s Project Seminar at the University of Portsmouth, 13 November 2008.
9. M. Dickinson, 'The State and the Consolidation of Monopoly' *op. cit.*, p. 93.
10. L. Friedman and S. Stewart, 'Keeping His Own Voice: Interview with Stephen Frears,' in W.W. Dixon (ed), *Reviewing British Cinema 1900–1992: Essays and Interviews* (New York: State University of New York Press, 1994), pp. 221–240, p. 234.
11. *Ibid.*
12. PR production file, *Carry On England*, correspondence between H.J Nimwegen of Film Producers Association to Geoff Rice at Equity, letters dated 20 and 27 August 1976.
13. D. Petrie, *The British Cinematographer* (London: BFI Publishing, 1996), p. 58.
14. *Ibid.*
15. D. Gordon, '10 Points about the Crisis in the Film Industry' *Sight and Sound*, Volume 43, Number 2 (1974), pp. 67–72, p. 70.
16. S. Neale and F. Krutnik, *Popular Film and Television Comedy* (London: Routledge, 1990), p. 210.
17. Figures from http://www.screenonline.org.uk and P. Goodwin, *Television under the Tories: Broadcasting Policy 1979–1997* (London: BFI Publishing, 1998), p. 12.
18. *Ibid.*, p. 14.
19. L. Wood, *British Films 1971–1981, op. cit.*, p. 5.
20. *Film Producers Association Annual Report*, 1970–1971, p. 7.
21. D. Docherty, D. Morrison and M. Tracey, *The Last Picture Show?: Britain's Changing Film Audiences* (London: BFI Publishing, 1987), p. 28.
22. P. Perelli, 'Statistical Survey of the British Film Industry,' in J. Curran and V. Porter (eds), *British Cinema History* (London: George Weidenfeld and Nicholson, 1983), p. 372.
23. S. Hanson, *From Silent Screen to Multi-Screen: A History of Cinema Exhibition in Britain since 1896* (Manchester: Manchester University Press, 2007), p. 102 and A. Sutcliffe, *An Economic and Social History of Western Europe Since 1945* (Harlow: Longman, 1996), p. 143.

24. CTV Report, *Screen Digest*, December 1976, p. 222.
25. *Ibid.*
26. D. Gordon 'Ten Points about the Crisis in the Film Industry,' *Sight and Sound*, Volume 43, Number 2 (1974), pp. 67–72, p. 70. Figures from http://www.screenonline.org.uk/film/facts/fact1.html.
27. *Film Production Association Annual Report*, 1970–1971, p. 7.
28. D. Gordon, 'Ten Points about the Crisis in the Film Industry,' *op. cit.*, p. 70.
29. Parliamentary debates (Hansard) House of Commons official report. Written question from Mr Faulds. Volume 867, 21 January 1974, p. 212.
30. Estimated costs from Gwyneth Dunwoody from her speech in House of Commons. Parliamentary debates (Hansard) House of Commons official report. Volume 871, 4 April 1974, p. 1586. Additional figures are taken from the Joseph Losey papers and Peter Rogers papers held within the BFI Special Collections.
31. D. Freeman, *Television Policies of the Labour Party 1951–2001* (London: Frank Cass Publishers, 2003), p. 49 and P. Goodwin, *Television under the Tories, op. cit.*, p. 16.

7   Production, Genre and Popular Taste

1. D. Gifford, *British Film Catalogue: Fiction Film 1895–1994*, Volume 1, 3rd Edition (London: Fitzroy Dearborn Publishers, 2001).
2. J. Chapman, 'From Amicus to Atlantis: The Lost Worlds of 1970s British Cinema,' in R. Shail (ed), *Seventies British Cinema* (London: Palgrave Macmillan, 2008), pp. 56–64.
3. *EMI Annual Report*, 1975, p. 36.
4. L. Friedman and S. Stewart, 'Keeping His Own Voice: Interview with Stephen Frears,' in W.W. Dixon (ed), *Reviewing British Cinema 1900–1992: Essays and Interviews* (New York: State University of New York Press, 1994), pp. 221–240, p. 233.
5. S. Street, *Transatlantic Crossings: British Feature Films in the United States* (London: Continuum International Publishing, 2002), p. 187.
6. Figures taken from data supplied by James Tilmouth, Manager of Odeon Southampton. Analysis of this data is included in S. Barber, 'Beyond Sex, Bond and Star Wars: Exhibition data from the Southampton Odeon 1972–1980,' *POST SCRIPT: Essays in Film and the Humanities*, Volume 30, Number 3 (2011), pp. 77–90.
7. Comments taken from unpublished interview with David Puttnam conducted by the author via telephone on 17 August 2009.
8. L. Jodanova, *History in Practice* (London: Hodder Headline, 2000), p. 96.

8   *Sunday Bloody Sunday*: Authorship, Collaboration and Improvisation

1. All archival material taken from the Schlesinger papers held within the BFI Special Collections and will hereafter be referred to as JRS. JRS/7/19 Publicity and Financial file, John Schlesinger to his solicitor Michael Oliver (undated).
2. *Ibid.*

3. JRS/7/19 Publicity and Financial file.
4. JRS/7/20 Correspondence file, John Terry at NFFC to John Schlesinger, letter dated 23 October 1969.
5. JRS/7/23 Expenses and Finances file.
6. JRS/7/16 Casting and Crew suggestions file, John Schlesinger to Penelope Gilliatt, letter dated 1 March 1968.
7. *Ibid.*
8. JRS/7/14 Schlesinger/Gilliatt Correspondence file, Joseph Janni to Penelope Gilliatt, letter dated 28 July 1969.
9. *Ibid.*
10. *Ibid.*
11. *Ibid.*
12. *Ibid.*
13. JRS/7/9 Character breakdown and notes file, character synopses by Penelope Gilliatt (undated).
14. JRS/7/4 Annotated shooting script, script note, p. 8.
15. M. Riley, ' "I Both Hate and Love What I Do:" An Interview with John Schlesinger,' *Literature/Film Quarterly*, Volume 6, Number 2 (1978), p. 109.
16. D. Spiers, 'John Schlesinger interview,' *Screen*, Volume 11, Number 3 (1970), p. 16.
17. JRS/7/16 Casting and Crew suggestions file, John Schlesinger to Joseph Janni, letter dated 22 January 1969 and JRS/7/15 Janni/Schlesinger correspondence file, Joseph Janni to Penelope Gilliatt, letter dated 24 June 1969.
18. JRS/7/14 Schlesinger/Gilliatt correspondence file, John Schlesinger to Penelope Gilliatt, letter dated 15 August 1969.
19. Comments taken from an interview with Glenda Jackson conducted by the 1970s project team. Full text of interview included in Appendix 1.
20. JRS/7/4 Annotated shooting script, script note, page 12.
21. A. Walker, *National Heroes* (London: Harrap, 1985), p. 18.
22. JRS/7/19 Publicity and Financial file, John Schlesinger to his solicitor Michael Oliver (undated).
23. *Ibid.*
24. JRS/7/16 Casting and Crew suggestions file, Miriam Brickam, casting agent for *Sunday Bloody Sunday* to John Schlesinger, letter dated 30 October 1969.
25. JRS/7/16 Casting and Crew suggestions file, John Schlesinger to Joseph Janni, letter dated 31 October 1968.
26. *Ibid.*
27. JRS/7/20 Correspondence file, John Schlesinger to Albert Finney, letter dated 20 November 1969.
28. JRS/7/14 Schlesinger/Gilliatt correspondence file, John Schlesinger to Penelope Gilliatt, letter dated 15 May 1970.
29. E. Dundy, *Finch, Bloody Finch* (London: Michael Joseph, 1980), p. 310.
30. *Ibid.*, p. 309.
31. *Ibid.*, p. 310.
32. JRS/7/9 Character breakdown and notes file, character synopses by Penelope Gilliatt (undated).
33. JRS/7/16 Casting and Crew suggestions file, John Schlesinger to Joseph Janni, letter dated 31 October 1968 and John Schlesinger memo dated 12 November 1969.

34. JRS/7/14 Schlesinger/Gilliatt correspondence file, John Schlesinger to Penelope Gilliatt, letter dated 15 May 1970.
35. J.R. Taylor, 'Bloody Sunday,' *Sight and Sound*, Volume 39, Number 4 (1970), p. 200.
36. E. Dundy, *Finch, Bloody Finch, op. cit.*, p. 310.
37. JRS/7/20 Correspondence file, Joseph Janni to John Schlesinger undated letter (circa August 1971).
38. M. Riley, 'An interview with John Schlesinger', *op. cit.*, pp. 109–110.
39. Billy Williams cited in D. Petrie, *The British Cinematographer* (London: BFI Publishing, 1996), p. 156.
40. Jocelyn Rickards cited in E. Dundy, *Finch, Bloody Finch, op. cit.*, p. 308.
41. Jocleyn Rickards cited in S. Harper, *Mad, Bad and Dangerous to Know: Women in British Cinema* (London: Continuum Press, 2000), p. 216.
42. J.R. Taylor 'Bloody Sunday,' *op. cit.*, p. 200.
43. *Ibid.*, p. 201.
44. Comments taken from interview with Glenda Jackson conducted by the 1970s project team.
45. P. Gilliatt, *Sunday Bloody Sunday* (London: Secker and Warburg, 1972), pp. 133–134.
46. JRS/7/9 Character breakdown and notes file, character synopses by Penelope Gilliatt (undated).
47. P. Gilliatt, *Sunday Bloody Sunday, op. cit.*, pp. 122–123.
48. JRS/7/20 Correspondence file, Joseph Janni to John Schlesinger undated letter (circa August 1971).
49. T. Milne, 'Sunday Bloody Sunday,' *Monthly Film Bulletin*, Volume 28, Number 450 (1971), pp. 146–147.
50. JRS/7/9 Character breakdown and notes file, character synopses by Penelope Gilliatt (undated).
51. JRS/7/4 Annotated shooting script, script notes from p. 16.
52. Penelope Gilliatt entry in *Dictionary of National Biography* accessed from http://www.oxforddnb.com.
53. JRS/7/4 Annotated shootings script, script notes from pp. 28 and 6.
54. Penelope Gilliatt and John Schlesinger entries in *Dictionary of National Biography* accessed from http://www.oxforddnb.com.
55. JRS/7/21, Screenings file.
56. JRS/7/21, Screenings file.
57. JRS/7/15 Janni/Schlesinger correspondence file, Charles Berman to Joseph Janni, letter dated 11 June 1971.
58. JRS/7/19, Financial file, the cost for this specific objective was $5,000 over a period of six months.

9 *The Go-Between*: The Past, the Present and the 1970s

1. The Losey papers at the BFI Special Collections have been extensively used for this work and will hereafter be abbreviated to LPGB for *The Go-Between* and LPRE for *The Romantic Englishwoman*. LPGB, L.P Hartley to Harold Pinter letter dated 4 February 1969.
2. L.P. Hartley, *The Go-Between* (Middlesex: Penguin Books, 1975), p. 33.

3. Harold Pinter quoted by J.R. Taylor in 'The Go-Between,' *Sight and Sound*, Volume 39, Number 4 (1970), p. 203.
4. S. Harper, 'History and Representation: The Case of 1970s British Cinema,' in J. Chapman, M. Glancy and S. Harper (eds), *The New Film History* (Basingstoke: Palgrave Macmillan, 2007), p. 34.
5. M. Ciment, *Conversations with Losey* (London: Methuen, 1985), p. 303.
6. LPGB, L.P Hartley to Harold Pinter letter dated 4 February 1969.
7. M. Ciment, *Conversations with Losey, op. cit.*, p. 304.
8. Transcript from Film Time Radio Programme Number 66, broadcast on 9 October 1971 on Radio 4 taken from BBC written archives at Caversham.
9. LPGB, Notes on Melton Constable dated December 1969.
10. Carmen Dillon quoted by J.R. Taylor in 'The Go-Between,' *Sight and Sound, op. cit.*, p. 202.
11. *Ibid.*
12. D. Petrie, *The British Cinematographer* (London: BFI Publishing, 1996), p. 92.
13. J. Dawson, 'The Go-Between,' *Monthly Film Bulletin*, Volume 38, Number 453 (1971), p. 196.
14. L.P Hartley, *The Go-Between, op. cit.*, p. 276.
15. LPGB, Joseph Losey to Carmen Dillon letter dated 15 October 1970.
16. Alan Bates quoted in D. Spoto, *Otherwise Engaged: The Life of Alan Bates* (London: Hutchinson, 2007), p. 123.
17. LPGB, Script notes (undated).
18. LPGB, Script notes (undated).
19. M. Ciment, *Conversations with Losey, op. cit.*, p. 240.
20. LPGB, Casting notes included the names of Nigel Havers and Peter Duncan (undated).
21. LPGB, Joseph Losey to Dominic Guard letter dated 25 November 1970.
22. M. Ciment, *Conversations with Losey, op. cit.*, p. 208.
23. *Ibid.*, p. 156.
24. *Ibid.*, p. 146.
25. *Ibid.*, p. 155.
26. G. Gow, 'The Go-Between', *Films and Filming*, Volume 18, Number 1 (1971), p. 53.
27. *Ibid.*, p. 262.
28. *Ibid.*, p. 233.
29. *Ibid.*, p. 265.
30. *Ibid.*, p. 279.
31. *Ibid.*, p. 45.
32. R. Roud, 'Going Between,' *Sight and Sound*, Volume 40, Number 3 (1971), p. 158.
33. L.P Hartley, *The Go-Between, op. cit.*, p. 187. From the text on page 187 when Marcus confides to Leo that his mother has taken to her bed with nerves as she is unsure if Marian will 'stick to her engagement,' it is clear that Mrs Maudsley has some prior knowledge of the affair. Also, Leo begins to privately wonder how much other people know about the affair between Marian and Ted.
34. *Ibid.*, p. 277.
35. M. Ciment, *Conversations with Losey, op. cit.*, p. 240.

36. LPGB, Casting suggestions from 1969 and 1970.
37. Julie Christie quoted in T. Eubank and S. Hildred, *Julie Christie: The Biography* (London: Andre Deutsch, 2000), p. 175.
38. C. Gardner, *Joseph Losey* (Manchester: Manchester University Press, 2004), p. 168.
39. L.P. Hartley, *The Go-Between, op. cit.*, p. 92. Leo looks up to Hugh but his youthful adoration is tempered by his belief that Hugh's superiority is in part due to his position as a Viscount.
40. LPGB, Casting suggestions from 1969 and 1970.
41. LPGB, Joseph Losey to Alan Bates letter dated 22 September 1970 and Joseph Losey to Julie Christie letter dated 22 September 1970.
42. LPGB, Julie Christie to Joseph Losey letter dated 18 May 1971.
43. LPRE, Julie Christie to Joseph Losey letter dated 18 January 1974.
44. LPGB, Financial information taken from memo dated 31 July 1973.
45. LPGB, Peter Sainsbury to Joseph Losey letter dated 13 May 1971.
46. LPGB, Script notes (undated).

10 *Confessions of a Window Cleaner*: Sex, Class and Popular Taste

1. I.Q. Hunter, 'Take an Easy Ride: Sexploitation in the 1970s,' in Robert Shail (ed), *Seventies British Cinema* (London: Palgrave Macmillan, 2008), pp. 3–13, p. 3.
2. A. Medhurst, *A National Joke: Popular Comedy and English Cultural Identity* (London: Routledge, 2007), p. 1–40.
3. I.Q. Hunter, *op. cit*, Matthew Sweet, *Shepperton Babylon: The Lost Worlds of British Cinema* (Chatham: Faber and Faber, 2005), Ian Conrich 'Forgotten Cinema: The British style of Sexploitation,' *Journal of Popular British Cinema*, Volume 1, Number 1 (1998), pp. 87–100 and David McGillivray, *Doing Rude Things: History of the British Sex Film, 1957–81* (London: Sun Tavern Fields, 1992).
4. L. Hunt, *British Low Culture: From Safari Suits to Sexploitation* (London: Routledge, 1998).
5. A. Stuart, 'Review of *Confessions of a Window Cleaner*,' *Films and Filming*, September 1974, p. 62.
6. Robin Askwith quoted by A. Needham 'Robin Askwith interview' in *Left Lion Nottingham Culture* [online/undated]. Available at: http://www.leftlion. co.uk/articles.cfm/id/761 (accessed 7 January 2009).
7. C.H.B. Williamson, 'Box Office,' *CinemaTV Today* 26 October 1974, p. 4.
8. Figures taken from the Michael Klinger Papers accessed from University of the West of England, Bristol. These papers have recently been catalogued and the online catalogue can be located at http://michaelklingerpapers.uwe. ac.uk/cat3.htm. When the papers were consulted for the purposes of this chapter they had yet to be catalogued and so for this purpose are quoted here in full with the abbreviation MKP to indicate that they come from the Klinger collection. MKP, Swiftdown Company file, payments made for the film from the British Film Fund Agency.
9. L. Hunt, *British Low Culture, op. cit.*, pp. 117–118.

10. MKP, *Confessions of a Window Cleaner* file 1, RMR Eckart from Star Group Ltd to Michael Klinger, letter dated 14 May 1973.
11. MKP, *Confessions of a Window Cleaner* file 1, Ed Gerenson comments on Christopher Wood's screenplay, letter dated 16 February 1973.
12. MKP, *Confessions from a Holiday Camp* file, Michael Klinger to Greg Smith, Clive Parsons and Norman Cohen, letter dated 7 January 1977.
13. *Ibid.*
14. *Ibid.*
15. MKP, *Confessions of a Window Cleaner* file 1, Clive Parsons to Michael Klinger letter dated 12 December 1973.
16. S. Frith, 'Best Sellers,' *English in Education*, Volume 12, Number 3 (1978), pp. 20–26, p. 5.
17. MKP, *Confessions of a Pop Performer* file, Greg Smith memo dated 5 February 1974.
18. MKP, *Confessions of a Pop Performer* file, Christopher Wood memo undated (circa 1974).
19. MKP, *Confessions of a Window Cleaner* file, Val Guest to Michael Klinger and Greg Smith, letter dated 5 July 1973.
20. MKP, *Confessions of a Window Cleaner, Confessions of a Pop Performer Confessions from a Holiday Camp* and *Confessions of a Plumber's Mate* files, comments from Michael Klinger, Christopher Wood and Greg Smith about these aspects of the series.
21. MKP, *Confessions of a Window Cleaner* file, letter from *Film and Filming* (undated).
22. MKP, *Confessions of a Window Cleaner* file, Michael Klinger to Tom Nicholas at Columbia, letter dated 1 October 1975.
23. MKP, *Confessions of a Window Cleaner* file 1, Ed Gerenson's comments on Christopher Wood's screenplay, dated 16 February 1973.
24. Robin Askwith quoted in interview from http://www.leftlion.co.uk/articles.cfm/id/761.
25. MKP, *Confessions of a Window Cleaner* file 1, Michael Klinger to Ken Maidment at Columbia, letter dated 19 September 1973.
26. MKP, *Confessions of a Pop Performer* file, Christopher Wood memo undated (circa 1974).
27. MKP, *Confessions of a Window Cleaner* file, Val Guest to Michael Klinger and Greg Smith letter dated 5 July 1973.
28. S. Frith, 'Best Sellers,' *op cit*, p. 20.
29. L. Hunt, *British Low Culture, op. cit.*, p. 142.
30. Robin Askwith quoted in interview from http://www.leftlion.co.uk/articles.cfm/id/761.
31. L. Hunt, *British Low Culture, op. cit.*, p. 57.
32. MKP, *Confessions of a Window Cleaner file*, Val Guest to Michael Klinger and Greg Smith letter dated 5 July 1973.
33. *Ibid.*
34. MKP, *Further Confessions* file, details on unmade *Confessions* projects.
35. MKP, *Further Confessions* file, Michael Klinger to David Puttnam, telex dated 9 July 1986.
36. Michael Klinger Obituary, *The Times*, 20 September 1989.

11 *Stardust*: Stardom, Performance and Masculinity

1. S. Lieberson interviewed by Sue Harper and Justin Smith for the 1970s Project on 6 March 2008.
2. A. Medhurst, 'It sort of Happened Here: A Brief Life of the British Pop Film,' in J. Romney and A. Wootton (ed), *Celluloid Jukebox: Pop Music and the Movies since the 50s* (London: BFI Publishing Ltd, 1995), p. 61.
3. L. Wood, *British Films 1971–1981* (London: British Film Institute Library Services, 1983) and D. Gifford, *British Film Catalogue: Fiction Film 1895–1994*, Volume 1, 3rd Edition (London: Fitzroy Dearborn Publishers, 2001).
4. M. Kermode, 'Twisting the Knife,' in J. Romney and A. Wootton (eds), *Celluloid Jukebox: Pop Music and the Movies since the 50s* (London: BFI Publishing Ltd, 1995), p. 9.
5. K. Donnelly, *Pop Music in British Cinema: A Chronicle* (London: BFI Publishing Ltd, 2001), p. 61.
6. A. Higson, 'Renewing British Cinema in the 1970s,' in B. Moore-Gilbert (ed), *The Arts in the 1970s: Cultural Closure?* (London: Routledge, 1994), p. 222. and A. Medhurst, *op. cit.*, p. 62.
7. *Ibid.*, p. 51.
8. N. Gearing, '*Stardust* review,' *Monthly Film Bulletin*, 41, 489, 1974, p. 230.
9. Ray Connolly interviewed via email by the author on 28 April 2009.
10. David Puttnam comments via email to the author on 2 May 2009.
11. Comments taken from unpublished interview with David Puttnam conducted by the author via telephone on 17 August 2009.
12. D. Essex, *A Charmed Life* (London: Orion Books, 2003), p. 144.
13. N. Gearing, *Monthly Film Bulletin*, Volume 41 (October 1974), p. 229.
14. A. Stuart, '*Stardust* review,' *Films and Filming*, December 1974, p. 39.
15. R. Connolly interviewed via email by the author on 28 April 2009.
16. Videos available of 'Rock On,' 'Hold Me Close' and 'Gonna Make You A Star' on http://www.youtube.com/?gl=GB&hl=en-GB.
17. C. Lindholm, *Charisma* (Oxford: Blackwell Publishers, 1990), p. 7.
18. R. Dyer, *Stars* (London: BFI Publishing Ltd, 1998), p. 99, p. 129.
19. E. Goffman, *Interaction Rituals: Essays on Face to Face Behaviour* (Middlesex: The Penguin Press, 1972), p. 50.
20. *Ibid.*, p. 51.
21. F. Dellar, *NME Guide to Rock Cinema* (Middlesex: Hamlyn Paperbacks, 1981), p. 153.
22. Description offered by screenwriter Ray Connolly on his website http://www.rayconnolly.co.uk/pages/films_tv_and_radio/screenplays_for_the_cinema.htm.
23. A. Spicer, *Typical Men: Representations of Masculinity in the Popular British Culture* (London: I.B. Tauris and Co, 2001), p. 157.
24. *Ibid.*, p. 215.
25. Ray Connolly interviewed via email by the author on 28 April 2009.
26. D. Malcolm 'Review of *Stardust*,' *Cosmopolitan*, November 1974, p. 9.
27. D. Essex, *A Charmed Life, op.cit.*, p. 140.
28. Ray Connolly interviewed via email by the author on 28 April 2009.
29. *Ibid.*

30. M. Luckett, 'Performing Masculinities: Dandyism and Male Fashion in 1960s–1970s British Cinema,' in S. Bruzzi and P. Church Gibson (eds), *Fashion Cultures: Theories, Explorations and Analysis* (London: Routledge, 2000), p. 316.
31. *Ibid.*, p. 316.
32. L. Hunt, *British Low Culture, op. cit.*, p. 4. and p. 57.
33. N. McLaughlin, 'Rock, Fashion and Performativity,' in S. Bruzzi and P. Church Gibson (eds), *Fashion Cultures: Theories, Explorations and Analysis* (London: Routledge, 2000), p. 271.
34. P. Church Gibson and A. Hill, ' "Tutto e Marchio!": Excess, Masquerade and Performativity in 70s Cinema,' in R. Murphy (ed), *The British Cinema Book*, 2nd Edition (London: BFI, 2001), p. 268.
35. *Ibid.*
36. M. Luckett, 'Performing Masculinities,' *op. cit.*, p. 321.
37. Ray Connolly interviewed via email by the author on 28 April 2009.
38. L. Hunt, *British Low Culture, op.cit.*, p. 19.
39. *Variety Film Reviews, 1971–1974*, Volume 13, 4 September 1974.
40. BBFC file for *Stardust*.
41. *Ibid.*
42. *Ibid.*
43. *Ibid.*
44. *Ibid.*
45. *Ibid.*
46. *Ibid.*
47. *Ibid.*
48. Sample letter to be sent to respondents from VPS (subsidiary of Goodtimes) contained within BBFC file for *Stardust*.
49. BBFC file for *Stardust*.
50. D. Malcolm, 'Review of *Stardust*,' *Cosmopolitan* (November 1974), p. 9. and *Variety Film Reviews, 1971–1974*, 13, 4 September 1974.
51. A. Stuart, 'Stardust review,' *Films and Filming*, December 1974, p. 39.
52. *Variety Film Reviews, 1971–1974*, 13, 4 September 1974.
53. C.H.B. Williamson, 'Box Office Facts and Figures,' *CinemaTV Today*. Saturday 9 November 1974, p. 2.

12 *Scum:* Institutional Control and Patriarchy

1. Comments made by Alasdair Milne quoted on Radio 4 programme on *Scum* broadcast 4 November 2009.
2. Comments made by Alan Clarke quoted on Radio 4 programme on *Scum* broadcast on 4 November 2009.
3. Comments made by Clive Parsons in an interview conducted with members of the production team and included on DVD of the film released in 2005.
4. Comments made by David Threlfall in an interview conducted with cast members and included on DVD of the film released in 2005.
5. Comments made by Phil Daniels in an interview conducted with cast members and included on DVD of the film released in 2005.

6. Information taken from the Don Boyd collection of papers held at the Bill Douglas Centre at the University of Exeter hereafter referred to as DB. DB041, Production file, details of rejections from production companies and studios.

7. Comments made by Don Boyd when interviewed by the author via email on 11 June 2012.

8. DB304, Correspondence file, Roy Minton to Don Boyd and Clive Parsons letter dated 1 December 1978 and Roy Minton to Alan Clarke dated 1 December 1978.

9. DB304, Correspondence file, Roy Minton to Clive Parsons letter dated 12 December 1978.

10. DB304, Correspondence file, Clive Parsons to Frances Purdell of Dennis Davidson Associates letter dated 7 January 1979.

11. Comments made by Don Boyd quoted on Radio 4 programme on *Scum* broadcast on 4 November 2009.

12. Comments made by Don Boyd when interviewed by the author via email on 30 June 2009.

13. BBFC file on *Scum*.

14. *Ibid.*

15. *Ibid.*

16. A. Walker, *National Heroes: British Cinema in the 70s and 80s* (London: Harrap, 1985).

17. Comments made by Don Boyd when interviewed by the author via email on 30 June 2009.

18. *Ibid.*

19. DB304, Correspondence file, Don Boyd to Alan Clarke letter dated January 1979.

20. Comments made by Don Boyd quoted on Radio 4 programme on *Scum* broadcast on 4th November 2009.

21. Comments made by an ex-Borstal boy quoted on Radio 4 programme on *Scum* broadcast on 4th November 2009.

22. DB041, Production file, Michael Relph to Roy Tucker letter dated 18 January 1979.

23. DB018, Distribution file, Terry Glinwood at Osprey Films to Don Boyd letter dated 1 November 1979.

24. *Ibid.*

25. Don Boyd comments taken from an interview conducted with the author via email on 11 June 2012.

26. Detail taken from an interview with Don Boyd conducted by the author via email on 30 June 2009.

27. M. Garnett, *From Anger to Apathy: The Story of Politics, Society and Popular Culture in Britain since 1975* (London: Vintage Books, 2008), p. 8.

28. E. Goffman, *Asylums: Essays on the Social Situation of Mental Patients and Other Inmates* (Middlesex: Penguin Books, 1968).

29. *Ibid.*

30. *Ibid.*, p. 24.

31. M. Douglas, *How Institutions Think* (London: Routledge and Kegan Paul, 1987), p. 102.

32. Goffman, *Asylums, op. cit.*, p. 61.

33. DB047, Publicity and Distribution file, Results from C. Drakeford Survey of audience response to the film.
34. DB304, Correspondence file, Michael Relph to Bill Dunn of GTO Film Distributors letter dated 15 August 1979.
35. DB304, Correspondence file, Laurence Myers at GTO Film Distributors to Michael Relph letter dated 20 August 1979.
36. DB304, Correspondence file, Michael Relph to Bill Dunn of GTO Film Distributors letter dated 15 August 1979.
37. DB304, Correspondence file, Laurence Myers at GTO Film Distributors to Michael Relph letter dated 20 August 1979.
38. DB304, Correspondence file, Michael Relph to Bill Dunn of GTO Film Distributors letter dated 15 August 1979.
39. G. Gow, 'Review of *Scum,*' *Films and Filming*, Volume 25, Number 11 (1979), p. 31. and J. Dawson, 'Review of *Scum,*' *Monthly Film Bulletin*, Volume 46, Number 548 (1979), pp. 201–202.

13   *The Tempest*: A Brave New World of Creative Endeavour?

1. B. Green, 'Review of *The Tempest,*' *Punch*, 21 May 1980.
2. Don Boyd comments taken from an interview conducted with the author via email on 11 June 2012.
3. G. Bluestone, *Novels into Film* (Berkeley, CA: University of California Press, 1968), p. 62.
4. Don Boyd comments taken from an interview conducted with the author via email on 30 June 2009.
5. Material from the papers of Derek Jarman has been accessed from the BFI Special Collections and will hereafter be referenced as DJ. DJ, box 5, item 1b, note to *The Tempest* (undated).
6. *Ibid.*
7. Toyah Willcox comments from DVD commentary to accompany the DVD release of the film by Second Sight Films Ltd.
8. J. A Gomez, 'The Process of Jarman's *War Requiem*: Personal Vision and the Tradition of Fusion in the Arts,' in C. Lippard (ed), *By Angels Driven: The Films of Derek Jarman* (Trowbridge: Flicks Books, 1996), p. 90.
9. T. Biga, 'The Principle of Non-narration in the Films of Derek Jarman,' in C. Lippard (ed), *By Angels Driven: The Films of Derek Jarman* (Trowbridge: Flicks Books, 1996), p. 23.
10. Peter Middleton comments from DVD commentary to accompany the DVD release of the film by Second Sight Films Ltd.
11. Material from the papers of Don Boyd, has been accessed from the Bill Douglas Centre at the University of Exeter and will hereafter referred to as DB. DB433, Production file.
12. DJ, box 28, item 5, Christopher Hobbs to Derek Jarman letter (undated, circa 1976).
13. *Ibid.*
14. DB158, Publicity file, Derek Jarman comments taken from Press Book for *The Tempest.*

15. D. Hawkes, 'The Shadow of This Time: The Renaissance Cinema of Derek Jarman,' in C. Lippard (ed), *By Angels Driven: The Films of Derek Jarman* (Trowbridge: Flicks Books, 1996), p. 106.
16. D. Harris and M. Jackson, 'Stormy Weather, Derek Jarman's *The Tempest*,' *Literature/Film Quarterly*, Volume 25, Number 2 (1997), pp. 90–91.
17. Derek Jarman 1993 interview 'There We Are John,' contained on the DVD of *The Tempest* released by Second Sight Films Ltd.
18. Derek Jarman quoted in *Time Out*, 2 May 1980, p. 33.
19. *Ibid.*
20. DJ, box 7, item 12, Toyah Willcox interview (undated).
21. Don Boyd comments taken from an interview conducted with the author via email on 30 June 2009.
22. *Ibid.*
23. Derek Jarman in interview 'There We Are John,' contained on the DVD of *The Tempest* released by Second Sight Films Ltd.
24. Peter Middleton comments from DVD commentary to accompany the DVD release of the film by Second Sight Films Ltd.
25. *Ibid.*
26. DJ, box 5, item 4, comments taken from personal notebook dated Autumn 1974.
27. DJ, box 5, item 1c, comments taken from personal notebook dated Autumn 1974.
28. Peter Middleton comments from DVD commentary to accompany the DVD release of the film.
29. DB433, Production notes file, comments from a scenario for the film, (undated).
30. Details on Yolanda Sonnabend taken from biographical information contained on website for the Chambers Gallery http://www.thechambersgallery.co.uk/artists.html?artID=13 accessed July 2009.
31. Anonymous, '*Tempest* Review,' *The Financial Times*, 2 May 1980.
32. P. French, 'Such Camp as Dreams are made on,' *The Observer*, 4 May 1980 and 'Review of *The Tempest*,' *Screen International*, 7 June 1980, p. 15.
33. DJ, box 28, item 1, comments taken from notebook dated August 1975.
34. R. Wymer, *Derek Jarman* (Manchester: Manchester University Press, 2005), p. 6.
35. DJ, box 5, item 4, comments taken from annotated notebook with costume sketches and character notes dated Autumn 1974.
36. Toyah Willcox comments from DVD commentary to accompany the DVD released by Second Sight Films Ltd.
37. DJ, box 7, item 12, Toyah Willcox interview (undated).
38. R. Wymer, *Derek Jarman, op. cit.*, p. 78.
39. Toyah Willcox comments from DVD commentary to accompany the DVD released by Second Sight Films Ltd.
40. DJ, box 5, item 4, comments taken from annotated notebook with costume sketches and character notes dated Autumn 1974.
41. DJ, box 5, item 4, comments taken from annotated notebook with costume sketches and character notes dated Autumn 1974.
42. DJ, box 5, item 4, comments taken from annotated notebook with costume sketches and character notes dated Autumn 1974.

43. Toyah Willcox comments from DVD commentary to accompany the DVD released by Second Sight Films Ltd.
44. DJ, box 28, item 1, comments taken from notebook of designs and character notes dated August 1975.
45. *Ibid.*
46. *Ibid.*
47. P. French, *The Observer, op. cit.*
48. D. Hawkes, 'The Shadow of this Time: The Renaissance Cinema of Derek Jarman,' in C. Lippard (ed), *By Angels Driven: The Films of Derek Jarman* (Trowbridge: Flicks Books, 1996), p. 107.
49. DJ, box 7, item 11, notes from page 45 of annotated script (undated) but based on copy of script dated 20 December 1975.
50. DJ, box 7, item 12, Toyah Willcox interview (undated).
51. DJ, box 5, item 4, comments taken from annotated notebook with costume sketches and character notes dated Autumn 1974 and DJ, box 7, item 12, Toyah Willcox interview (undated).
52. DJ, box 5, item 4, comments taken from annotated notebook with costume sketches and character notes dated Autumn 1974.
53. DB085, Production notes file.
54. *Ibid.*
55. Don Boyd comments taken from an interview conducted with the author via email on 30 June 2009.
56. DJ, box 29, item 1, Derek Jarman interview with Clive Hodgson (undated).
57. B. Green, 'Review of *The Tempest*,' *Punch*, 21 May 1980. A. Walker 'Review of *The Tempest*,' *Evening Standard*, 23 June 1980. D. Malcolm, 'Review of *The Tempest*,' *The Guardian*, 1 May 1980.
58. DB392 and DB1086, Correspondence files, British Council to Don Boyd letter dated 16 January 1985.
59. DB3030, '*The Tempest* Review,' *New York Times* 22 September 1980.
60. Derek Jarman 1993 interview 'There We Are John,' contained on the DVD of *The Tempest* released by Second Sight Films Ltd.
61. Toyah Willcox comments from DVD commentary to accompany the DVD released by Second Sight Films Ltd.
62. C. Auty, '*The Tempest*,' *Time Out*, 6 June 1980.

Bibliography

Primary, Archival and Unpublished Sources

Bill Douglas Centre, University of Exeter

Don Boyd Collection, papers on *Scum*. Files covering correspondence, publicity, marketing and production, DB002, DB009, DB013, DB021, DB041,DB109, DB144, DB158, DB196, DB272, DB304, DB329, DB380, DB495

Don Boyd Collection, papers on *The Tempest*. Files covering correspondence, publicity, marketing and production, DB017, DB018, DB145, DB293, DB303, DB392, DB433

Bower Ashton Campus, University of the West of England, Bristol

Michael Klinger papers. Files on *Confessions of* films (un-catalogued) relating to sales, marketing production, pre-production, casting and finance. Files consulted, *Confessions of a Window Cleaner*, *Confessions of a Pop Performer*, *Confessions from a Holiday Camp*, *Confessions of a Driving Instructor*, *Confessions of a Plumber's Mate*, *Confessions from a Haunted House*, Further Confessions, Swiftdown Ltd

BBC written archives, Caversham

Transcript of Film Time Radio Programme (selected)

British Board of Film Classification, London

Film files for:

Scum
Stardust

British Film Institute, London

ACTT Report *Nationalising the Film Industry* August 1973
British Lion Holdings Ltd, Reports and Accounts 1969–1972
CinemaTV Today 1971–1975 (selected articles)
EMI, Reports and Accounts 1969–1979
Film co-production agreement between the Government of the United Kingdom of Great Britain Northern Ireland and the Government of the French Republic, (1965) Cmnd 2781
Film co-production agreement between the Government of the United Kingdom of Great Britain Northern Ireland and the Government of the Italian Republic, (1967) Cmnd 3434

Film co-production agreement between the Government of the United Kingdom of Great Britain Northern Ireland and the Government of the Federal Republic of Germany, (1975) Cmnd 6155

Film Production Association, Annual Reports 1970–1980

Film Production Association of Great Britain *Co-production guide to the Anglo-French and the Anglo-Italian co-production treaties* 1971

Future of the British Film Industry: Report of the Prime Minister's working party (1976) Cmnd 6372

Monopolies Commission, *Films; A report on the Supply of Films for Exhibition in Cinemas* (London: HM Stationary office, 1966)

National Film Finance Corporation, Annual Reports 1969–1980

Variety Film Reviews, 1971–1974

British Film Institute, Special Collections, London

Derek Jarman Collection, pre-production and production files on *The Tempest,* boxes 5, 6, 7, 28 and 29 containing script notes, treatments, sketches and publicity material (1974–1980)

John Schlesinger Collection, pre-production, production and correspondence notes for *Sunday Bloody Sunday,* files JRS/7/4–JRS/7/23 inclusive (1967–1972)

Joseph Losey Collection, pre-production, production and correspondence notes for *The Go-Between,* box 18, *A Doll's House,* box 20, *The Romantic Englishwoman,* box 22 (1968–1977)

Peter Rogers Collection, Production files for *Carry On up the Jungle, Carry On Loving, Carry On Henry, Carry On at your Convenience, Carry On Matron, Carry On Abroad, Carry On Girls, Carry On Dick, Carry On Behind, Carry On England, Carry On Emmannuelle* (1968–1978)

British Library, London

British Board of Film Censorship Bulletins for 1976 (Reports 1–12), 1977 (Reports 1–12), 1978 (Reports 1–12) and 1979 (Reports 1–3)

Hansard

House of Commons official report, call for Cinematograph Films Levy Bill to be approved, Volume 821, 15 July 1971

House of Commons official report, questions about levy on films sold to television, Volume 867, 21 January 1974

House of Commons official report, Adjournment debate about the future of the Film Industry, Volume 871, 4 April 1974

Parliamentary debates, House of Commons official report, question about a review of film censorship. Written answer, Volume 856/857, 24 May 1974

House of Commons official report, Prime Minster's statement about setting up the Working Party, Volume 892, 17 June 1975

House of Commons official report, question about the role of the British Board of Film Censors. Written Answer, Volume 911, 20 May 1976

House of Commons official report, question about a Bill on film censorship. Written answer, Volume 917, 21 October 1976

House of Commons official report, statement about proposed National Film Finance Corporation Bill, Volume 959, 27 November 1978

House of Commons official report, statement about financial assistance to the Film Industry, Volume 969, 2 July 1979

House of Commons official report, reading of the Films Bill, Volume 983, 25 April 1980

National Archives, London

BT 335/31 Films Bill 1969

BT 335/11 Levy on cinema takings: review of policy and regulation and a history of the levy

BT 383/14 British Film Fund Agency: minutes of meetings 1970

BT 383/15 British Film Fund Agency: minutes of meetings 1971

BT 383/16 British Film Fund Agency: minutes of meetings 1972

BT 383/17 British Film Fund Agency: minutes of meetings 1973

BT 383/18 British Film Fund Agency: minutes of meetings 1974

BT 383/19 British Film Fund Agency: minutes of meetings 1975

BT 383/20 British Film Fund Agency: minutes of meetings 1976

BT 383/21 British Film Fund Agency: minutes of meetings 1977

BT 383/22 British Film Fund Agency: minutes of meetings 1978

BT 383/23 British Film Fund Agency: minutes of meetings 1979

ED 245/54 Cinematograph Films Council: finance of the film industry

FV 81/93 Prime Minister's Working Party on the Future of the British Film Industry: implementation of report (Terry Report)

FV 81/95 Cinematograph Films Council: Minister's special meeting to discuss the report of the Prime Minister's Working Party on the future of the British film industry (Terry Report), 26 January 1976; minutes

HO 265/85 Committee on Obscenity and Film Censorship: evidence and Papers. Letters from Public

HO 265/2 Committee on Obscenity and Film Censorship: evidence (BBFC)

HO 265/7 Committee on Obscenity and Film Censorship: evidence (Portsmouth)

HO 300/166 Summary of film censorship and opposing views: legislation and local authority responsibilities

HO 300/171 Communication with Greater London Council on film censorship: summary of background to legislation on censorship and Home Office position

Portsmouth City Records Office, Portsmouth

Minutes of Fire Services and Public Control Committee Meetings 1971–1974, books CCM1/54 and CCM1/55

Portsmouth University Library, Portsmouth

Kinematograph Weekly 1968–1971 (selected articles) microfilm holdings

The Guardian online 1968–1980 (selected articles)

Secondary Sources

Books

Aldgate, Anthony, Chapman, James and Marwick, Arthur, *Windows on the Sixties: Exploring Key Texts of Media and Culture* (London: IB Tauris, 2000)

Aldgate, Anthony and Robertson, James, *Censorship in the Theatre and the Cinema* (Edinburgh: Edinburgh University Press, 2005)

Allen, Robert C and Gomery, Douglas, *Film History: Theory and Practice* (New York: McGraw-Hill, 1985)

Ashby, Justine and Higson, Andrew, *British Cinema, Past and Present* (London: Routledge, 2000)

Auty, Martin and Roddick, Nick, *British Cinema Now* (London: BFI Publishing, 1985)

Baillieu, Bill and Goodchild, John, *The British Film Business* (Chichester: John Wiley and Sons Ltd, 2002)

Barber, Sian, *Censoring the 1970s: The BBFC and the Decade that Taste Forgot* (Newcastle: Cambridge Scholars Press, 2011)

Barker, Martin and Petley, Julian, *Ill-Effects: The Media Violence Debate* (London: Routledge, 2001)

Barnwell, Jane, *Production Design: Architects of the Screen* (London: Wallflower Press, 2004)

Barnes, Alan and Hearn, Marcus, *The Hammer Story* (London: Titan Books, 1997)

Baxter, John, *An Appalling Talent: Ken Russell* (London: Joseph, 1973)

Beckett, Andy, *When the Lights went out: Britain in the 1970s* (London: Faber and Faber Ltd, 2009)

Betts, Ernest, *The Film Business* (London: George Allen and Unwin Ltd, 1973)

Bloch, Marc, *The Historians Craft* (Manchester: Manchester Universtiy Press, 1992) 7th Edition

Bluestone, George, *Novels into Film* (Berkeley, CA: University of California Press, 1968)

Bond, Ralph, *Monopoly: The Future of British Films* (London: Association of Cine-Technicians Publishing, 1946)

Booker, Christopher, *The 70s: Portrait of a Decade* (London: Penguin Books Ltd, 1980)

Bourdieu, Pierre, *Distinction: A Social Critique of the Judgement of Taste* (London: Routledge and Kegan Paul, 1956)

Bracewell, Michael, *Re-make/Re-model: Art, Pop, Fashion and the Making of Roxy Music, 1953–1972* (London: Faber and Faber, 2007)

Bright, Morris and Ross, Robert, *Carry On Uncensored* (London: Boxtree 1999)

Brody, Stephen, *Screen Violence and Film Censorship* (London: Crown Copyright, 1977)

Bruzzi, Stella and Church Gibson, Pamela (eds) *Fashion Cultures: Theories, Explorations and Analysis* (London: Routledge, 2000)

Chapman, James, *Past and Present: National Identity and the British Historical Film* (London: IB Tauris and Co Ltd, 2005)

Chapman, James, *A License to Thrill: A Cultural History of the James Bond Film* (London: I B Tauris and Co Ltd, 2007)

Chapman, James, Glancy, Mark and Harper, Sue (eds) *The New Film History*, (Basingstoke: Palgrave Macmillan, 2007)

Chibnall, Steve, *Get Carter* British Film Guides Series (London: IB Tauris and Co Ltd, 2003)

Chibnall, Steve, *Quota Quickies: The Birth of the British 'B' Film.* (London: BFI, 2007)

Chibnall, Steve and Petley, Julian (eds) *British Horror Cinema* (London: Routledge, 2002)

Ciment, Michel, *Conversations with Losey* (London: Methuen, 1985)

Curran, James and Porter, Vincent, *British Cinema History* (London: George Weidenfeld and Nicholson, 1983)

Deeley, Michael and Field, Matthew, *Blade Runners, Deer Hunters and Blowing the Bloody Doors Off: My Life in Cult Movies* (London: Faber and Faber, 2008)

Dellar, Fred, *NME Guide to Rock Cinema* (Middlesex: Hamlyn Paperbacks, 1981)

Dhavan, Rajeev and Davies, Christie, *Censorship and Obscenity* (London: Martin Robertson and Co Ltd, 1978)

Dickinson, Margaret and Street, Sarah, *Cinema and State: The Film Industry and the British Government, 1927–1984* (London: BFI Publishing, 1985)

Docherty, David, Morrison, David and Tracey, Michael, *The Last Picture Show? Britain's Changing Film Audiences* (London: BFI Publishing, 1987)

Donnelly, Kevin, *Pop Music in British Cinema: A Chronicle* (London: BFI Publishing Ltd, 2001)

Douglas, Mary, *How Institutions Think* (London: Routledge and Kegan Paul, 1987)

Dundy, Elaine, *Finch, Bloody Finch* (London: Michael Joseph, 1980)

Durgnat, Raymond, *A Mirror for England: British Movies from Austerity to Affluence* (London: Faber and Faber Ltd, 1970)

Dyer, Richard, *Stars* (London: BFI Publishing Ltd, 1998)

Eberts, Jake and Ilot, Terry, *My Indecision is Final: The Rise and Fall of Goldcrest Films* (London: Faber and Faber, 1990)

Essex, David, *A Charmed Life* (London: Orion Books, 2003)

Eubank, Tim and Hildred, Stafford, *Julie Christie: The Biography* (London: Andre Deutsch, 2000)

Forster, Laurel and Harper, Sue (eds) *British Culture and Society in the 1970s: The Lost Decade* (Newcastle: Cambridge Scholars, 2010)

Foucault, Michel, *The History of Sexuality Volume 1: The Will to Knowledge.* Translated by Robert Hurley (London: Penguin Books, 1978)

Freeman, Des, *Television Policies of the Labour Party, 1951–2001* (London: Frank Cass Publishers, 2003)

Gardner, Colin, *Joseph Losey* (Manchester: Manchester University Press, 2004)

Garnett, Mark, *From Apathy to Anger: The Story of Politics, Society and Popular Culture in Britain since 1975* (London: Vintage Books, 2008)

Gifford, Denis, *British Film Catalogue: Fiction Film, 1895–1994* Volume 1, 3rd Edition (London: Fitzroy Dearborn Publishers, 2001)

Gilliatt, Penelope, *Sunday Bloody Sunday* (London: Secker and Warburg, 1972)

Glancy, Mark, *When Hollywood Loved Britain: The Hollywood 'British' Film, 1939–1945* (Manchester: Manchester University Press, 1999)

Glucksmann, Andre, *Violence on the Screen* (London: BFI, 1971)

Goffman, Erving, *Asylums: Essays on the Social Situation of Mental Patients and Other Inmates* (Middlesex: Penguin Books, 1968)

Goffman, Erving, *Interaction Rituals: Essays on Face to Face Behaviour* (Middlesex: The Penguin Press, 1972)

Goodwin, Peter, *Television under the Tories: Broadcasting Policy, 1979–1997* (London: BFI Publishing, 1998)

Hanson, Stuart, *From Silent Screen to Multi-Screen: A History of Cinema Exhibition in Britain since 1896* (Manchester: Manchester University Press, 2007)

Harper, Sue, *Mad, Bad and Dangerous to Know: Women in British Cinema* (London: Continuum Press, 2000)

Harper, Sue and Porter, Vincent, *British Cinema of the 1950s: The Decline of Deference* (Oxford: Oxford University Press, 2003)

Harper, Sue and Smith, Justin (eds) *British Film Culture in the 1970s: The Boundaries of Pleasure* (Edinburgh: Edinburgh Universtiy Press, 2011)

Hartley, L.P, *The Go-Between* (Middlesex: Penguin Books, 1975)

Hewison, Robert, *Too Much: Art and Society in the Sixties, 1960–1975* (London: Methuen, 1986)

Hill, John, *British Cinema in the 1980s* (Oxford: Clarendon Press UOP, 1999)

Hobsbawm, Eric, *Age of Extremes: The Short 20th Century, 1914–1991* (London: Michael Joseph, 1984)

Hunt, Leon, *British Low Culture: From Safari Suits to Sexploitation* (London: Routledge. 1998)

Hutchings, Peter, *Hammer and Beyond: The British Horror Film* (Manchester: Manchester University Press, 1993)

Jordanova, Ludmilla, *History in Practice* (London: Hodder Headline, 2000)

Kelly, Terence, Norton, Graham and Perry, George, *A Competitive Cinema: An IEA Research Report* (London: Institute of Economic Affairs Ltd, 1966)

Kracauer, Siegfried, *From Caligari to Hitler A Psychological Study of the German Film* (Princeton, NJ, Oxford: Princeton University Press, 2004)

Lanza, Joseph, *Phallic Frenzy: Ken Russell and his Films* (London: Aurum Press Ltd, 2008)

Lea, Timothy, *Confessions of a Window Cleaner* (London: Macdonald Futura, 1977)

Leach, Jim, *British Film* (Cambridge: Cambridge University Press, 2004)

Lindholm, Charles, *Charisma* (Oxford: Blackwell Publishers, 1990)

Lovell, Alan, *The BFI Production Board* (London: BFI Publishing, 1976)

Marr, Andrew, *A History of Modern Britain* (London: Macmillan Press, 2007)

Marwick, Arthur, *Culture in Britain since 1945* (Oxford: Basil Blackwell Ltd, 1991)

Marwick, Arthur, *The Sixties: Cultural Revolution in Britain, France, Italy and the United States* (Oxford: Oxford University Press, 1998)

Mathews, Tom Dewe, *Censored: What they Didn't Allow You to See and Why: The Story of Film Censorship in Britain* (London: Chatto and Windus Ltd, 1994)

McCabe, Colin, *Performance* BFI Film Classics (London: BFI Publishing, 1998)

McGillivray, David, *Doing Rude Things: The History of the British Sex Film, 1957–1981* (London: Sun Tavern Fields, 1992)

Medhurst, Andy, *A National Joke: Popular Comedy and English Cultural Identity*. (London: Routledge, 2007)

Moore-Gilbert, Bart (ed) *The Arts in the 1970s: Cultural Closure?* (London: Routledge, 1994)

Mullally, Frederic, *Films: an Alternative to Rank. An Analysis of Power and Policy in the British Film Industry* (London: The Socialist Book Centre, 1946)

Murphy, Robert, *Sixties British Cinema* (London: BFI Publishing, 1992)

Murphy, Robert, *The British Cinema Book*, 2nd Edition (London: BFI, 2001)

Neale, Steve and Krutnik, Frank, *Popular Film and Television Comedy* (London: Routledge, 1990)

Newland, Paul (ed), *Don't Look Now: British Cinema in the 1970s* (Bristol: Intellect Books, 2010)

O'Higgins, Paul, *Censorship in Britain* (London: Thomas Nelson, 1972)

Palmer, James, *The Films of Joseph Losey* (Cambridge: Cambridge University Press, 1993)

Perks, Robert and Thomas, Alastair, *The Oral History Reader* (London: Routledge, 1998)

Petrie, Duncan, *The British Cinematographer* (London: BFI Publishing, 1996)

Phelps, Guy, *Film Censorship* (London: Victor Gallancz Ltd, 1975)

Richards, Jeffrey, *The Age of the Dream Palace: Cinema and Society, 1930–1939* (London: Routledge and Kegan Paul, 1984)

Roberts, Geoffrey, *Obscenity: An Account of Censorship Laws and their enforcement in England and Wales* (London: Weidenfeld and Nicholson, 1979)

Robertson, Patrick, *The Guinness Book of Film Facts and Feats* (Enfield: Guinness Superlatives, 1980)

Robertson, James, *The British Board of Film Censors: Film Censorship in Britain, 1896–1950* (London: Croom Helm, 1985)

Robertson, James *The Hidden Cinema: British Film Censorship, 1913–1972* (London: Routledge, 1989)

Samuel, Raphael, *Theatres of Memory: Volume 1, Past and Present in Contemporary Culture* (London: Verso, 1994)

Sandbrook Dominic, *State of Emergency. The way we were: Britain, 1970–1974* (London: Penguin Books, 2011)

Sanderson, Mark, *Don't Look Now* (London: BFI Publishing, 1996)

Sargeant, Amy, *British Cinema: A Critical History* (London: BFI, 2005)

Sellers, Robert, *Always Look on the Bright Side of Life: The Inside Story of Handmade Films* (London, Metro Books, 2003)

Shail, Robert (ed) *Seventies British Cinema* (London: BFI/Palgrave Macmillan, 2008)

Sheridan, Simon, *Keeping the British End Up: Four Decades of Saucy Cinema* (Richmond: Reynolds and Hearn Ltd, 2005)

Shrapnel, Norman, *The 70's: Britain's Inward March* (London: Constable, 1980)

Sinyard, Neil, *The Films of Nicolas Roeg* (London: Letts, 1991)

Smith, Gary A, *Uneasy Dreams: The Golden Age of British Horror Films, 1956–1976* (London: McFarland and Company Inc, 2000)

Sounes, Howard, *Seventies: The Sights, Sounds and Ideas of a Brilliant Decade* (London: Simon & Schuster UK Ltd, 2006)

Spicer, Andrew, *Typical Men: Representations of Masculinity in the Popular British Culture* (London: IB Tauris and Co, 2001)

Spoto, Donald, *Otherwise Engaged: The Life of Alan Bates* (London: Hutchinson, 2007)

Sproas, John, *The Decline of the Cinema: An Economist's Report* (London: George Allen and Unwin Ltd, 1962)

Street, Sarah, *British National Cinema* (London: Routledge: 1997)

Street, Sarah, *British Cinema in Documents* (London: Routledge, 2000)

Street, Sarah, *Transatlantic Crossings: British Feature Films in the Unites States* (London: Continuum International Publishing Group, 2002)

Sutcliffe, Anthony, *An Economic and Social History of Western Europe Since 1945* (Harlow: Longman Limited, 1996)

Sweet, Matthew, *Shepperton Babylon: The Lost Worlds of British Cinema* (Chatham: Faber and Faber, 2005)

Swern, Phil and Childs, Mike, *The Guinness Book of Box Office Hits* (Enfield: Guinness, 1995)

Tosh, John, *The Pursuit of History*, 4th Edition (Harlow: Pearson Education, 2006)

Trevelyan, John, *What the Censor Saw* (London: Michael Joseph Ltd, 1973)

Turner, Alwyn W, *Crisis? What Crisis? Britain in the 1970s* (London: Aurum Press Ltd, 2008)

Walker, Alexander, *National Heroes: British Cinema in the 70s and 80s* (London: Harrap, 1985)

Walker, Alexander, *Hollywood England: The British Film Industry in the 1960s*, 2nd Edition (London: Harrap, 1986)

Walker, John, *The Once and Future Film: British Cinema in the Seventies and Eighties* (London: Methuen, 1985)

Walker, John A, *Left Shift: Radical Art in 1970s Britain* (London: IB Tauris, 2002)

Weight, Richard, *Patriots: National Identity in Britain, 1940–2000* (London: Macmillan Press, 2002)

Williams, Raymond, *Problems in Materialism and Culture* (London: Verso Editions and NLB, 1980)

Wistrich, Enid, *'I Don't Mind the Sex, It's the Violence': Film Censorship Explored* (London: Marion Boyars Publishers Ltd, 1978)

Wood, Linda, *British Films, 1971–1981* (London: British Film Institute Library Services, 1983)

Wymer, Rowland, *Derek Jarman* (Manchester: Manchester University Press, 2005)

Yule, Andrew, *Enigma: David Puttnam, the Story So Far* (Edinburgh: Mainstream, 1988)

Chapters in books

Biga, Tracy, 'The Principle of Non-narration in the Films of Derek Jarman' in C. Lippard (ed), *By Angels Driven: The Films of Derek Jarman* (Trowbridge: Flicks Books, 1996), pp. 12–30

Chapman, James, 'From Amicus to Atlantis: The Lost Worlds of 1970s Britisjh Cinema' in R. Shail (ed), *Seventies British Cinema* (London: BFI/Palgrave Macmillan, 2008), pp. 56–64

Chibnall, Steve, 'A Heritage of Evil: Pete Walker and the Politics of Gothic Revisionism' in S. Chibnall and J. Petley (eds), *British Horror Cinema* (London: Routledge, 2002), pp. 156–171

Church Gibson, Pamela and Hill, Andrew, ' "Tutte e Marchio!": Excess, Masquerade and Performativity in 70s Cinema' in R. Murphy (ed), *The British Cinema Book*, 2nd Edition (London: BFI, 2000), pp. 263–269

Dickinson, Margaret, 'The State and the Consolidation of Monopoly' in J. Curran and V. Porter (eds), *British Cinema History* (London: Weidenfeld and Nicholson, 1983), pp. 74–95

Eyles, Alan, 'Exhibition and the Cinema-Going Experience' in R. Murphy (ed), *The British Cinema Book*, 2nd Edition (London: BFI Publishing, 2001), pp. 163–169

Gomez, Joseph. A, 'The Process of Jarman's *War Requiem*: Personal Vision and the Tradition of Fusion in the Arts' in C. Lippard (ed), *By Angels Driven: The Films of Derek Jarman* (Trowbridge: Flicks Books, 1996), pp. 84–102

Harper, Sue, 'History and Representation: The Case of 1970s British Cinema' in J. Chapman, M. Glancy and S. Harper (eds), *The New Film History* (Basingstoke: Palgrave Macmillan, 2007), pp. 27–40

Hawkes, David, 'The Shadow of this Time: The Renaissance Cinema of Derek Jarman' in C. Lippard (ed), *By Angels Driven: The Films of Derek Jarman* (Trowbridge: Flicks Books, 1996), pp. 103–116

Higson, Andrew, 'A diversity of Film Practices: Renewing British Cinema in the 1970s' in Bart Moore-Gilbert (ed), *The Arts in the 1970s: Cultural Closure?* (London: Routledge, 1994), pp. 216–239

Hunter I.Q., 'Take an Easy Ride: Sexploitation in the 1970s,' in Robert Shail (ed), *Seventies British Cinema* (London: BFI/Palgrave Macmillan, 2008), pp. 3–13

Hutchings, Peter, 'The Problem of British Horror' in M. Jancovich (ed), *Horror: The Film Reader* (London: Routledge, 2002), pp. 117–124

Kermode, Mark, 'Twisting the Knife' in J. Romney and A. Wootton (ed), *Celluloid Jukebox: Pop Music and the Movies since the 50s* (London: BFI Publishing Ltd, 1995), pp. 8–19

Leggott, James, 'British Realist Cinema of the 1970s' in R. Shail (ed), *Seventies British Cinema* (London: BFI/Palgrave Macmillan, 2008), pp. 94–104

Luckett, Moya, 'Performing masculinities: Dandyism and Male Fashion in 1960s–1970s British Cinema' in S. Bruzzi and P. Church Gibson (eds), in *Fashion Cultures: Theories, Explorations and Analysis* (London: Routledge, 2000), pp. 315–330

Marwick, Arthur, 'Locating Key Texts Amid the Distinctive Landscape of the Sixties' in A. Aldgate, J. Chapman and A. Marwick (eds), *Windows on the Sixties: Exploring Key Texts of Media and Culture* (London: IB Tauris, 2000), pp. xi–pxxi

McLaughlin, Noel, 'Rock, Fashion and Performativity' in S. Bruzzi and P. Church Gibson (eds), *Fashion Cultures: Theories, Explorations and Analysis* (London: Routledge, 2000), pp. 264–285

Medhurst Andy, 'Music Hall and British Cinema' in C. Barr (ed), *All Our Yesterdays: Ninety Years of British Cinema* (London: BFI, 1986), pp. 168–188

Medhurst, Andy, 'It Sort of Happened Here: A Brief Life of the British Pop Film' in J. Romney and A. Wootton (eds), *Celluloid Jukebox: Pop Music and the Movies since the 50s* (London: BFI Publishing Ltd, 1995), pp. 60–71

Murphy, Robert, 'Three Companies: Boyd's Co, Handmade and Goldcrest' in M. Auty and N. Roddick (eds), *British Cinema Now* (London: BFI Publishing, 1985), pp. 43–56

Napper, Laurence, 'A Despicable Tradition? Quota Quickies in the 1930s' in R. Murphy (ed), *The British Cinema Book* (London: BFI, 2001), pp. 45–52

North, Dan, 'Don Boyd: The Accidental Producer' in R. Shail (ed), *Seventies British Cinema* (London: BFI/Palgrave Macmillan, 2008), pp. 139–149

Petley, Julian, 'Us and Them' in J. Petley and M. Baker (eds), *Ill-Effects: The Media Violence Debate* (London: Routledge, 2001), pp. 87–101

Porter, Vincent, 'The Context of Creativity: Ealing Studios and Hammer Films' in J. Curran and V. Porter (eds), *British Cinema History* (London: George Weidenfeld and Nicholson. 1983), pp. 179–207

Porter, Vincent, 'Methodism verses the Marketplace: The Rank Organisation and British Cinema' in R. Murphy (ed), *The British Cinema Book*, 2nd Edition (London: BFI Publishing, 2001), pp. 85–92

Richards, Jeffrey, 'Rethinking British Cinema' in J. Ashby and A. Higson (eds), *British Cinema, Past and Present* (London: Routledge, 2000), pp. 21–34

Richards, Jeffrey, 'Film and TV: The Moving Image' in S. Barber and C.M Penniston-Bird (eds) *History Beyond the Text: A Student's Guide to Approaching Alternative Sources* (Abingdon: Routledge, 2009), pp. 72–86

Shaw, Sally, 'Picking up the Tab' for the Whole Black Community?: Industrial, Social and Institutional Challenges as Exemplified in Babylon' in S. Harper and J. Smith (eds) *British Film Culture in the 1970s: The Boundaries of Pleasure* (Edinburgh: EUP, 2011), pp. 75–84

Smith, Justin 'Glam, Spam and Uncle Sam: Funding Diversity in British Film Production during the 1970s' in R. Shail (ed), *Seventies British Cinema* (London: BFI/Palgrave Macmillan, 2008), pp. 67–80

Trevelyan, John, 'Film Censorship and the Law' in R. Dhavan and C. Davies (eds), *Censorship and Obscenity* (London: Martin Robertson and Co Ltd, 1978), pp. 98–108

Journal articles

Anderson, Margaret, 'Stop Messing About: The Gay Fool in Carry On Films' *Journal of Popular British Cinema*, Volume 1, Number 1, 1998, pp. 37–47

Barber, Sian, 'Beyond Sex, Bond and Star Wars: Exhibition data from the Southampton Odeon 1972–1980' *POST SCRIPT: Essays in Film and the Humanities*, Volume 30, Number 3, Summer 2011, pp. 77–90

Barr, Charles, '*Straw Dogs, A Clockwork Orange* and the Critics,' *Screen*, Volume 13, Number 2, 1972, pp. 17–31

Conrich, Ian, 'Forgotten Cinema: The British style of Sexploitation' *Journal of Popular British Cinema*, Volume 1, Number 1, 1998, pp. 87–100

Edson, Barry, 'Commercial Film Distribution and Exhibition in the UK' *Screen*, Volume 21, Number 3, 1980, pp. 36–44

Ellis, John, 'Art, Culture and Quality: Terms for a Cinema in the 1940s and 1970s' *Screen*, Volume 19, Number 3, 1978, pp. 9–49

Eves, Vicki, 'The Structure of the British Film Industry' *Screen*, Volume 11, Number 1, 1970, pp. 41–54

Firth, Simon, 'Best Sellers' *English in Education*, Volume 12, Number 3, 1978, pp. 20–26

Harper, Sue, 'A Lower-Middle-Class Taste Community in the 1930s: Admission Figures at the Regent, Portsmouth' *The Historical Journal of Film, Radio and Television*, Volume 24, Number 4, 2004, pp. 565–588

Harper, Sue, 'Fragmentation and Crisis: 1940's Admissions Figures at the Regent Cinema, Portsmouth, UK,' *The Historical Journal of Film, Radio and Television*, Volume 26, Number 3, 2006, pp. 361–394

Harper, Sue and Porter, Vincent, 'Beyond Media History: The Challenge of Visual Style' *Journal of British Cinema and Television*, Volume 2, Number 1, 2005, pp. 1–17

Harris, Diana and Jackson, Mackenzie, 'Stormy Weather, Derek Jarman's *The Tempest*' *Literature/Film Quarterly*, Volume 25, Number 2, 1997, pp. 90–98

Higson, Andrew 'The Concept of a National Cinema' *Screen*, Volume 30, Number 4, 1989, pp. 36–46

Houston, Penelope, 'New Man at the NFFC' *Sight and Sound*, Volume 48, Number 2, 1979, pp. 70–73

James, Robert, 'Kinematograph Weekly in the 1930s: Trade Attitudes Towards Audience Taste,' *Journal of British Cinema and Television*, Volume 3, Number 2, 2006, pp. 229–243

Medhurst, Andy, 'Carry On Camp' *Sight and Sound*, Volume 2, Number 4, 1992, pp. 16–19

Petley, Julian, 'Clockwork Crimes' *Index on Censorship*, Volume 24, Number 6, 1995, pp. 48–52

Pirie, David, 'New Blood' *Sight and Sound*, Volume 40, Number 2, 1971. pp. 73–75

Porter, Vincent, 'Film Policy for the 80s: Industry or Culture?' *Sight and Sound*, Volume 48, Number 4, 1979, pp. 221–223 and p. 266

Riley, Michael, ' "I Both Hate and Love What I Do": An interview with John Schlesinger' *Literature/Film Quarterly*, Volume 6, Number 2, 1978, pp. 104–115

Sainsbury, Peter, 'Financial Base of Independent Film Production in the UK' *Screen*, Volume 22, Number 1, 1981, pp. 41–53

Spicer, Andrew, 'Film Studies and the Turn to History' in the *Journal of Contemporary History*, Volume 39, Number 1, 2004, pp. 147–155

Newspaper and magazine articles

Anonymous, 'Review of *The Tempest*' *Screen International* 7 June 1980

Anonymous, '*The Tempest* review' *The Financial Times*, 2 May 1980

Anonymous, '*The Tempest*' *Sight and Sound*, 49, 2, 1980

Anonymous, 'Michael Klinger Obituary' *The Times*, 20 September 1989

Auty, Chris, 'Interview with Derek Jarman' *Time Out*, 2 May 1980

Auty, Chris, 'Review of *The Tempest*' *Time Out*, 6 June 1980

Canby, Vincent, '*The Tempest* review' *New York Times*, 22 September 1980

Cashin, Fergus, 'Review of *Straw Dogs*' *The Sun*, 7 January 1972

Caulkin, Simon, 'Movie Moguls look to Brussels for Fresh Aid' *The Times*, 19 April 1972

Cooper, Rod, 'Production Review for 1970' *Kinematograph Weekly*, 19 December 1970

Courte, Kenneth, 'The Dollar and Film' *Today's Cinema*, 20 August 1971

Courte, Kenneth, 'No Longer the Kindly Money Lenders' *Today's Cinema*, 3 September 1971

Dawson, Jan, 'Review of *The Go-Between*' *Monthly Film Bulletin*, 38, 453, 1971

Dawson, Jan, 'Review of *Scum*' *Monthly Film Bulletin*, 46, 548, 1979

Ewbank, Tim, 'What the Censors of Southend Ban and Why' *CinemaTV Today*, 19 February 1972

Falk, Quentin, 'Just How Far Should the Government be Involved in the Film Industry?' *CinemaTV Today*, 23 March 1974

French, Philip, 'Such Camp as Dreams Are Made on' *The Observer* 25 March 1980

Gearing, Nigel, 'Stardust' *Monthly Film Bulletin*, 41, 489, 1974

Gordon, David, 'Ten points about the crisis in the film industry' *Sight and Sound*, 43, 2, 1974

Gow, Gordon, 'The Go-Between' *Films and Filming*, 18, 10, 1971
Gow, Gordon, 'Review of *Scum*' *Films and Filming*, 25, 11, 1979
Green, Benny, 'Review of *The Tempest*' *Punch* 21 May 1980
Malcolm, Derek, 'Review of *Stardust*' *Cosmopolitan*, November 1974
Malcolm, Derek, 'Review of *The Tempest*' *The Guardian*, 1 May 1980
McGrath, Terry, 'The Market Place Changes – So Must We' *Kinematograph Weekly*, 29 August 1970
Milne, Tom, '*Sunday Bloody Sunday*' *Monthly Film Bulletin*, 28, 450, 1971
Mooney, Bel, 'Censorship' *Cosmopolitan* March 1977
Murari, Tim, 'Nat King Cohen' *The Guardian* 17 November 1973
Roud, Richard, 'Going Between' *Sight and Sound*, 40, 3, 1971
Spiers, Daniel, 'Interview with John Schlesinger' *Screen*, 11, 2, 1970
Stuart, Alexander, '*Confessions of a Window Cleaner*' *Films and Filming*, 20, 12, September 1974
Stuart, Alexander, '*Stardust*' *Films and Filming*, 21, 3, 1974
Taylor, J.R, 'Bloody Sunday' *Sight and Sound*, 39, 4, 1970
Taylor, J.R, '*The Go-Between*' *Sight and Sound*, 39, 4, 1970
Todd, Derek, 'The Stable Door After the (US) Force Has Gone' *Kinematograph Weekly* 6 December 1969
Todd, Derek, 'Freedom for the Flicks' *Kinematograph Weekly*, 19 December 1970
Walker, Alexander, 'Review of *Straw Dogs*' *Evening Standard* 25 November 1971
Walker, Alexander, 'Review of *The Tempest*' *Evening Standard*, 23 June 1980
Waymark, Peter, 'Close GLC Look at Film Violence When Public Comment Is Aroused' *The Times*, 1 March 1972
Wilcox, Herbert, 'Preserving the Film Finance Corporation: Letter to the Editor' *The Times*, 21 July 1969
Williamson, C.H.B, 'Box Office' *CinemaTV Today*, 26 October 1974
Williamson, C.H.B, 'Box Office' *CinemaTV Today*, 9 November 1974

DVD sources

Interviews with cast members of *Scum* on DVD to accompany the film's release in 2005
Derek Jarman in interview *There We Are John* (1993) contained on the DVD of *The Tempest* released by Second Sight Films Ltd
Comments from Toyah Willcox and Peter Middleton from *The Tempest* DVD released by Second Sight Films Ltd

Radio

Radio 4 programme on *Scum* broadcast on 4 November 2009

Websites

http://www.screenonline.org.uk
http://www.bbfc.co.uk

http://csedmac01.prs.uea.ac.uk:8080/Plone/bchrp-bectu-oral-history-project/document_view
http://www.youtube.com/?gl=GB&hl=en-GB
http://www.rayconnolly.co.uk/pages/films_tv_and_radio/screenplays_for_the_cinema.htm
http://www.oxforddnb.com/view/article/52076

Select filmography

Apted, Michael (dir), *Stardust* (UK, Goodtimes Enterprises/EMI Film Productions, 1974).

Clarke, Alan (dir), *Scum* (UK, Kendon Films/Berwick Street Films 'A', 1979).

Guest, Val (dir), *Confessions of a Window Cleaner* (UK, Swiftdown/Columbia [British] Pictures Corporation, 1974).

Jarman, Derek (dir), *The Tempest* (UK, Boyd's Company, 1979).

Losey, Joseph (dir), *The Go-Between* (UK, EMI Film Productions/Columbia Pictures Corporation/Associated British Productions/World Film Services Ltd, 1971).

Schlesinger, John (dir), *Sunday Bloody Sunday* (UK/US, Vectia Films/Vic Films [London]/United Artists, 1971).

Index